I0810707

SACRAMENTO'S HISTORIC JAPANTOWN

SACRAMENTO'S HISTORIC JAPANTOWN

LEGACY OF A LOST NEIGHBORHOOD

KEVIN WILDIE

THE History PRESS

Published by The History Press
Charleston, SC 29403
www.historypress.net

First published 2013

Manufactured in the United States

ISBN 978.1.62619.186.0

Library of Congress CIP data applied for.

In Memory of Wayne Maeda
(1947–2013)

CONTENTS

Foreword, by Jill Shiraki and Donna Graves 9
Acknowledgements 11
Introduction 13

1. The Settlement of Japanese in California: An Introduction 15
2. The Rise of Japantown in Sacramento, 1890–1940 29
3. Sacramento's Japanese American Community and Forced Evacuation, 1941–1942 83
4. Postwar Resettlement, Urban Redevelopment and the End of Japantown, 1945–1960 115
5. Conclusion 157

Appendix. Sacramento's Japantown Business Establishments, 1940 161
Notes 167
Bibliography 179
Index 187
About the Author 191

FOREWORD

No longer does the Tripper or "Tokyo Express" travel down Fourth Street to pick up the students going to school; no longer do people walk down Japanese Alley greeting neighbors near homes located behind the stores or finding children playing kick-the-can; no longer is Kabuki performed or Japanese movies with live narration screened at the Nippon theater or the Boxing Hall. No physical reminders are left of Sacramento's Japantown that was not once, but twice abruptly disrupted—first by the mass removal and incarceration of Japanese Americans during World War II and then by the complete obliteration of the streetscape in the name of redevelopment in the late 1950s. Only through hearing the memories of those who lived and worked in the area surrounding Fourth Street does the vigor of the neighborhood come back to life. Through family photographs, archival documents and a lively narration from Nisei interviews, Kevin Wildie's *Sacramento's Historic Japantown: Legacy of a Lost Neighborhood* creates a moving picture of what once was.

Having visited remnants of former Japantowns throughout the state and having met community members who shared their memories with the "Preserving California's Japantowns" project, we relish the stories from Nisei that infuse us with understanding of the resiliency and strength that helped them endure, rebuild and sustain community. For agricultural workers in the Delta and Northern California region in the 1930s and '40s, Sacramento's Japantown was the anchor. For the Japantown residents who returned after the war, it was their hometown. Sacramento native Fred Matsuda reflected, "There was something rich about the way we all lived. You can't get that now."

Sacramento's Japantown is erased but not forgotten.

—Jill Shiraki and Donna Graves,
Preserving California's Japantowns

ACKNOWLEDGEMENTS

My first thanks go to Cheryl Anne Stapp, author of *Sacramento Chronicles: A Golden Past*, for helpful advice and connecting me to Aubrie Koenig, commissioning editor at The History Press. Without Aubrie's invaluable insights, creative vision, patient guidance and wise suggestions, this book would never have been published.

This book was formed over two phases: 1994–1998 and the summer of 2013. Over this long stretch of time, I have become indebted to a number of people. First, my deep appreciation goes to Dr. Joseph Pitti and Wayne Maeda, my two graduate advisors at California State University–Sacramento, who provided guidance in the early formation of this book. I would never have been able to write this book if it were not for Toko Fujii, Kanji Nishijima, Fred Ouye, Alice Hayashi, Frank Hiyama, James Kubo, Jerry Miyamoto, Dean Itano, Karri Yagi, Eugene Okada, Sooky Lee, Kan Sanui, Jerome Lipp, Michiko Takahashi, Fred Matsuda, Amy Wong and April Adachi. Their willingness to share their experiences greatly enriched my life and made this project all the more rewarding.

I would like to thank all those who were willing to share memories and photos, identify people and places and connect me with others, including Sybil Miyamoto, Hideko Oya, Yomisu Oya, Marielle Tsukamoto, JoAnn Fujikawa, Fred and Katie Shirasago, the Shimono family, Melvin Okamoto, Mike Sawamura, Carolyn Ishii, Cindy Kitade, Joseph Fukuda, Victor Shibata, Gene Itogawa, Terry Kornelly, Barbara Zweig, Douglas Kubo,

Lloyd Ouye, David Taketa, George Hisatomi, Jane Komure, Bonnie Okamoto, Donna Komure-Toyama, Keiko Komura and Ben Pease of Pease Press Maps.

My deep appreciation goes to Jill Shiraki and Donna Graves of Preserving California's Japantowns for proofreading the manuscript and writing the foreword. Marian Uchida, Christine Umeda and Donna Komure-Toyama played a memorable and cherished role in this project. They reviewed the manuscript, offered valuable suggestions on layout and accurate terminology for the World War II experience, hunted down photos, identified individuals and shared their experiences. I also want to thank my father-in-law, Yoshimitsu Yajima, for translating Japanese and Chinese characters on documents and images.

I extend thanks to the helpful staff and individuals from many institutions, including those at the Sacramento Room, Sacramento Central Library; the Center for Sacramento History; the California History Room, California State Library; Susan Snyder at the Bancroft Library, University of California–Berkeley; and Julie Thomas at Special Collections and University Archives, California State University–Sacramento.

Lastly, I want to thank my mom and dad, Nordell and Terri Wildie; my wife, Vanessa; and my two girls, Maddie and Allie. Their patience and accommodations throughout the formation of this project carried me to the end.

INTRODUCTION

On June 15, 1954, Henry Taketa, a prominent Japanese American attorney in Sacramento, California, appeared before the Sacramento City Council with more than one hundred Japanese American supporters. They were concerned about a proposed redevelopment project in downtown Sacramento that threatened the very existence of their neighborhood. Taketa opened his remarks with a sentimental appeal:

> *We have our whole heart and soul in what will take place here. Our fathers and mothers came here in their youth, and now they are reaching the twilight years of their lives. But in the meantime, they have worked hard, industriously, and provided a foundation for us, for the young generation. We have a considerable fondness for our community. For that reason, after our wartime dislocation, we always dreamt of coming back here. I would say 90 percent of us have returned.*

The community of which Henry Taketa spoke so fondly dated back to the late nineteenth century, a time when Sacramento stood as one of the most important distribution points for Japanese laborers throughout the California Delta region. By 1910, Sacramento had become the fourth most Japanese-populated city in the state. During slow periods of the agricultural season, many Issei (first-generation) field laborers gathered in downtown Sacramento, in a six-block section bound by L and O and Third and Fifth Streets. A Japanese population settled in this neighborhood, while enterprising

Issei families established more than two hundred businesses to serve the needs of this growing population. Colorful lanterns and flying windmills decorated "Japanese Town Alley," a strip in the heart of Japantown well known for its sumo tournaments. "In the olden days in the evening," recalls Chikaji Teramoto, "twelve or one o'clock, you could walk down Japanese Town Alley and hear the shamisen and some ladies and men singing. And that was natural every night." Ai Miyasaki was surprised when she arrived in Sacramento in 1918: "It was like Japan...The groceries, like in Japan, were displayed outside the store...There was even a Japanese bathhouse and a few Japanese doctors."

Other smaller Japanese enclaves developed throughout the Sacramento valley, but Sacramento's Japantown served as the hub that pulled others together. By 1940, some 3,500 persons of Japanese descent were living in the city. Here, doctors, lawyers, dry goods dealers, Delta fishermen, Yolo County truck farmers and Clarksburg ranchers gathered for religious services, classes in traditional Japanese flower arrangement and tea ceremony, authentic Japanese meals, baseball and basketball games, judo and sumo tournaments, New Year celebrations and Obon festivals, a Japanese Buddhist holiday to honor the spirits of one's ancestors. Such vernacular contours cultivated a sense of place and provided a seedbed for a lively Nikkei culture in Sacramento. While Sacramento's Japanese American community remains vibrant to this day, this historic neighborhood has disappeared from Sacramento's urban landscape. This book is an attempt to trace the origins of Sacramento's Japantown and uncover the story of its demise.

CHAPTER 1
THE SETTLEMENT OF JAPANESE IN CALIFORNIA

AN INTRODUCTION

Japan stood isolated from the rest of the world for over two centuries, until 1854, when the United States forced Japan to open its borders to migration and trade under the Treaty of Kanagawa. At first, the Japanese government permitted only Japanese students and the upper classes to emigrate. As a result of a rapid economic shift away from agriculture to industrial production during the Meiji Restoration beginning in 1868, Japan accumulated a surplus of unemployed farmers and extended emigration rights in 1884 to the laboring and farming classes. Most of these new emigrants served as contract laborers on Hawaiian sugar plantations prior to their settlement on the West Coast. Nearly 30,000 of these *dekasegii* or "birds of passage" had arrived before the turn of the century. Between 1890 and 1940, some 200,000 Japanese traveled to the United States.[1]

The first generation of these "birds of passage," the Issei, concentrated in the West Coast states of California, Oregon and Washington and worked in a narrow range of occupations. In 1920, 65 percent of Japanese emigrants had settled in California, 16 percent in Washington and 4 percent in Oregon.[2] By 1930, there were over ninety thousand Japanese in California, a population that comprised 75 percent of the total Japanese population in the United States. More than half clustered in the four counties of Los Angeles, San Francisco, Fresno and Sacramento.[3] Although significant, the heavy concentration of Japanese in California is not surprising considering that California represents the area of first major contact for the Japanese immigrants. Like Washington and Oregon, California required manual labor for railway construction and other types of intensive physical work that young, single immigrants could provide. With the passage of anti-Chinese immigration laws after 1882, labor positions that had previously been filled by Chinese were soon filled with ambitious Japanese immigrants. This rapidly developing state also provided conditions that later opened opportunities to engage in economic pursuits to which they were accustomed, such as farming and small business operations.[4]

Unlike the majority of European immigrants who arrived in family groups, the first wave of Japanese immigrants was predominantly made up of single males, a status that enabled them to accept work as migratory laborers such as lumberjacks, seasonal field hands, farmers, fishermen and laborers on railroads. Although oftentimes risking disease and death from unsanitary conditions and hard work, they could live as bachelors outdoors, in makeshift tents and bunkhouses, and could afford to take lower wages and still save some money to either start a small business catered to their own countrymen or return to Japan.[5] The experience of Nisuke Mitsumori, who eventually settled in Sacramento, provides a glimpse of the migratory life of a Japanese laborer in 1905:

> *On the farm, I was paid only a dollar and a half for ten hours of work, although this was better in San Francisco. The work on this farm was also seasonal. When Strawberry season was over, my work was over, too. Some of us decided to go to Fresno, hoping to get a job there. We thought we could earn three or four dollars, at least, in Fresno, however, we were afraid of getting sick in Fresno since malaria was quite widespread and it was hot there without many trees in those days. Yet, we decided to go…*
>
> *First, I worked in a vineyard in Fresno. It was so hot that I could not see things on the other side. We started working early in the morning and came back to camp at night, which was just a barrack. It was a terrible place. One morning we got up early as usual, finished breakfast and found that one* [in] *our group was still sleeping. We tried to wake him up, but found him dead…He worked all day the night before, came back tired, and went to bed. He never woke up. This incident made me aware of a conflict. Making money was fine. But I started to think that it would be meaningless if I died in this struggle.*
>
> *After that…I worked only in the early morning and late in the afternoon, and took a rest under a fig tree during the day. After I finished work in this vineyard, I went to another vineyard in Fowler…The grape season was over in October. I needed some money to go back to San Francisco. Luckily,*

> *I saw an advertisement for railroad men. I immediately became a rail man and went back to San Francisco...From San Francisco I went down to Los Angeles, got on the ship and went to the Gulf of Mexico, came back to San Francisco again, and then took a boat again to Los Angeles. I also went to Fresno in the same year. During this whole year, I experienced a lot.*[6]

Because Japan offered few opportunities for social mobility and financial success, most Issei laborers came to the United States with the hope of becoming rich and then returning to Japan to live a more comfortable life; permanent settlement in North America had little appeal to most of the early immigrants. "In those days two or three thousand dollars meant quite a lot to a Japanese person," said Riichi Satow of Sacramento. "Anybody coming back to Japan with that kind of money could do whatever he wanted to do—say, build a new house or buy some farmland. This was the dream that most Japanese emigrants had."[7] The desire to learn a trade outside of farming and return to Japan on a greater financial standing motivated James Kubo's father to travel to the United States. A Nisei (first American-born generation) born in Sacramento in 1916, James Kubo recalled:

> *My dad and mom were farmers. At that time in Japan the prospect of making money or getting anywhere beyond farming was almost impossible. Once you're a farmer, you're a farmer. So when* [my dad] *was seventeen years old, he had just enough money to take a boat to Hawaii. He worked in the sugar canes until he got enough money to go to the United States. He landed in Seattle and worked on the railroads all over the Northwest. He learned how to cook...and eventually opened up a candy store in Sacramento on Fourth and N* [Streets].[8]

While some did achieve great prosperity—such as George Shima, the "potato king of California," who established a $17 million farm empire in the California Delta and stands as a classic example of the "Horatio Alger" path to the American dream—the vast majority of the first generation found moderate gains in their financial standing, moving from a wage laborer to self-employment in farming or city trades.[9] However, because of growing racial hostility against them and their unfamiliarity with the English language, many found accumulating enough money in order to move from a labor position or tenant farming to independent employment much more difficult than they had anticipated. Frank Hiyama, born in Fresno in 1915, was a child of Issei farmers in the Sacramento and San Joaquin Valley.

He remembered the racial antagonism and obstacles to financial success that faced most Japanese farmers at this time: "If you were a farmer, you had to buy the farm, had mortgages and hired people to work. The farm usually never made enough money to pay its own mortgage. Very few people made enough money to go back to Japan, including my parents."[10] At age eleven, Hiyama and his family moved to Sacramento's Japanese American neighborhood near Third and O Streets. A 1911 United States Immigration Commission report substantiates his family's personal experience:

> *The race prejudice against them, a prejudice in part due to that earlier exhibited against the Chinese, has prevented their employment in many branches of industry and, in those in which they have been employed, has cooperated with the lack of command of English and of technical knowledge to retard their occupational progress...These limitations upon their occupational advance have placed a premium upon engaging in petty business and farming on their own account.*[11]

Failing to discover their dreams of enduring wealth and good fortune, and unable to save the necessary sums required to make the trip back to Japan, many of the first generation were forced to stay much longer than they had anticipated. Others decided to plant permanent roots in America and exchanged photographs with Japanese women who were willing to marry by correspondence and join their new husbands in the United States. A wave of *shashin-kekkon* or "picture brides" reached the shores of California in the first quarter of the twentieth century.[12] The practice of picture brides emerged as a response to circumvent the Gentlemen's Agreement of 1908, an agreement championed by the racially paranoid Asiatic Exclusion League. This new immigration agreement between Japan and the United States restricted the immigration of Japanese laborers but allowed their wives who were living in Japan to join their husbands in the United States. By 1921, the Asiatic Exclusion League had succeeded in eliminating this immigration loophole for Japanese women and, in effect, sealing America's borders to all new Japanese settlers. Despite racial exclusionist efforts to prevent Japanese from permanently settling in the United States, the picture bride arrangement fostered a more settled family life. In California, between 1900 and 1920, the ratio of Japanese women to men went from one to seventeen to about one for every two and had almost reached par by 1930.[13] In the 1910s and 1920s, Japanese women joined their matrimonial partners, established families and worked alongside their husbands as field workers or domestic aids. Perhaps

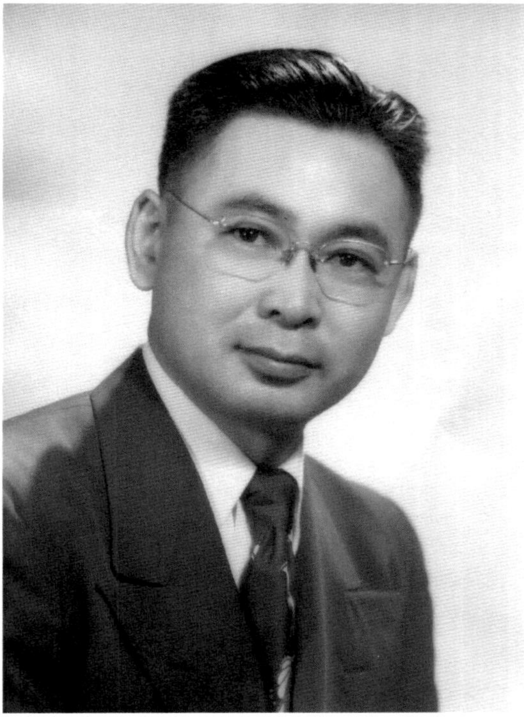

Frank Hiyama. *Courtesy Barbara (Hiyama) Zweig.*

even more intensely, Japanese women discovered the toil that their husbands had been enduring on the American frontier. Kane Kozono, who helped her husband on their Sacramento Delta farm, recalls those trying early days: "I was young then and could do the hard work. From time to time, however, it was so difficult that I often thought I should have stayed in Japan. I had to cook for a lot of the field hands, too." Raising children was another added responsibility. She continued:

> *When I went to work, I took* [my children] *with me to the ranch, and I would leave them sleeping under a tree. And when the day's work was over, I would carry one of them on my back to our home. Men had to work only while they were out in the field, whereas I had to do all of those things besides my share of the work in the field. I did their laundry after work, too. It was a really grueling, hard time for me.*[14]

Apart from such trying difficulties, by 1910, the men and women of the first generation had advanced as farmers, establishing themselves as one

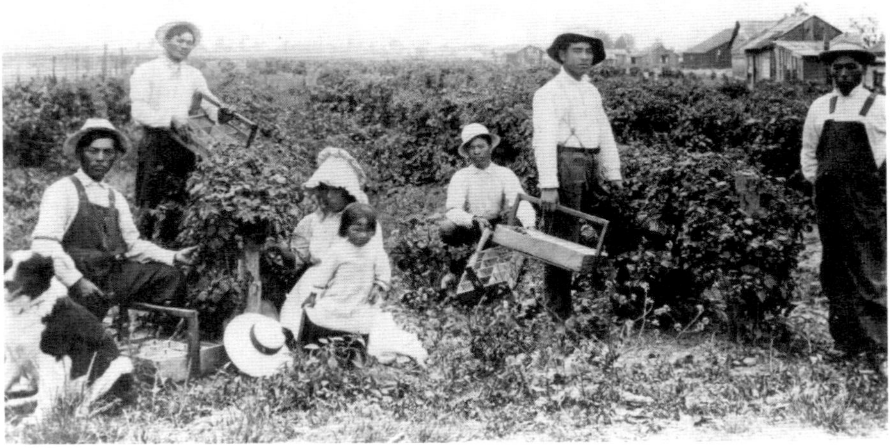

Uchida family strawberry farm in Florin. *Courtesy Japanese American Archival Collection. Department of Special Collections and University Archives, California State University–Sacramento.*

of the most skilled groups of agriculturalists in the United States. Some six thousand Japanese families owned or leased more than 210,000 acres in the western states, Texas and Florida. Skill, persistence and optimism, rather than initial wealth, determined the success of most of these family-operated farms. Those families who did rise to the top and become independent farmers were indeed "self-made."[15] Frank Hiyama recalls the older generation's persistence: "I remember as a child listening to adults talk. I remember one Japanese man who owned a pear orchard and said, 'One of these days, I'm gonna hit it big!'"[16]

The fertile Delta lands along the Sacramento and San Joaquin Rivers serve as an example of one of the earliest areas of extensive Japanese agricultural activity in California. The farms of the Delta were practically all reclaimed from swamplands by the building of levees and the construction of seepage and drainage ditches. Chinese laborers had cleared much of the land in the 1860s and 1870s for the production of grain, hay and vegetables, all of which went to Sacramento and San Francisco.[17] With the availability of better markets, reliable transportation and dependable Chinese labor, farmers began to produce onions, beans, asparagus, celery and deciduous fruits. All of these crops required intensive physical labor in ditch digging, planting, hoeing and harvesting. By the end of the first decade of the twentieth century, tenant farmers, mostly Chinese, Japanese, Italian and Portuguese, dominated the Delta, cultivating 9 out of every 10 acres.[18] Because of the Chinese Exclusion Act of 1882, subsequent anti-Chinese immigration laws and the willingness of Japanese laborers to work for less and pay higher rents for land, Japanese tenants came to outnumber the Chinese.[19] For example, in 1909, of the 305 tenants who farmed 70,000 acres in the Sacramento Delta, 112 were Japanese, 48 were Chinese, 40 were Portuguese, 60 were Italian and 45 were either Swiss, German, Swedish or native-born whites. Japanese immigrants also occupied the largest share of this land—17,500 acres. An immigration report stated that "for ten years or more the Japanese engaged in work of this kind have been more numerous throughout this large district than all other races combined."[20]

The Delta Issei did not achieve their dominant position without their share of pain, misery and sacrifice. Most settled in camps along the Sacramento River in the small farm towns of Clarksburg, Freeport, Courtland, Pearson, Walnut Grove, Isleton, Grand Island and Sutter. Within these camps, malaria and typhoid fever were rampant, living quarters were poorly constructed and the furniture was cheap, crude and inadequate for comfortable living. Oftentimes, especially during harvest seasons, overcrowded housing forced some to find shelter in barns with horses and cows. One report stated that thirty-six Japanese laborers were occupying an eight-room house. In another instance, sixty-one were occupying an eleven-room house.[21] Further, the Delta offered few opportunities for a social life. Access to the small, dilapidated churches, schools or bar rooms near the little villages at boat landings remained difficult. The absence of wagon roads and bridges forced travelers to use ferries and steamboats, both of which required money. "We didn't have any recreation at all," said Osuke Takizawa, a Delta farmer who settled in Sacramento. "If you wanted to go to town, you had to travel 40 miles to Sacramento on a river boat. The river boat was the only transportation."[22] An immigration agent added, "The older ranchers have tended to move away from their ranches to other places where as a result of 40 years of progress, normal living is possible, as it is not for the ordinary farmers residing on the Delta lands."[23]

Searching for more comfortable living and employment during slower periods of the season, Issei laborers traveled either south to Stockton or back up the river to Sacramento. In Sacramento, seasonal laborers found comfort in Japanese-owned lodging, bathhouses, saloons, billiard halls and provision stores. Authentic Japanese meals and lively entertainment offered an ambiance reminiscent of their lives in Japan and fostered a greater sense of companionship with others who were equally struggling to keep body

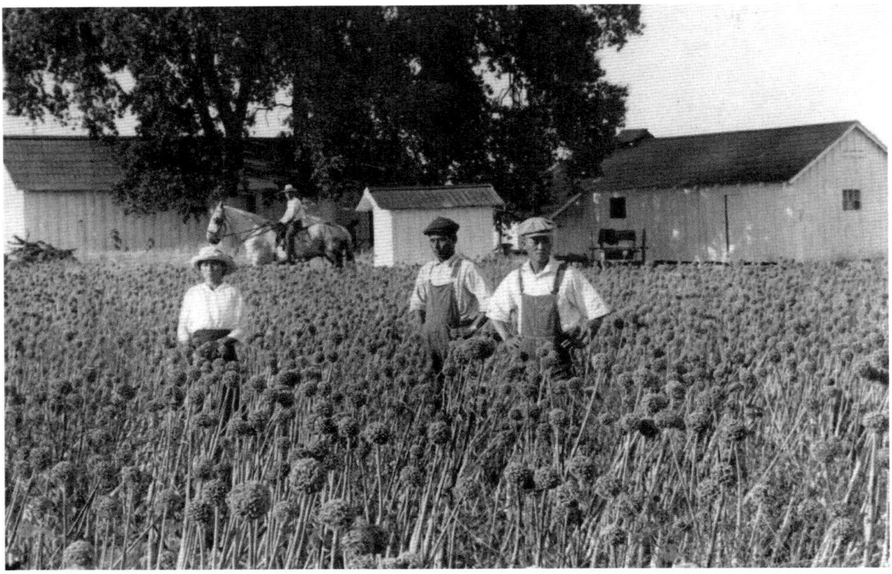

Sawamura family onion farm in West Sacramento. *Courtesy Japanese American Archival Collection. Department of Special Collections and University Archives, California State University–Sacramento.*

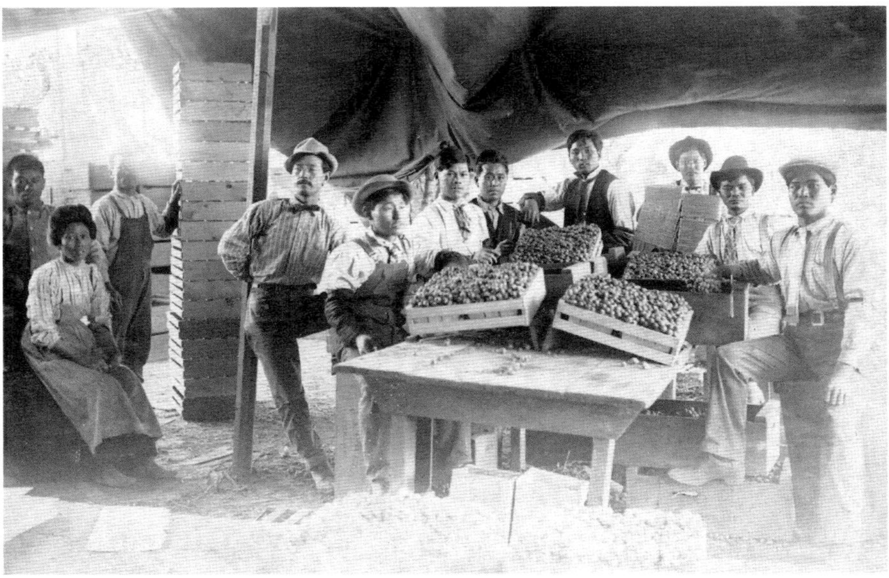

Florin grape-packing shed. *Courtesy Japanese American Archival Collection. Department of Special Collections and University Archives, California State University–Sacramento.*

and soul intact. Fred Matsuda, whose father owned Tamagawa-Do Manju bakery near Fourth and N Streets, remembers farmers coming into town in the evenings. "We had the manju business, so a lot of the farmers who were relatives and kenjinkai people who were big farmers in West Sacramento would come into town in the evening to play Hana [Japanese card game] at my dad's place."[24] Throughout the year, some 200 to 2,500 Japanese transient laborers would travel to Sacramento.[25]

However rugged life may have been on the Delta, it failed to break the first generation's pioneering spirit. Building levees and constructing drainage ditches, they helped reclaim seventy thousand acres of swampland.[26] Commenting on their formidable determination, agricultural historian Masakazu Iwata wrote, "Every Japanese tenant farmer in the Delta region anticipated becoming a part of a small group of five percent who made $2,500 in profit. To them, it might be the next year when they too could rightfully say '*Atatta*!' [Struck it!]. The gold at the end of the rainbow induced the Issei to plod ahead year after year despite discouragement; not to achieve success would imply *haji* [shame]."[27] Japanese labor organizations contributed to their success in the Delta. The majority of tenant farmers held membership in either the Japanese Producers' Association or the Japanese Farmers Association of California, both of which had offices in Stockton and Sacramento. These organizations facilitated land leases, assisted in drawing up lease contracts and mediated landlord and tenant disputes.[28]

World War I greatly expanded American agriculture as warring European nations increased their reliance on U.S. staple food imports. Between 1914 and 1918, agricultural profits increased from $8 billion to $18 billion. Sharing in the general prosperity of American agriculturalists, Japanese farmers throughout the United States more than doubled their land between 1914 and 1920.[29] Frank Sakata was one of those farmers. Sakata's daughter, Alice Hayashi, born in Clarksburg, California, and raised in Sacramento, recalls that her father, after saving enough money while working on a Hawaii sugar cane plantation, sailed to the shores of San Francisco in the late 1890s and immediately began working for a railroad company. In 1910, Frank Sakata moved his family to Yolo County, where he collaborated with a white farmer to transform a plot of swampland into a highly lucrative asparagus farm. The high demand for food during the First World War catapulted Sakata into almost instantaneous wealth. By the early 1920s, Frank Sakata, crowned the "Asparagus King," had generated enough money to lease other farmlands in the area and open a property investment firm, Highland Investment, in Sacramento's Japantown business

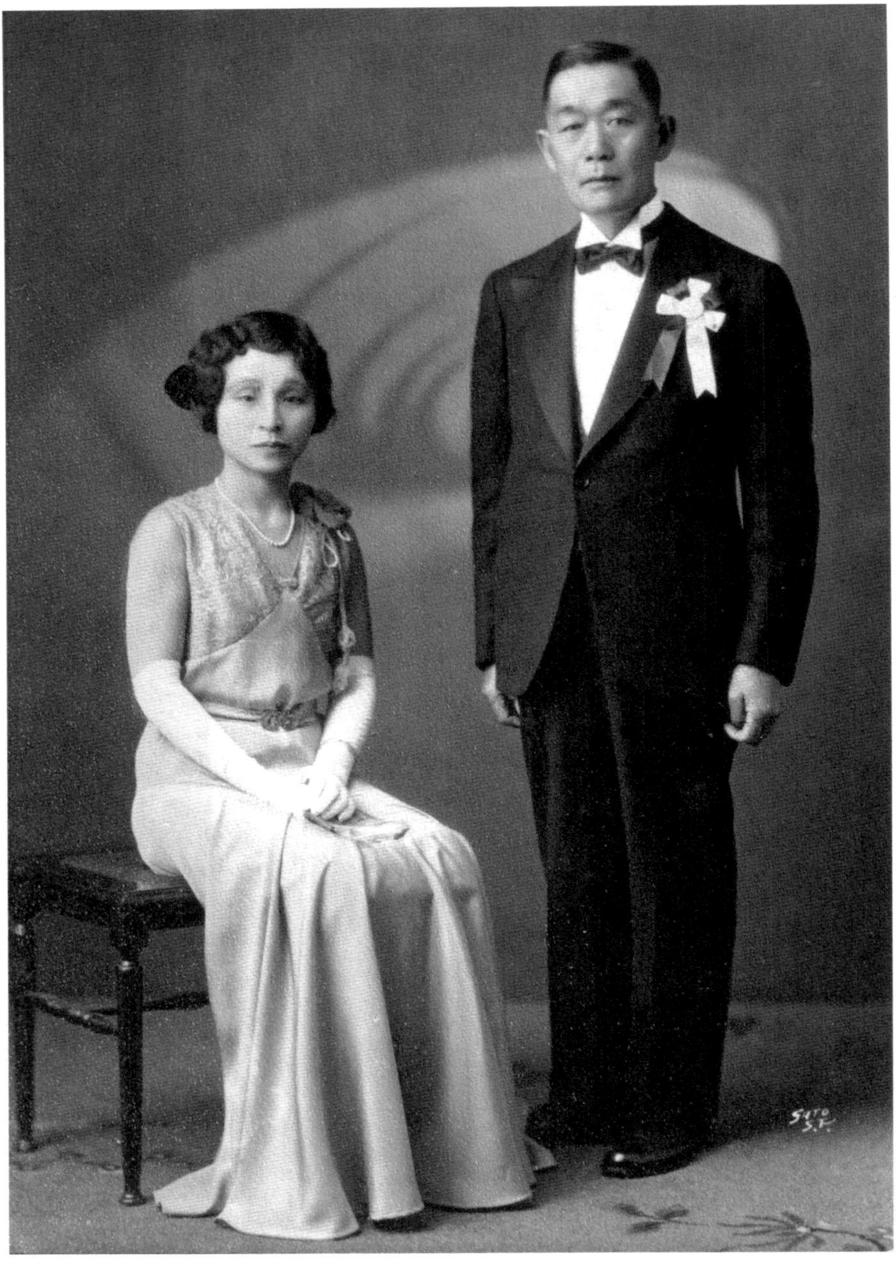

Frank and Matsuye Sakata. *Courtesy Sybil (Hayashi) Miyamoto.*

district. From his headquarters in Sacramento, Sakata managed thousands of acres all throughout Yolo County and the Clarksburg-Courtland Delta region. Sakata's success not only established him as one of the most financially successful and most well-respected farmers in the Sacramento area but also provided him with a position of influence and prominence within Sacramento's emerging Japanese American community. He later became president of the Sacramento chapter of the Japanese Association, an organization to assist new immigrants in employment, housing and legal matters.[30] Even if few Japanese immigrants reached the level of Sakata's success during World War I, most early settlers found moderate gains in their financial standing.

In addition to the economic difficulties they encountered, the first generation confronted a xenophobic white supremacist mentality that whites had previously developed against Chinese immigrants who arrived in the 1850s during California's gold rush. Many whites in the western states claimed that Asians threatened American society in general because they were too culturally inbred into their own way of life to adopt American culture. Asians would "Orientalize" the United States. Other white exclusionists argued that racially inferior Asians would socially and racially amalgamate with whites, producing an unclassifiable and degraded offspring.[31] In the western states in general, and California most severely, Asian exclusionists feared the economic competition posed by Asian immigrants.

Anti-Japanese sentiments first emerged in the 1890s when Japanese immigrants began to arrive in significant numbers and quickly demonstrate their outstanding skills in agriculture. Such skills induced fear within their white competitors. Anti-Japanese movements in California sprang from paranoid predictions that Japanese farmers, with their "unfair" use of family labor, would diminish wages and produce widespread unemployment for whites.[32] As a child, Frank Hiyama worked on his father's ranch in Fresno. He recalls the racial hostility of the anti-Japanese labor movement and the Farm Bureau: "I remember that the Japanese workers would work from sun-up 'til sundown. That's how they were able to survive. But the white [farmers] would say that the Japanese had [used] unfair labor practices because the women worked out in the field. My mom worked out in the field in the '20s in Fresno. But this was out of necessity."[33] Issei farming proved to be an economic asset to the West Coast states and particularly California. Historian Roger Daniels states, "If California and other Westerners had been 'rational economic men' of nineteenth century classical economic theory, there would have been no anti-Japanese movement. The Issei subeconomy neither lowered wages nor put white men out of work. Its major effect in fact was a lowering of the cost of fresh fruit and vegetables for the general population, and Issei agriculture was one of the bases which allowed California's population to expand as rapidly as it did."[34] But white farmers held little value in classical economic theory. By the end of the nineteenth century, a "yellow peril" mentality also had feverishly engulfed the white farm labor movements. The language in this *Industrial Commission Report* illustrates the predatory image white labor cast on the Japanese:

> *Close upon the retreat of the Chinese coolie, however, came the Japanese, equally menacing to the laboring interests of the country. Almost unnoticed, and without exciting either suspicion or alarm, has Japanese coolie labor crept into the country…Every vessel from the Orient that touched at our western ports left large numbers of these little brown toilers upon our shores. They were sent out in gangs to the farming and fruit-growing districts, and almost before the white labor of the coast was aware that this new foe was among them, it found itself displaced by a new rival more dangerous than the Chinese.* [The Japanese] *are more servile than the Chinese, but less obedient and far less desirable. They have most of the vices, with none of their virtues. They underbid the Chinese in everything, and are as a class tricky, unreliable, and dishonest.*[35]

In 1905, various labor unions in California had joined forces to establish the Asiatic Exclusion League. White city laborers in Sacramento opened a chapter in 1908. With headquarters in San Francisco, the league strove to end all Japanese immigration to America and circumscribe the right to a livelihood among those already in the country. During this period, the American Federation of Labor, led by Samuel Gompers, practiced a policy of racial superiority, refusing charters to California agricultural workers' unions whose membership consisted mainly of Mexican and Japanese laborers. As already mentioned, white exclusionists won a national victory with the passage of the Gentlemen's Agreement of 1908. The State of California passed a series of racial exclusion laws. In 1909, it barred Japanese from marrying whites. In 1913, the state prevented Japanese immigrants from owning property with the passage of the Alien Land Act. In 1921, the California legislature succeeded in amending the state's school code to specifically name Japanese as a group eligible for segregation in public schools. Only the four districts of Florin, Courtland, Isleton and Walnut Grove took advantage of the amended law to create separate "oriental" schools. Communities provided segregated schools, social clubs, sports teams, swimming pools and movie theaters for Japanese.[36]

Although the anti-Japanese movement pointed to the expansion of Issei farming with paranoid racist overtones and apocalyptic predictions about the end of "white civilization," the growth of Issei farming was real. At the time of the passage of California's Alien Land Act in 1913, Japanese farmers owned about twenty-six thousand acres. By 1920, they held almost seventy-five thousand and owned 80 percent of all nonwhite farms but only 4 percent of all farms in California.[37] However, Japanese tenant farmers occupied more valuable land than their white neighbors, particularly in counties such as Alameda, Orange, Sacramento and Solano. For example, in Sacramento County in 1920, white agriculturalists held 141 farms with an average value per acre of $128, compared to Japanese, who held 259 farms worth $380 per acre. Japanese farmers defied California's white exclusionist campaigns, circumventing the 1913 Alien Land Act by purchasing land either in the names of their American-born children or through joint land companies with whites. But as Robert Higgs reports in his study of Japanese farmers in California, Japanese generally paid higher rents relative to land values than did their white counterparts. According to Higgs, "Landlords as late as 1920 effectively discriminated against the Japanese in the land rental market."[38]

One of the greatest factors that contributed to the failure of anti-Japanese forces to completely rid California of all Japanese was the arrival of over sixty-six thousand Japanese women between 1908 and 1924. Not only did this influx provide fertile soil for the formation of numerous Japanese families, but the offspring of these families were guaranteed birthright citizenship as declared by the Fourteenth Amendment of the U.S. Constitution. The Nisei generation stabilized Japanese American society by discouraging their families' return to Japan. By 1940, 64 percent of all Japanese in the United States were American-born citizens. Also, Japanese men tended to move out of the transient labor force and into more settled agriculture by leasing or purchasing their own land. White farmers, who had been content with Japanese as seasonal transient laborers, vigilantly turned against them when they became competitors.[39]

By 1920, white farmers, together with the California State Federation of Labor (CSFL), helped form the Japanese Exclusion League of California. Whereas the Asiatic Exclusion League had been led by big-city labor in San Francisco, the CSFL was composed of small-scale farmers and local businessmen. These small business elements within the CSFL became the dominant pressure group behind the enactment of the second Alien Land Law in 1920, legislation that barred the Issei from registering their property in their children's names; and the National

Origins Immigration Act of 1924, which barred primarily all Asian and Eastern European immigration to the United States.[40] The California press acted as one of the main catalysts in amassing public support for the Alien Land Law. One study reports that fifty-six out of sixty daily and weekly California newspapers supported the Land Law measure, with the *Sacramento Bee* and *Union* "militantly" leading the campaign.[41] The land acts and anti-immigration laws symbolized the white racism that prevailed on the West Coast. Historian Yuji Ichioka points to the far-reaching effect the post–World War I slump in agriculture, the 1920 Alien Land Law and the 1924 Immigration Act had on the Issei: "It was a part of a series of events which culminated in their rejection by American society. [The Land Law and the Immigration Act] combined to produce a profound sense of rejection among Japanese immigrants, a feeling that they were deemed racially inferior and hence undesirable by white America. This left a legacy of bitter resentment which ranked in their hearts well into the decade of the thirties."[42] Anti-Japanese crusades succeeded in slowing down the growth of landownership among Issei farmers but failed to drive them out of agriculture. Determined to succeed, the first generation entered into many of their own smaller labor unions, solidified their work in various crops by organizing into gangs that dealt through one spokesman and continued to open up new farmland such as in the Imperial Valley in California.[43] In 1920, they were producing up to 35 percent, by value, of all commercial truck crops grown in California.[44] And the number of farm operators (5,152) in 1920 remained virtually the same by 1940.[45] Issei farming proved to be an economic asset to the larger population, but the prevailing "yellow peril" mentality blinded Californians from recognizing the positive contribution the first generation made to the growth of the state.

The Japanese immigrants who settled along the West Coast states in North America, most of whom arrived as laborers, struggled intensely not only with the physical challenges that accompanied life as a railroad worker, a miner, a lumberjack or a cannery laborer but also against organized discrimination and prohibition. Much like their Irish, Italian, Chinese and Hindu predecessors, the Japanese Americans experienced bitter racial hostility. Despite such obstacles, the Issei had sunk their roots deep into the soil of the Pacific West Coast, reclaiming swampland and converting thousands of acres of uncultivated land in valleys and deltas with names like Imperial, Yakima, Puyallup, San Joaquin, Yolo and Sacramento into productive agricultural sectors. The influx of Japanese women between 1908 and 1924 helped to create a more settled life, sparking the development of small rural farm communities throughout the West Coast states. They also made inroads into city trades, firmly imprinting their unique identity on the urban mosaic landscape.

CHAPTER 2

THE RISE OF JAPANTOWN IN SACRAMENTO, 1890–1940

Issei city trades first emerged in the United States in the 1880s and generally catered to both American and Japanese American clientele. But because of racial discrimination against them, and because they preferred food and living conditions to which they were accustomed, most Japanese trades to arise were those that fulfilled the primary needs of their fellow countrymen. These included Japanese provision stores, boardinghouses, barbershops and bathhouses.[46] In 1887, 8 percent of the Japanese residing in the United States worked in mercantile activity.[47] By the 1910s, Japanese American settlements began to rapidly develop, spawning an efflorescence of ethnic urban enterprises. As the Japanese American population grew, the scope of their trade enlarged to include places of amusement, newspaper and magazine publishing, doctors, dentists and optometrists. The *Nihonmachi* or Japantown became an important sector to the first generation because it served as a refuge from the anti-Asian hostility that prevailed in the outside community.

By the 1890s, the city of Sacramento had evolved into an important distributing point for Japanese laborers throughout the Sacramento and San Joaquin Delta. By 1910, the city had become the top distributing point for agricultural laborers in California and stood as the fourth most Japanese-populated city in California.[48] This was because of its strategic location at the confluence of the Sacramento and American Rivers and its proximity to one of California's major entry ports, San Francisco. Sacramento's earliest Japanese settlers, largely single male laborers, clustered in a six-block section

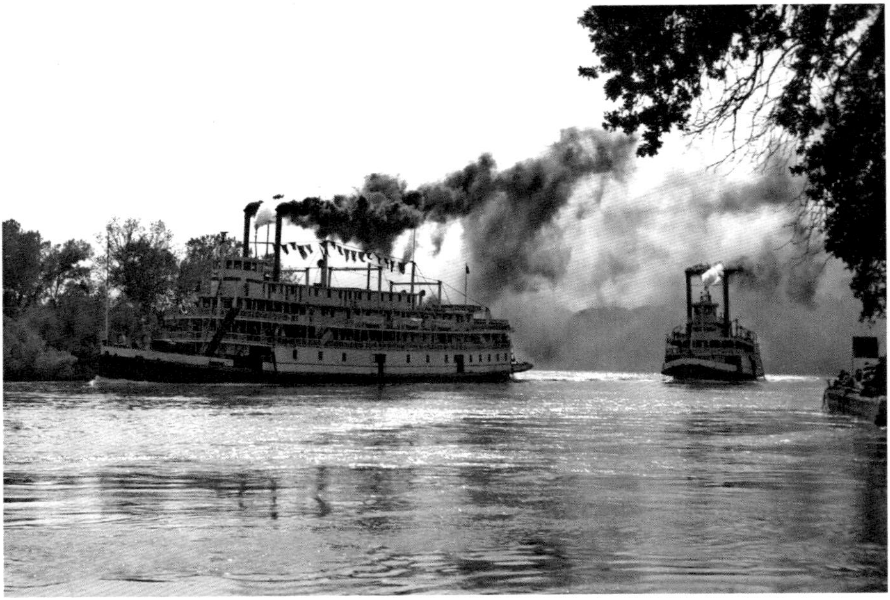

Pride of Paducah riverboat. *Courtesy Sacramento Room, Sacramento Public library.*

bound between I Street and Capitol Avenue and Second and Fourth Streets, located in the city's West End, where farmers and food producers recruited seasonal laborers to work in the outlying farm areas.[49] During slow periods of the agricultural season, many of these laborers spent their time in the city of Sacramento. By 1900, 336 Japanese settlers were living in the city and 1,209 in the county of Sacramento. Steam and electric railroads transported many of these laborers to Oroville, Marysville, Newcastle, Woodland, Vacaville, Stockton and Fresno. Riverboats carried them down the Sacramento Valley to Walnut Grove, Clarksburg, Isleton, Antioch and the islands of the San Joaquin Delta. Most of the Issei famers and migratory laborers along the Sacramento and American Rivers produced citrus fruits, berries, vegetables, sugar beets, hops and other commodities that required intensive hand labor and represented a sizable portion of those who were engaged in agriculture in the Sacramento Valley.[50]

Sacramento's Japantown became the hub that connected the Delta laborers and smaller farm communities. "[Japantown] gradually built up out of necessity because a lot of our parents could not speak English that well," recalled Toko Fujii, who was born in Stockton, California, in 1920 but grew up in Sacramento's Japantown neighborhood: "They were very reluctant

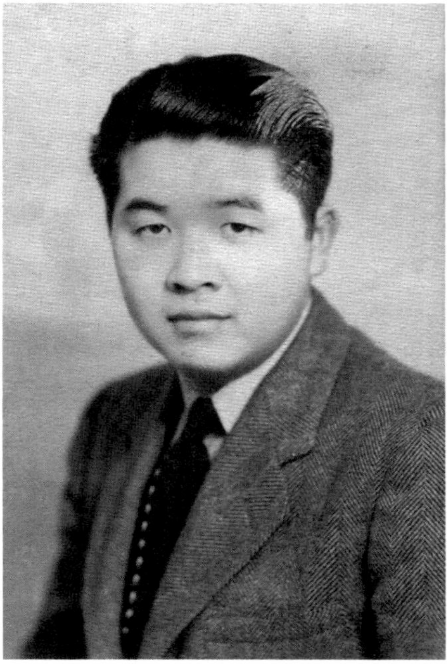

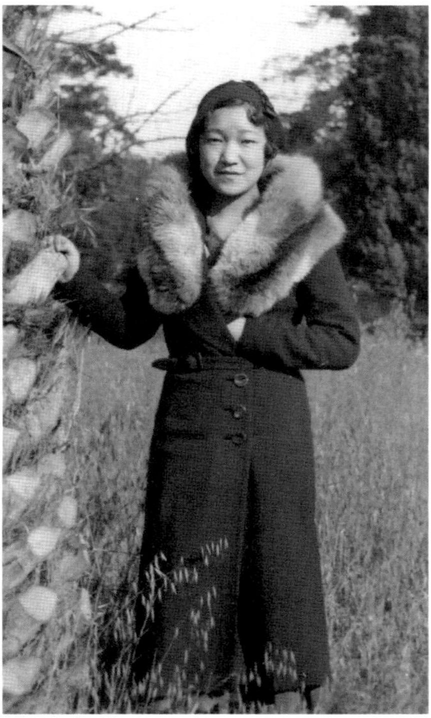

to go outside of the community for services. If there was a need, they would fill it, like clothing stores, drugstores, poultry and groceries. They felt more comfortable dealing with Japanese merchants rather than going outside of the community. There was substantial Japanese population in the farm areas, and they used to come in once or twice a week and shop in Japantown."[51] Notwithstanding Toko Fujii's insight, Japantown was not simply an outgrowth of Issei necessity; it also reveals the extent of white racism and racial zoning commonly practiced by white real estate companies. As another Sacramento resident, Frank Hiyama, put it, "Prewar Japanese could not live anyplace else. There was no other choice."[52] As a child, Alice Hayashi, who grew up around Sacramento's Japantown, rarely ventured beyond the artificial boundaries of her Japanese American neighborhood. "When I was growing up," she said, "the only street I knew was Fourth Street. I went to Lincoln Grade School and Junior High. I took the streetcar to Sacramento High for school. That was it."[53]

Top: Toko Fujii. *Courtesy Terry (Fujii) Kornelly.*

Bottom: Alice (Sakata) Hayashi. *Courtesy Sybil (Hayashi) Miyamoto.*

As the number of transient Japanese Americans increased in the Delta, the number of Japanese Americans engaged in business in Sacramento increased. A Japanese American lodging house, a bathhouse and two hotels opened in the area in 1891, and more than four of these lodging houses appeared in 1896. The first store providing Japanese merchandise, the first restaurant serving American and traditional Japanese meals and the first Japanese American barbershop all opened in 1893. And by 1909, Issei businessmen had established twelve dry goods stores in Japantown.[54] Japanese newspapers *Nichi Bei Shimbum* (*Japanese-American Newspaper*) located at 1216 Third Street and the *Shin Sekai* (*New World*) at 1313 Third Street held offices in Sacramento in 1906, and the *Ofu Nippon* (*Sakura City Japanese Daily*) began to circulate one year later. Some Japanese Americans worked as gardeners or porters in saloons and clubs, while others held domestic positions that brought them into the houses and establishments of whites. By the end of the first decade, Sacramento's Japanese American population had reached 3,874 in the county and 1,437 in the city and had opened up 207 businesses. These pioneering Issei of Sacramento constructed a well-organized ethnic subculture with various churches, doctors, associations, clubs, guilds and prefecture societies.[55] Japantown's wide range of small businesses appears as its most striking feature. Pool rooms, shoe repair shops, barber and beauty shops, grocery stores, bakery shops, drugstores, restaurants, hotels, rooms for rent, bathhouses, cleaners, laundry stores, tofu manufacturers, jewelry and watch repair, photography galleries, fish markets, import companies and a movie theater were some of the enterprises located in Japantown. These merchants supplied their own needs as well as provided provisions and Japanese goods to those working not far from the city.[56] Such a well-developed community provided comfort to a young Ai Miyasaki when she arrived in Japantown in 1918: "When I came to Sacramento, it was like Japan, more so than now. The groceries, like in Japan, were displayed outside the store…There were many Japanese. There was even a Japanese bathhouse and a few Japanese doctors, so we decided to stay awhile. We bought a rooming house and we all moved in."[57] Arriving about the same time as Miyasaki, Toshiko Igarashi, wife of Reverend Kenzaburo Igarashi of the First Japanese Baptist Church at 1530 Fifth Street on the corner of Fifth and P Streets, recalls her first impression of Sacramento's Japantown: "When I landed here, I was first impressed with the big Japanese town. Japanese Issei were thriving then, having big stores with three or four employees; in some stores maybe even seven or eight of them. There were rows of such stores on Third and Fourth Streets. On Saturdays and Sundays, a lot of people from the country—farms were also thriving then—came to Japanese Town."[58]

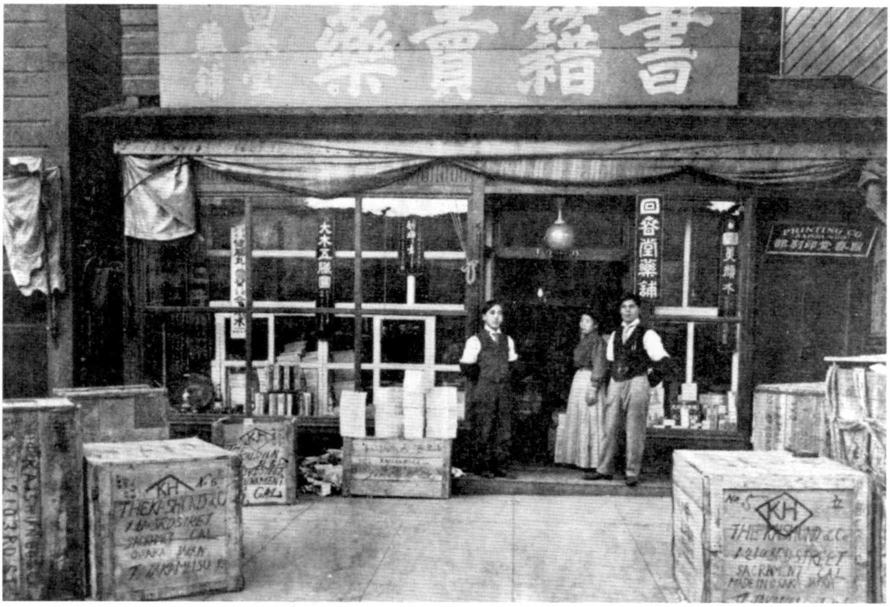

Hamai Kaishundo Drugs and Print Shop, 1210 Third Street. *Courtesy Center for Sacramento History, Sacramento Community Ethnic Survey Collection, 1983/146/1918.*

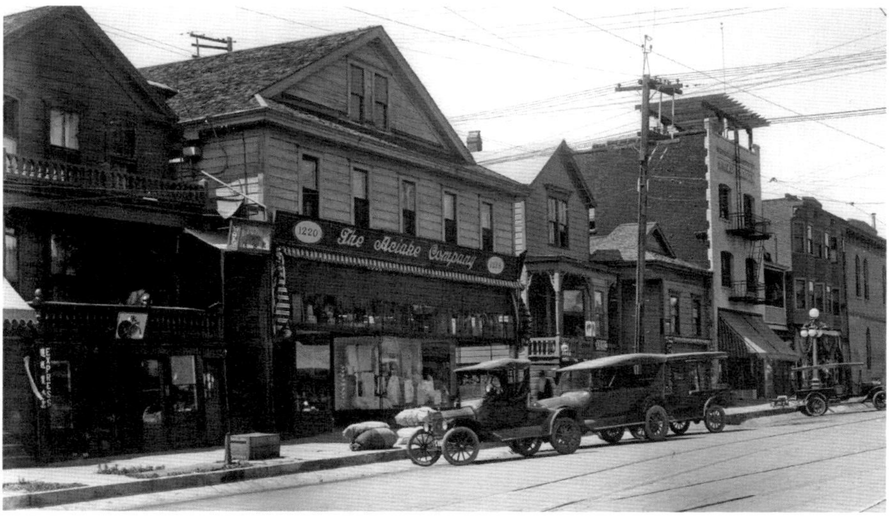

Third Street between L Street and Capitol Avenue, 1935. *Left to right:* Ohira Express Shipping, Higoya Boarding House, Ariake Dry Goods, Kitaura Taylor, Mikado Fish Market, Ishii's Eagle Drugs. *Courtesy California History Room. California State Library, 2008/3537.*

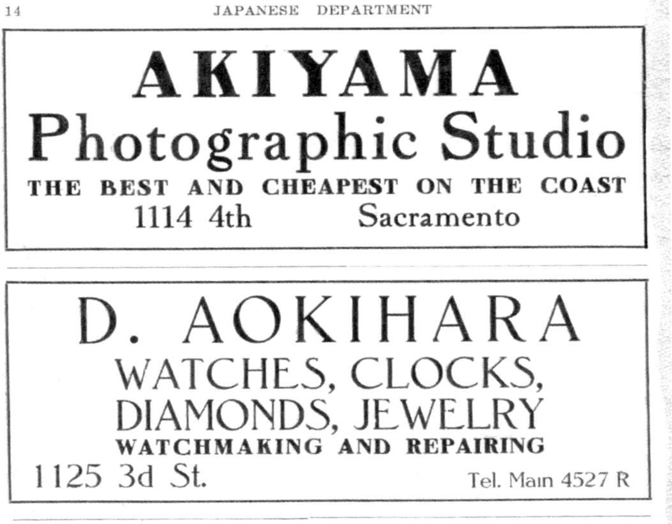

14 JAPANESE DEPARTMENT

AKIYAMA
Photographic Studio
THE BEST AND CHEAPEST ON THE COAST
1114 4th Sacramento

D. AOKIHARA
WATCHES, CLOCKS,
DIAMONDS, JEWELRY
WATCHMAKING AND REPAIRING
1125 3d St. Tel. Main 4527 R

Sacramento City Directory, 1913.

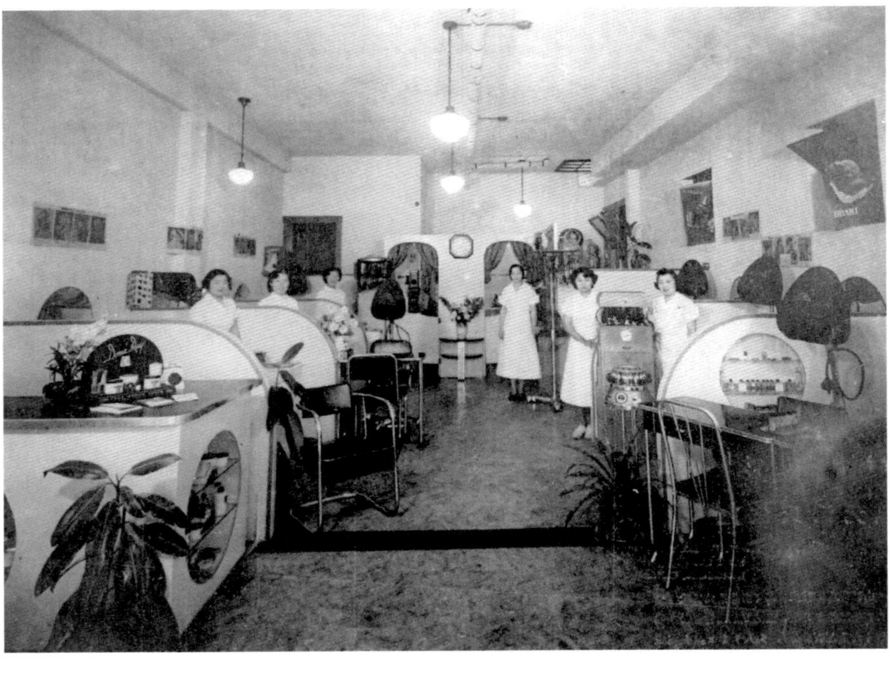

Ishima's beauty shop, 523 M Street. *Courtesy Center for Sacramento History, Sacramento Community Ethnic Survey Collection, 1983/146/1670.*

The first generation's success in small business stemmed from their devotion to their family and community and their dedication to individual thrift.[59] The variety of trades that existed to supply the needs of the urban sector provided many Japanese American laborers with opportunities to engage in various lines of trade or become self-employed small business owners, an occupation that enhanced their social prestige. Many became merchants, lodging house proprietors, tailors, shoemakers, cleaners and restaurant owners. One reporter revealed that a shoemaker in Sacramento had worked as a farmer, a grocer, a lumber dealer, a watchmaker, a photographer and a laundry proprietor since he had arrived in the city.[60]

This early period also witnessed the birth of various types of Japanese-owned medical facilities in the Sacramento area. In 1903, the Takeoka Ofu Byoin (Sakura City Hospital) opened at 410 O Street, becoming the first to dispense medical care, and six years later, Sacramento had five physicians and two dentists.[61] In 1915, pharmacist Miyakawa Tsunesaburo opened Eagle Hospital and Drug Company at 1210 Third Street, and ten years later, he built a new three-story Agnes Hospital at 1405 Fourth Street on the corner of Fourth and N Streets. Although the hospital was forced to close in 1933 during the depths of the Great Depression, Agnes offered Japanese Americans in the Sacramento area modern surgery rooms, X-ray equipment, private patient rooms and an interpreter service.[62] Even traditional Asian wellness practices made their appearance. It was not unusual for medical practitioners from Japan to hold special classes in traditional Eastern medicine. Michiko Takahashi, born in 1925, attended some of these classes held in the Naniwa Hotel at 1210 Fourth Street with her father, Shichiro Takahashi, who worked at Funahashi's Grocery store in the heart of Japantown: "People would come from Japan, and they wore the *hakama*. They would teach acupuncture and people would attend these classes, including my father. They all spoke in Japanese. Yuriko, my sister, she was very ill. So my papa thought maybe if he learned acupuncture he could help my sister."[63] Toshiko Igarashi recalled how important Japantown was to Japanese Americans who needed medical care at this time:

> *As for doctors, there were three or four Japanese doctors. One of them was from Tokyo University then called Tei-dai...I really didn't feel that I was in America. We Issei here in Sacramento still don't because we speak in Japanese. Yet, when people had to go to a doctor or had similar needs, those who could speak English, such as Christian store owners who spoke English and ministers...used to take care of them, nursing the sick,* [and

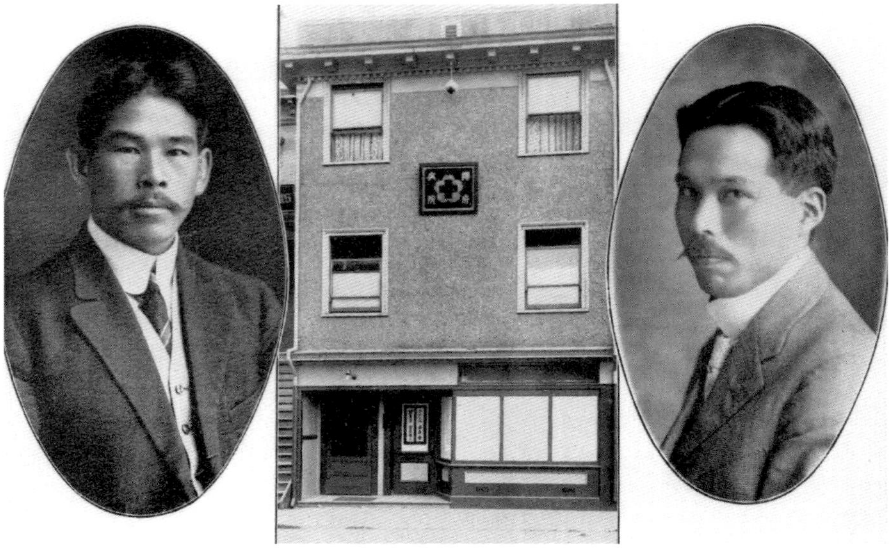

Takeoka Ofu Byoin (Sakura City Hospital), 314 M Street. *Translation courtesy Yoshimitsu Yajima. Image courtesy Center for Sacramento History, Sacramento Community Ethnic Survey Collection, 1983/146/2281.*

> taking them to the] *hospital. Few people knew how to go about getting general services of this nature.*[64]

Because they experienced much hostility among white boardinghouse owners who denied their services to them and because they naturally preferred to live among those who shared a similar culture and language, most of the Issei stayed in prefecture (*ken*) lodges run by other Japanese. Prefectures are regions in Japan with different dialects and customs. For example, immigrants from Hiroshima prefecture in Japan affiliated with the Hiroshima ken and referred to one another as *kenjinkai* or fellow *ken* people. Japanese prefecture boardinghouse keepers and hotel managers served as employment agents for Japanese lodgers. These prefecture houses also assisted in finding employment for other *ken* while serving as a common meeting ground for all Issei in the Sacramento Valley. Immigrants from Hiroshima opened a prefecture boardinghouse on Fourth Street in 1891 to serve their *ken* from Hiroshima, while those from the Kumamoto region housed their *ken* in the Kumamoto-Tamagawa Inn boardinghouse.[65] By 1909, Sacramento had thirty-seven of these boardinghouses, more than any other type of Japanese establishment.

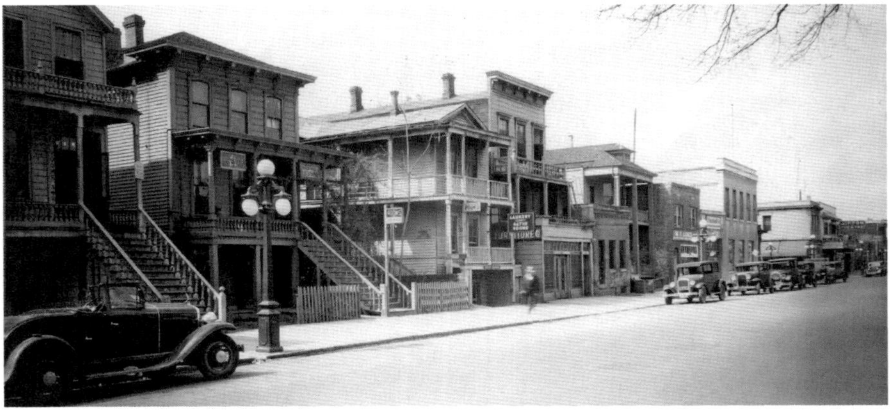

L Street between Fourth and Fifth Streets, 1935. *Left to right*: Kano Beauty Shop, Okamoto Rooms, Yamagata OK furniture, Nakamura Rooms, Okamoto Rooms, Funahashi Grocery, Sumitomo Bank. *Courtesy California History Room. California State Library, 2010/2348.*

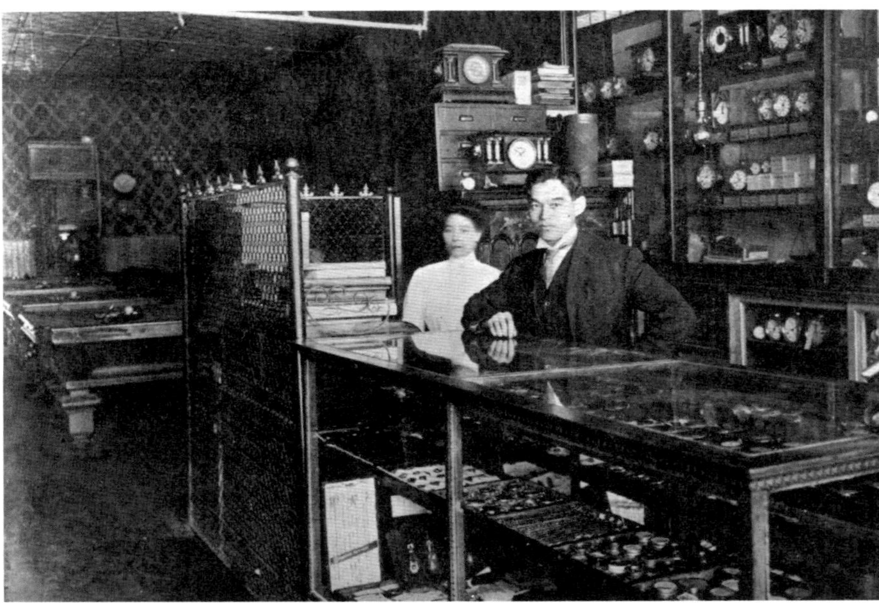

Aokihara's Watches, Clocks, Diamonds and Jewelry, 1125 Third Street, 1910s. *Courtesy Center for Sacramento History, Sacramento Community Ethnic Survey Collection, 1983/146/1896.*

The Hiroshima, Kochi, Wakayama, Yamaguchi, Kumamoto and Okayama prefecture housing lined both sides of Second, Third and Fourth Streets between L Street and Capitol Avenue and ranged from small cottages to three-story Victorian mansions. Residents took pride in the appearance of their housing. As an immigration reporter noted, "Almost without exception, the buildings are painted and in good repair and the premises are well kept. With very few exceptions the rooms are well furnished, having good beds and clean bedding, including pillow slips, counterpanes, etc., carpet or matting, and other furnishings of good quality."[66]

Because of the strong racial antagonism against the Japanese, whites refused to occupy houses near Japantown. As a general rule, Japanese American businessmen, their families and their employees lived in the rear or above the room used for business purposes. Because of these living arrangements, they were willing to pay high rents for the same structures in which they conducted business. This sparked a rise in the rental and market value of property occupied by them while the property value around Japantown fell as it became less desirable by whites. These areas remained low in value until they were occupied by Japanese American tenants or owners.[67] As the Japanese American population grew, Japanese lodging no longer held the distinction of serving exclusively their prefecture.[68]

During this early period of development, Sacramento's Japanese American neighborhood slowly began to shift from its previous location around Second and Fourth Streets and L Street and Capitol Avenue, close to where a large Chinese settlement stood, to form its own distinct neighborhood bound between Third and Fifth Streets and L and O Streets.[69] The formation of Japantown as a distinct ethnic community by 1910 was a response to the growing white exclusionist efforts that were gaining momentum throughout the city. The most notorious of the anti-Asian leaders, Dennis Kearney, who led the successful campaign to exclude Chinese in 1882, launched his attack against Japanese immigration as early as 1892, just as the nation was slipping into a recession. In the summer of 1892, he took his campaign to Sacramento, where, standing on a wooden crate on the corner of K and Fourth Streets, he gave a roaring speech to a cheering crowd of vigilant anti-Asian exclusionists. The next morning, the *Sacramento Daily Union* declared, "Dennis Kearney Is on the War Path Again." The writer continued: "Dennis Kearney, the well-known agitator, who won fame years ago on the 'sand lot' in San Francisco, has buckled on his armor again after a long rest. Dennis's slogan used to be 'the Chinese must go.' The Exclusion Act and other Chinese legislation quieted him, but now he is out with a new one. This time he says 'the Japs must go!'"[70] Along with Kearney, one of the earliest and most vocal anti-Japanese advocates in the nation was V.S. McClatchy, founder and owner of the *Sacramento Bee* newspaper. Between 1906 and 1945, McClatchy ran as many as ninety racially demeaning anti-Japanese editorial cartoons.[71]

Another reason for the geographical shift and creation of a separate neighborhood away from Chinatown was a response to the growing conflicts between Japan and China in the 1890s. The Sino-Japanese War between 1894 and 1895 caused violent tension in Sacramento among the residents of Chinatown and Japantown. Such violent altercations prompted a Sacramento newspaper to declare that a war had broken out between the two communities.[72] Hostilities between the two usually arose when Issei in the United States publicly celebrated their motherland's triumph, such as had happened in San Francisco and Honolulu.[73] However, such violence did not stop some seven hundred Japanese Americans from Sacramento from gathering in McKinley Park in the summer of 1895 to celebrate Japan's victory over China.[74]

Excluded from white trade unions, Japanese Americans established trade organizations to safeguard their economic standing. Confronting barriers that attempted to restrict them from white competition, just as they had in the agricultural field, they organized guilds to achieve their economic interests in city enterprises. When the Anti-Jap Laundry League boycotted Japanese Americans products, posted anti-Japanese advertisements and personally solicited white patrons, Issei businessmen organized their laundries as they did restaurants, boardinghouses, barbers, dry cleaners, tailors, grocery stores and carpenters, among other trades.[75] For example, Sacramento shoemakers organized their own guild to fix prices, control the location of shops, maintain a common supply house, handle apprenticeships and sustain a system of fraternal benefits. Because they were generally prohibited from joining American labor and fraternal organizations, Japanese Americans in Sacramento organized their own guilds, forming seven by 1909: the Boarding and Lodging House Keepers' Association, the Expressmen's Union, the Japanese Barbers' Union, two Japanese Restaurant Keepers' Associations, the Watchmakers' Union and the Carpenters' Union. The shoemakers belonged to a general organization of Japanese cobblers in various parts of California.[76]

As more Japanese immigrants began to arrive in significant numbers, a Sacramento chapter of the Japanese Association of America opened an office in 1900 in the Japanese American district, near Third and L Streets.

In the pre–World War II period, the Japanese Association of America served as the overriding political representative of the Japanese American population. Founded in San Francisco in 1895, the association, with help from the Japanese government, operated as a federation of state and local organizations to assist new arrivals at immigration stations. The association promoted social and educational programs, kept immigrant records, offered legal advice, provided translators and ultimately served as a mediator between the Japanese American community and the local authorities.[77]

During the 1920s and 1930s, cities across the West Coast witnessed an efflorescence of Japanese American enterprises. In 1929, Japanese Americans in Los Angeles operated 1,849 enterprises, and by 1940, 40 percent were self-employed, handling more than 60 percent of all small businesses in the city and grossing an estimated $26.5 million.[78] Two factors contributed to this development: first, anti-Japanese farm movements in California, Oregon and Washington; and second, the increase of Japanese women in the United States—over sixty-six thousand between 1908 and 1924. First, anti-Japanese farm movements, most notably embodied in the Alien Land Act of 1920, which completely barred the Issei from owning land or placing their property in the name of their American-born children, forced some Japanese Americans farmers to look for work in urban sectors. In part, urban anti-Japanese forces designed the Immigration Act of 1924 to halt this anticipated influx of Japanese Americans into the cities.[79] Second, and more significant, as increasing numbers of Japanese women immigrated to the United States and started families, the Japanese American population began to settle in urban centers, where better educational facilities existed for their children, and open up small businesses.[80] The United States Census reflected this rural-to-urban migration. In California in 1910, about 45 percent of Japanese Americans settled in urban centers, with only a 2 percent increase in this figure by 1920. By 1930, 55 percent settled in cities, with only a 1 percent increase by 1940.[81] Clearly, the largest migration, a 10 percent increase, occurred during the decade that witnessed the enactment of one of the most significant anti-Japanese legislative decrees: the Alien Land Law of 1920.[82] Washington and Oregon also passed similar land laws that were detrimental to Japanese American farming, and the migration shift from rural to urban in these two states paralleled California's. Therefore, during the 1920s, the Japanese immigration shifted from a single-male, migratory-dominated pattern to a more settled family-centered trend; second, the Japanese Americans settled in more urban environments. These two changes fostered the creation of many distinct, highly organized, self-sustaining Japanese American subcultures throughout the cities and towns of the West Coast states.

Social, Religious and Educational Organizations

Social institutions reinforced the economic foundations of Japantown. Sociologist John Modell points out that, in getting started, as few as one Issei in six received assistance from organizations such as churches or immigration companies.[83] This may reflect a strong cultural trait shared among the Issei that stressed hard work and self-reliance and shunned aid from the government, values they carried with them from the Tokugawa period in Japan (1600–1868). However, when Issei did need help, they could turn to their neighborhood prefecture *kenjinkai* or *ken*-affiliated social clubs, which bound the Issei into a mutually beneficial communal social-security system. The prefecture clubs supervised the social and economic welfare of the immigrants, published newspapers, offered legal advice to members, sponsored the finance-oriented *tanomoshi* and served as employment agencies. By 1909, Japanese Americans in Sacramento had organized at least eight of these societies.[84] The *kenjinkai* sponsored social and benevolent activities during both Japanese and American holidays.[85] James Kubo remembers his Sacramento *kenjinkai* throwing grand celebrations for its members, as well as providing charity to the less fortunate: "They would throw birthday parties for people. The biggest [celebration] was New Year's. The *kenjinkai* would also help out the transient fruit pickers who would travel from here to [Los Angeles]. When it got warmer, they came up north and picked cherries, plums, asparagus, and then go to Oregon and then come back to Sacramento. For thirty dollars a month, *kenjinkai* took care of room and board."[86]

The *kenjinkai* club appeared at the apex of a pyramid of traditional ethnic relief organizations expected to aid destitute Japanese Americans. The clubs encouraged individuals to be industrious and thrifty and make provisions for hard times. But the *kenjinkai* always provided assistance to their members, buried the indigent and helped to pay medical bills. Welfare demands were so few that pre–World War II Japanese Americans had an astounding record of virtually complete absence from public welfare services, even during the Great Depression.[87] But responsibility for ethnic community-based relief programs did not always fall on the *kenjinkai*. For example, during the Depression, the Sacramento chapter of the Japanese Association of America organized an emergency relief program, providing food to the destitute during the night so that recipients of the charity would not be embarrassed.[88]

Japanese American churches also helped in establishing a stable and diversified social life for Japanese immigrants. When not providing spiritual and moral guidance, they offered employment advice, provided instruction in Japanese and English, organized athletic events, sponsored Boy Scouts and assisted in child care. In 1891, Christian ministers from the Japanese Methodist Church in San Francisco traveled by riverboat to Sacramento to hold worship services. On February 12, 1892, Reverend Tonochichi Kihara helped to establish the first Japanese Methodist Church of Sacramento in a house at 501 I Street. This was the third Japanese Methodist church to appear in the United States. A few months later, the church moved to 310 Capitol Avenue, and thirteen years later, it moved to 417 P Street. From the beginning, the church served as a boardinghouse for young Japanese immigrants. Some of the converts among this group became the lay leaders of the church. Early in 1913, Dr. H.B. Johnson met with a group of Japanese immigrants to organize a branch Methodist Christian mission and Japanese school in the town of Florin. This mission evolved into the Florin Methodist Church in July of that same year.[89]

The first Buddhist Church in Sacramento appeared in 1899 when, on December 7, Reverend Shuye Sonoda and Reverend Kakuro Nishijima dedicated the temple at 1221 Third Street. Reverend Ryotetsu Hara, the first resident minister, led the congregation, which included many members of the Young Men's Buddhist Association. As church attendance swelled during the first year, the congregation relocated the temple in August 1900 to a much larger location at 418 O Street. In 1908, the temple inaugurated an English school that taught children's and adult classes. Most of the adult males learned English through evening classes offered by the Buddhist Mission, the Episcopal Mission, the Methodist Mission and the Independent Mission.[90] By 1912, the Buddhist

Opposite, top: Japanese Methodist Episcopal Church at 417 P Street on Easter Sunday, 1918. *Courtesy Japanese American Archival Collection. Department of Special Collections and University Archives, California State University–Sacramento.*

Opposite, bottom: Sakura City Honganji Buddhist Church, 1912. *Translation courtesy Yoshimitsu Yajima. Image courtesy Center for Sacramento History, Sacramento Community Ethnic Survey Collection, 1983/146/1921.*

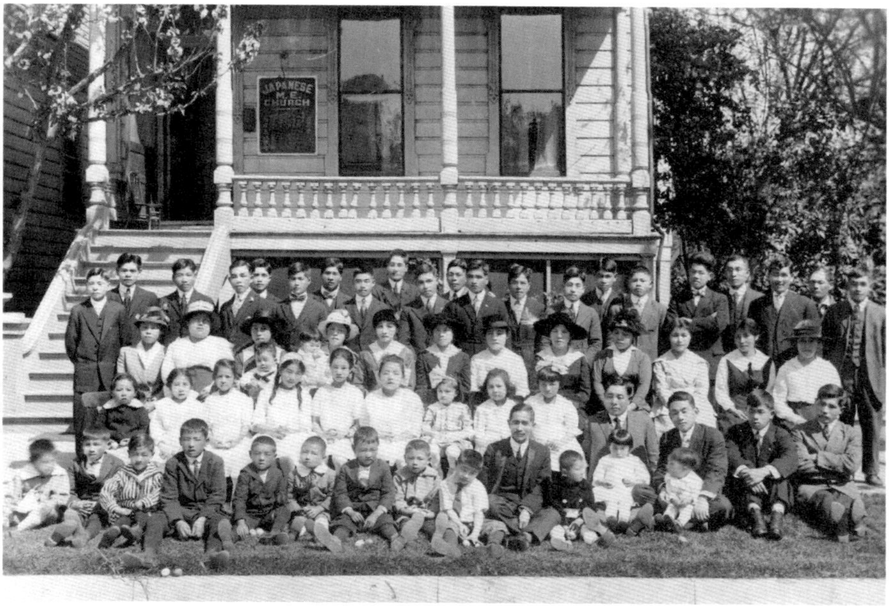
JAPANESE
M.E.
CHURCH

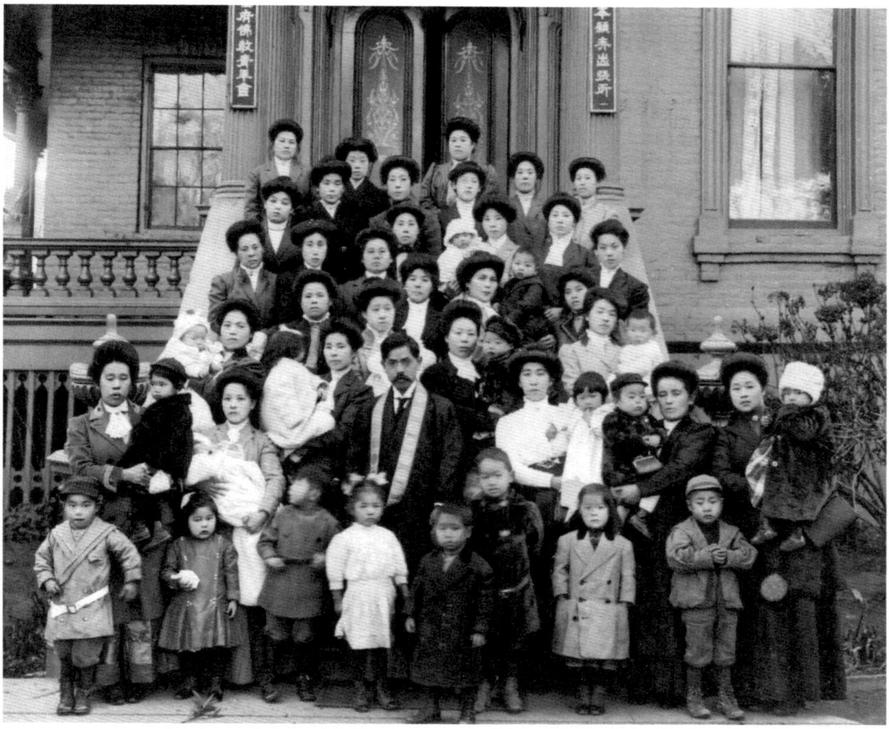
府佛教青年會
本願寺出張所

Temple had extended missionary services to such areas as Colusa, Chico, Oroville, Marysville and Penryn and had sponsored a number of lectures by a Buddhist missionary from India, Dr. Madhinand, attended by many whites. Also at this time, the first incorporated Young Buddhist Association of California appeared, as did the Sacramento Women's Association. By 1931, Buddhist missionaries in Sacramento had recruited enough followers to establish another Buddhist sect, the Nichiren Buddhist.[91]

A variety of Japanese religions had begun to make their appearance in Sacramento throughout the 1920s. Among the first were the Shingon sect, Daishi-Ko and the Tenrikyo Church. The Tenrikyo began as a missionary outpost near Third and L Streets in a hotel operated by Shonosuke Doi and his wife and grew under the enthusiastic and ambitious missionary efforts of Akira Iwama, who traveled as far as Stockton, Walnut Grove, Newcastle and Marysville. By the end of 1928, the success of their missionary work brought Mitsuzo Funo and Kumakichi Kojima to found a permanent church near Third and N Streets.[92] Another Japanese church, Konkokyo, appeared in 1930. In the summer of that year, the Reverend Yaukichi Yasumura began holding *toritsugi* meditation services in the Enkoji Hotel on Capital Avenue. One year later, he and his group of about one hundred followers established the Konko Church first at 522 O Street and then at a much larger facility at 604 O Street.[93]

Japanese immigrants also established a Baptist church in Sacramento. In November 1920, six Japanese Christians, under the leadership of Reverend Kiichi Hijikata, founded a *Seisho Gakuen* (Bible institute) at 1530 Fifth Street on the corner of Fifth and P Streets. After Reverend Hijikata left for Japan, the church began to grow under the leadership of Reverend H.Y. Shibata. In January 1922, the small congregation changed its name to First Japanese Baptist Church and was officially chartered in 1926. By the late 1920s, membership had increased dramatically, expanding church activities. They organized a Women's Society, a Boy Scouts chapter and a kindergarten school and established branch ministries in Woodland and Mayhew. The Japanese Baptist Church in Sacramento also sponsored the Camelia Mission, located four miles from Oak Park. The mission, under the guidance of Reverend and Mrs. Muraoka, ministered to about fifty families in the area. In the fall of 1930, the Northern Baptist Convention sent Reverend E.D. Sims to help establish a Japanese Christian Center next to the Baptist church. By the time of the dedication ceremony for the newly established Japanese Christian Center in July 1932, membership had grown to 96 people, with 126 Sunday school attendees and 25 youth group members.[94]

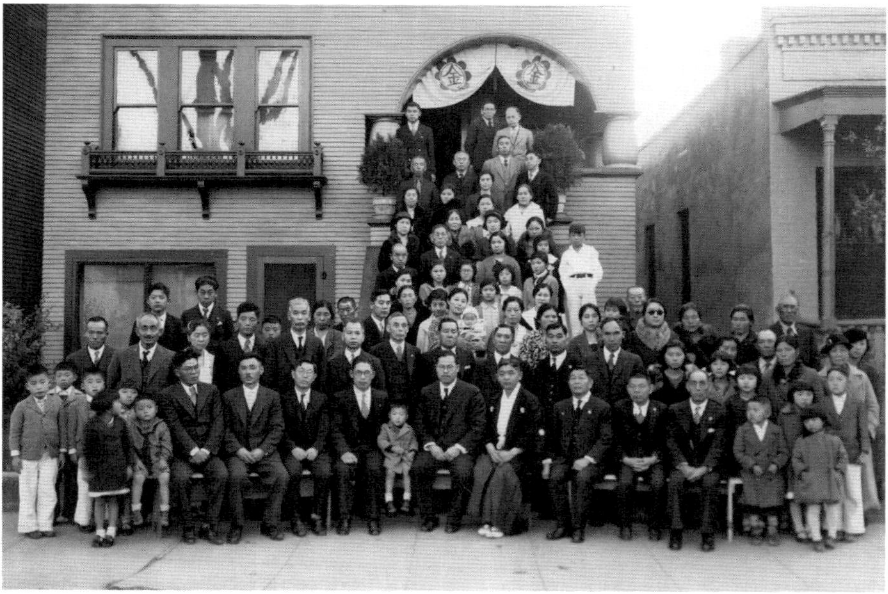

Konko Church. *Courtesy Reverends Hideo and Yomisu Oya.*

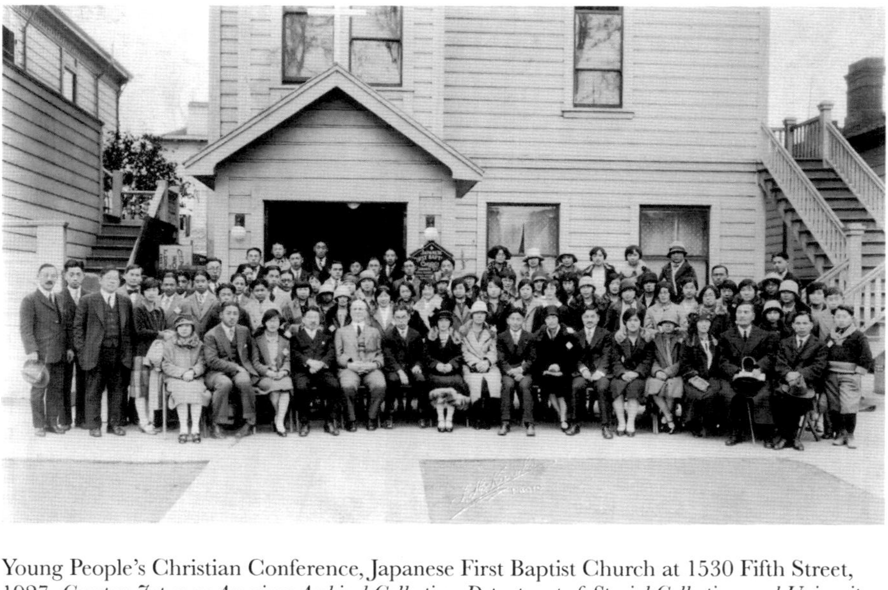

Young People's Christian Conference, Japanese First Baptist Church at 1530 Fifth Street, 1927. *Courtesy Japanese American Archival Collection. Department of Special Collections and University Archives, California State University–Sacramento.*

The Japanese Presbyterian Mission, which started as Japanese Church of Christ, began in 1912 on the corner of Fifth and Capitol Avenue. Like most Japanese Christian churches in Sacramento at this time, the Presbyterian Mission was a residence converted into a place of worship. Reverend Isamu Nakamura described the manse house behind the church as "an old and ghostly house with four or five rooms on the second floor, and the kitchen, dining room, and living rooms…on the first floor."[95] Some Issei also attended the Japanese Episcopal Mission from 1894 to 1917 and the Japanese Independent Mission from 1900 to 1930.[96] In 1940, while waiting for their new church to be built on the corner of Eighth and T Streets, members rented the Showa Hall on the corner of Third and O Streets. The Parkview Presbyterian Church has served Sacramento for over one hundred years.

As more Japanese women settled and had children in Sacramento, the cultural composition of Sacramento's public schools began to change. Foreign-born and native-born Japanese American children attended Sacramento's public schools regularly, even after the California legislature legalized Japanese American segregated schools in 1921. As an Immigration Commission reported, "All of the public schools of Sacramento are freely open to Japanese children of school age. The Japanese accept the educational opportunities offered, and the children are regular in their attendance."[97] In 1909, seventy-four Japanese American children were attending public schools in Sacramento. By the 1920s, most were attending Sacramento High School and Lincoln Primary and Junior High, which, because of its location at Fourth and P Streets, served as the southernmost boundary to Japantown. Japanese American students at Lincoln School formed a significant number of the student body, making up 33 percent by 1941.[98]

Japanese American churches also provided opportunities for education, particularly in Japanese subjects. Maintaining Japanese traditions—especially the language—among their American-born children became a central concern for the Issei. By 1940, the neighborhood had six Japanese language schools and twenty-three in the county. The Sakura language school, located behind the Buddhist Church at 418 O Street, had as many as ten teachers and almost five hundred students before the war. As Marian Uchida, who attended the Sakura School, said, "The parents didn't want their kids to forget their native tongue, so we all had to go to Japanese school. We had no choice."[99] The Buddhist Mission organized a supplementary school next to the Lincoln School to provide instruction in Japanese history, language and geography. This establishment served

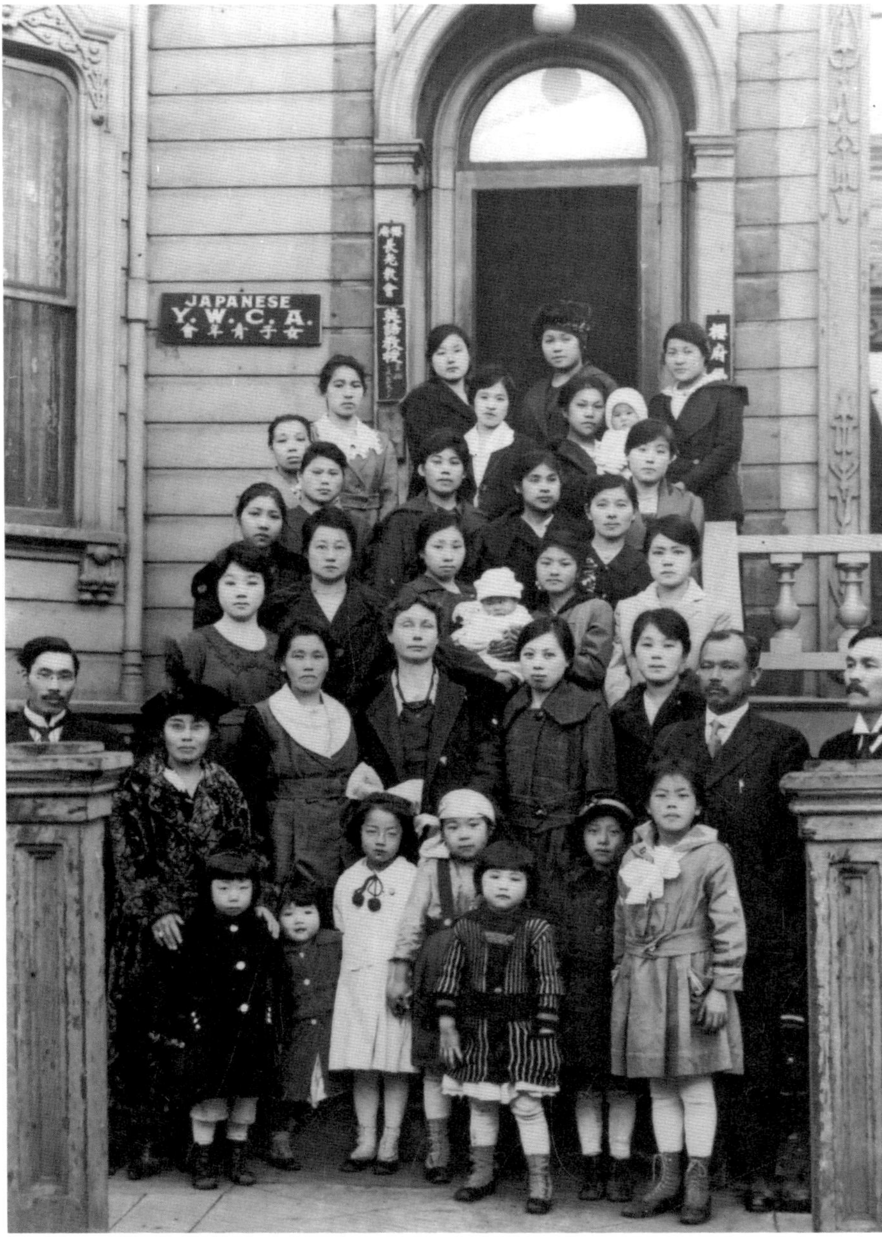

YWCA Sakura City English School. *Translation courtesy Yoshimitsu Yajima. Image courtesy Center for Sacramento History, Sacramento Community Ethnic Survey Collection, 1983/146/1907.*

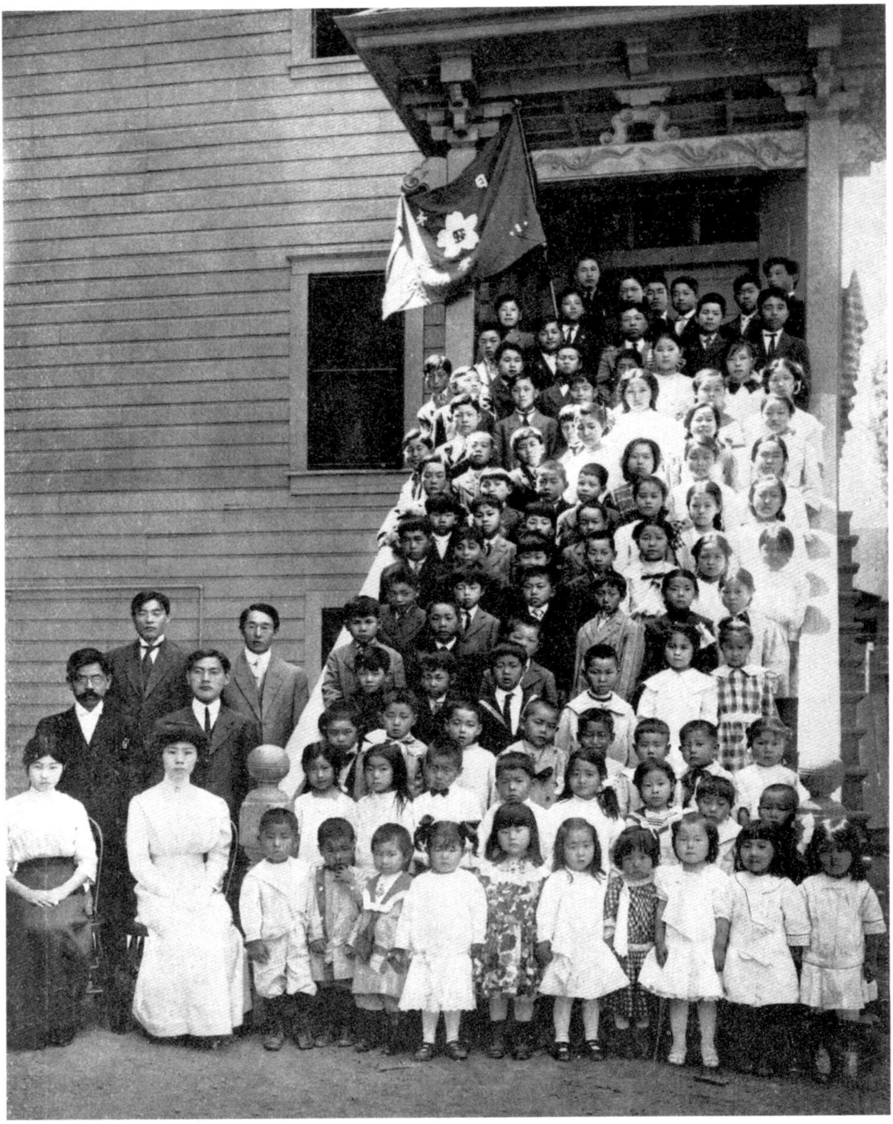

Sakura Japanese Language School, Buddhist Church. *Translation courtesy Yoshimitsu Yajima. Image courtesy Center for Sacramento History, Sacramento Community Ethnic Survey Collection, 1983/146/2270.*

mostly as a boarding school for children whose parents lived in the outlying farming communities such as Wheatland, Florin, West Sacramento, Acampo, Clarksburg, Freeport, Walnut Grove, Isleton and Oak Park.[100] Clearly, by the 1930s, Sacramento's Japanese American population had succeeded in creating a sense of place for themselves, fostering a vibrant, culturally rich, socially diversified community in the heart of Sacramento's downtown area.

Banks and the *Tanomoshi*

The first generation also made inroads into the field of banking, establishing the first Japanese bank, Ofu Kinyu Sha, in 1906 at 1007 Third Street near the intersection with J Street. As well as serving as a savings institution with a capital in excess of $65,000 by the end of 1910, the Ofu Bank financed Japanese enterprises and served as an agent in sending money abroad. In 1914, the Ofu Bank collapsed.[101] In its place appeared the Nippon Bank until it went under in 1923 as a result of the post–World War I recession.[102] The instability that characterized Sacramento's Japanese American banks at this time appeared in many other Japanese American banks in other cities in California. In fact, before 1930, most Asian banks in California had a mortality rate close to 100 percent, principally because of the California Banking Act of 1910. Prior to the law, nine Japanese American banks of various sizes were in operation in the United States. Afterward, all but two went out of existence. The two biggest casualties, the Golden Gate Bank and the Japanese-American Bank, folded in 1910. The two surviving banks were the Industrial Bank of Fresno and the Nippon Bank of Sacramento.[103] Issei in Sacramento were without a stable financial institution until the Japanese-incorporated Sumitomo Bank established a branch on the corner of Fourth and L Streets. The incorporated Yokohama and Sumitomo Banks had offices in San Francisco and Los Angeles as well.[104] However, these incorporated banks were interested exclusively in foreign exchange. Further, these banks had a reputation of being just as cautious as white-run credit institutions. Sacramento optometrist James Kubo commented, "At that time, the Sumitomo Bank was a very conservative bank. It wouldn't take any chances, wouldn't stick its neck out for anybody. That's its history. So, even at Sumitomo, you had a hell of a time getting money from them. But they were willing to take your deposit."[105]

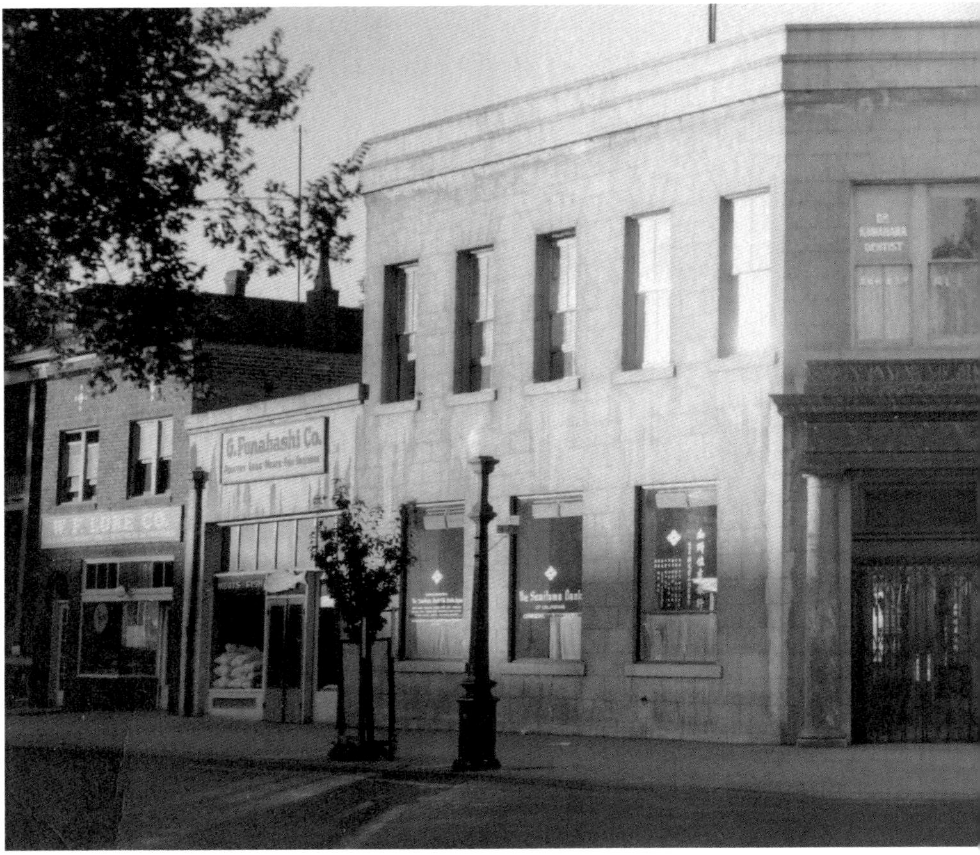

Corner of Fourth and L Streets. Sumitomo Bank, Funahashi Groceries, Kawahara Dentistry, Taketa Law Office, 1940. *Courtesy Sybil (Hayashi) Miyamoto.*

The incorporated banks' lack of support for Japanese Americans engaged exclusively in American markets encouraged the immigrants to rely on traditional rotating credit associations, or local money pools, as their principal device for capitalizing small businesses.[106] Variously called *ko* or *tanomoshi* (in Hawaii, the Pacific Northwest and Northern California) or *mujin* (in Southern California), these credit organizations, adapted from the thirteenth-century Chinese customs, were extremely popular in rural Japan as late as the 1930s.

In the United States, the membership of *tanomoshi* associations usually consisted of immigrants from the same prefecture or village in Japan. These

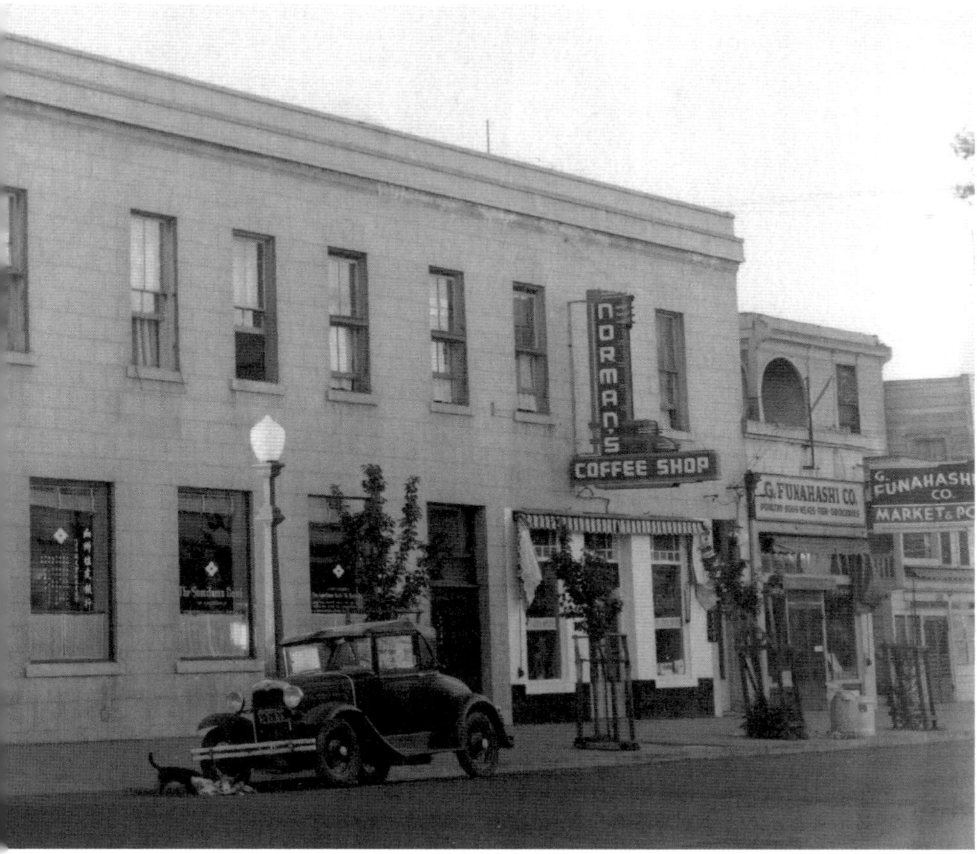

groups were called *kenjinkai*. Congruent with the Japanese tradition of neighborliness, neighborhood and friendship groups started *tanomoshi* clubs. Once an individual borrowed from the combined community fund, he was obligated to pay back at regular meetings the full stipulated contribution. Participants tendered interest payments as gifts rather than as payments for the use of money. Fred Matsuda, whose family belonged to the Kochi *kenjinkai*, recalled, "Everybody had their own line of credit. It was generated from dues, and each month someone would take it out. But you could only take it out once a month and you had to pay it back. It went to whoever needed help. It was a way of helping each other out without going to the bank, especially for

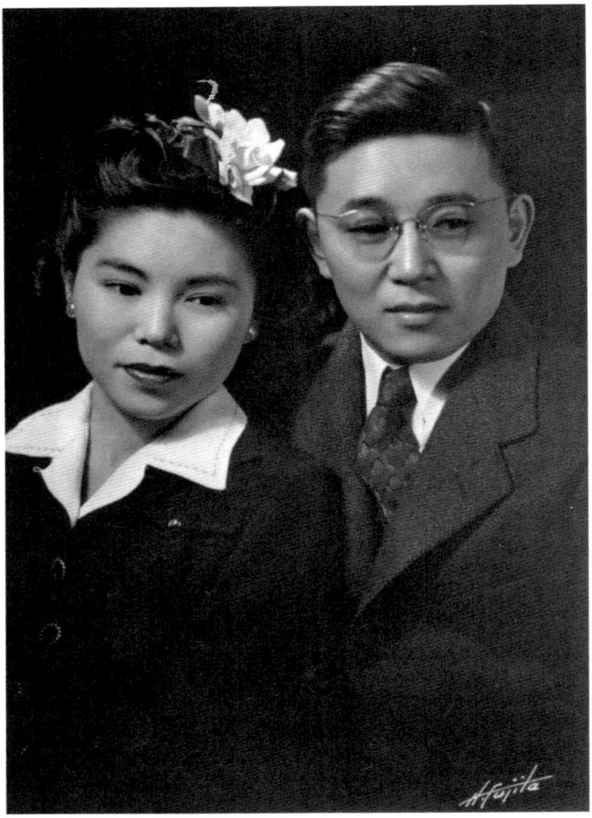

James and Tsugi Kubo.
Courtesy Douglas Kubo.

those who couldn't own property." Their meetings also served as social and business gatherings where members entertained one another with friendly conversation and discussed their financial concerns over sake and dinner. The *tanomoshi* circumvented racial barriers erected by white-owned banks and credit institutions in California by permitting Japanese, with or without credit, to obtain financing for business enterprises.[107] James Kubo's father held the position of treasurer for one such *tanomoshi* in Sacramento:

> *At that time, the Japanese weren't too welcome, especially the older people. It was very hard to get loans and insurance for their businesses. So, for their own protection, they formed their own organizations.* [The *tanomoshi*] *was basically a social club but helped out with finances as well. The members of the association would pay dues to build a kitty. If you wanted to start a business but had no money and you go to a bank, they are going to turn*

> *you down. So you come to a group. That's the way a lot of people started because they had no money and the banks weren't even an option. My dad had a little group, and he helped some doctors, dentists, some attorneys. The beauty is that nobody backed out or quit on them. They all paid their bills. The Japanese community is very small and very tight knitted. If you did something wrong, everybody knew about it. Even after the war started, people used to come over and pay off bills. They used to come out and pay my dad because he was treasurer of the organization.*[108]

A 1911 Immigration Commission report on Sacramento noted the prevalence of these local community financial partnerships: "The vast majority of the businessmen were first employed as laborers, primarily tenant farmers, before amassing enough capital to engage in business in the city. In many cases they were financially aided by partnerships and by securing loans from personal friends or credit from the unions they formed."[109]

Without the customary system of the *tanomoshi* and formation of trade guilds, the Issei would not have developed the sound economic structure found within the ethnic enclaves in cities such as Seattle, Portland, San Francisco, San Jose, Los Angeles and Sacramento.[110]

Ethnic Economy

Because of racial barriers erected against the Japanese, Issei settlers in North America developed an interdependent, rural-urban ethnic economy in which growers were linked to distributers, who in turn were linked to retailers. This entrepreneurial strategy was reinforced by Japanese cultural values of mutual support within the community.[111] Japanese pioneers in Sacramento also developed this type of economy. Japantown become an important business and social center to the outlying farmers and truck gardeners, providing them with entertainment, sports teams, language schools, religious instruction, Japanese meals, places to sell their fruits and vegetables and stores where they could purchase manufactured goods such as tea, soft drinks, rice, canned fish, meats and sauce—most of them purchased at Japanese provision stores.[112] Karri Yagi, a Nisei born in 1915 in Wheatland, California, remembers riding into Sacramento as a child with his parents and other Japanese American farmers on a horse-pulled wagon to stock up on provisions: "We used to come down across the I Street Bridge or Capitol Bridge into downtown. We had to come in about once a month for supplies. We grew our own vegetables and other foods, so we had to come into town to get rice, coffee, canned milk. We could stay all day until dusk so the horses could see to go back to the ranch."[113]

Issei living in Sacramento's rural surroundings also were tied to their city counterparts through a variety of friendly informal services, such as banking and mail distribution. These services reinforced urban-rural interdependence, binding the first generation into a tightly woven community. James Kubo recalls that many nights his father's candy store on Fourth Street served as an informal day-care center for farmers:

> *At that time when the Issei farmers would get married or have a birthday, the community would have a party which started around six in the evening and last until midnight. They would sit around and drink and sing until the early morning. So the farmers would bring their kinds into Japantown and give their kids a quarter or two and drop them off in front of the Nippon Theater to see a movie while they went to the celebration. After the kids got through with the movie, there was no place in town to go except my dad's candy store. So all these farmers would tell their kids to "wait for me over there." He never closed the store until all the kids were picked up.*[114]

Japanese American merchants were mutually dependent on those working in agriculture in the surrounding areas. Contact with truck gardeners assured the produce market owner of a regular supply of high-quality, select vegetables. In 1909, about 150 truck gardeners worked in the Sacramento area—55 percent were Japanese Americans who cultivated an average of ten acres each. Most of the gardens were located in the five areas around Y Street, Riverside Road, Brighton, Broderick and Florin. The Japanese American families who owned these gardens did all the work themselves, except when they hired extra help during the summer harvest months. Japanese American truck farmers brought to market their daily harvest in the central business district of Japantown, where they sold to fruit and vegetable stands, larger grocery stores and peddlers who served the country communities and small villages.[115] In addition, many of these wholesalers delivered fresh produce to grocers located in the foothills. Japanese Americans soon gained a favorable reputation among customers as "excellent gardeners," providing the best truck crops in town.[116] Produce and dry goods dealers, which could be found on every street corner in Japantown, conducted the largest volume of business among all Japanese

American traders in Sacramento. Chief among these establishments was the Aki Company (1908–38) at 1122–30 Fourth Street, on the corner of Fourth and L Streets. Like most Japanese American grocery stores, the Aki Company sold half Japanese imports and half American goods.[117] Another early enterprise was Koimori's Kii Company (1909–23) at 300 M Street on the corner of Third and M Streets. In 1926, the Japanese Association of the Sacramento Valley moved into the Kii Company location. Two other early landmark Japantown importers were the Nishimura family's Ariake Company (1909–32) at 1218–220 Third Street between L and M Streets and the Matsuho family's Inaka Company at 1225 Fourth Street (1913–32). When Inaka went under as a result of the Great Depression, the Kuroko family moved their photography studio from 1114 Third Street to a section of the Inaka building, while Matsuda's hardware (1933–42) moved into the remaining portion. While there were other smaller photography studios, such as Toyo and Oyama, Kuroko photography (1913–42) was one of the largest of its kind.[118]

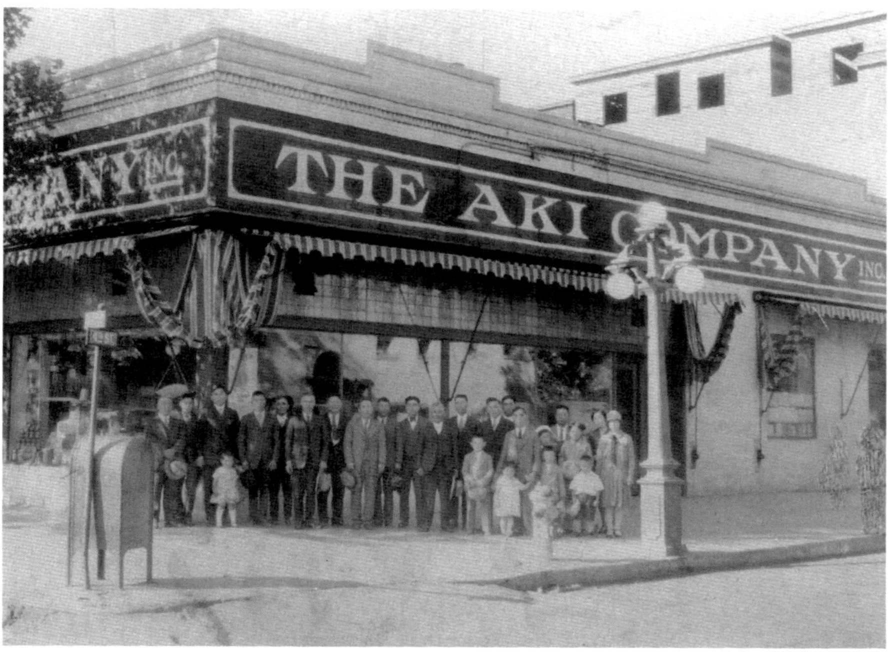

Okamoto, Katsumata and Omachi in front of Aki Co., corner of Fourth and L Streets. *Courtesy Okamoto family.*

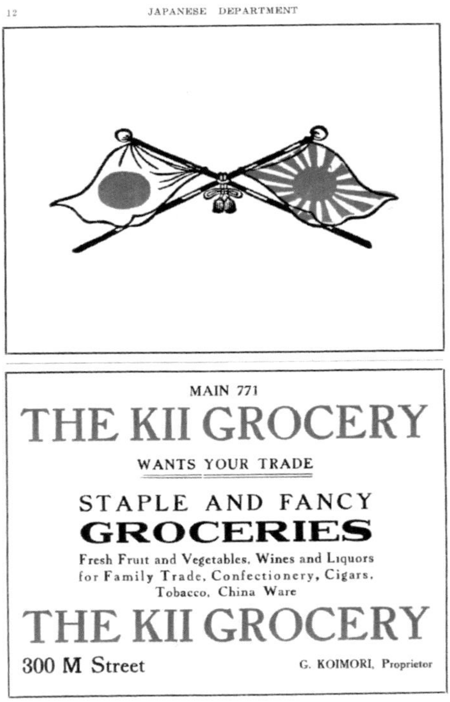

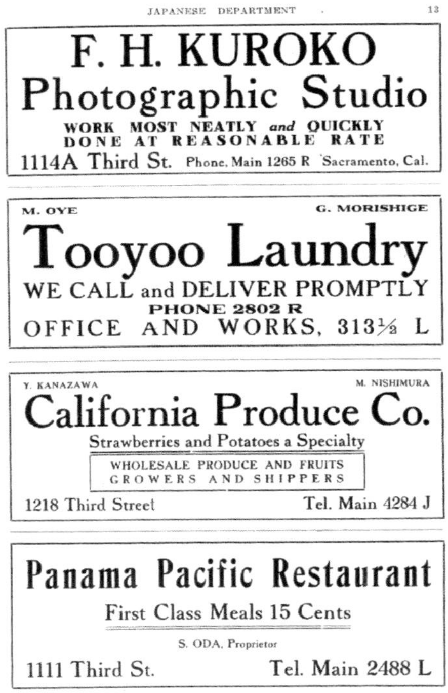

Left: Sacramento City Directory, 1913.

Right: Sacramento City Directory, 1909. "Tooyoo Laundry" should read "Toyo Laundry."

Japantown's interdependence with the smaller Japanese American rural communities that had developed in places like Isleton, Courtland, Clarksburg, Walnut Grove, Florin, Broderick, Franklin Boulevard, Pocket, Mayhew, West Sacramento and Wheatland was best illustrated in the recession years following World War I (1919–22) and again during the Great Depression of the 1930s. Because the community was interlocked both economically and socially, economic ripples generally affected everyone, rural or urban. At the close of World War I, war-torn Europe decreased its demand for American produce, driving price levels down for American crops. Further complicating problems, in 1920, heavy rains and dense fogs hovered over the crop fields in the Sacramento Valley during harvest time. Many farmers lost all their crops, and banks foreclosed on their loans. The enactment of the new Alien Land Law that same year made it even more difficult for many Japanese American farmers to regain a strong foothold in agriculture. The Nippon Bank in Sacramento went bankrupt in 1923 as a direct result of the failure of Japanese American farmers. Historians Audrie Girdner and Anne Loftis state:

> *Profits often depend on whether or not farmers did well enough to pay their bills. Weather and low crop prices could be calamitous for everybody. In the early nineteen twenties after a season of heavy rains in the Sacramento area, many farmers went into bankruptcy. Sacramento Nippon Bank was overextended and had to close, with consequent losses to depositors and borrowers, after which people used the Sumitomo Bank.*[119]

Economic recovery began by 1923, spawning a slow but steady growth in agricultural renewal. This recovery contributed to the success of businessmen in Japantown. Issei Toshiko Igarashi, who came to Sacramento in 1920 and opened a grocery and hardware store on the corner of Third and L Streets, remembers those promising times: "In those days, when Japanese people were thriving—since the people on the farm were also thriving—we piled up around one thousand bales of rice in front of the store on one New Year's Eve. Also eight hundred bottles of Kikkoman [soy sauce]."[120]

However, the stock market crash of 1929, an economic calamity that affected people in all ethnic and social groups to one degree or another, posed the greatest threat to Japantown's vibrant commercial district. Some of the grocery stores that depended on the surrounding agricultural sectors folded permanently. Chikaji Teramoto, who settled in Sacramento in 1920, recalled, "Gradually the picture or whole atmosphere of the Japanese community changed. It wasn't so lively as before, and the people started looking out for their own interests a little more seriously. Where the dry goods stores used to flourish, well, they dwindled down and most of them closed down after that."[121] The quantitative evidence substantiates this claim. The Japanese American population in the city of Sacramento declined during the decade of the 1930s from 3,240 to 2,800.[122] This demographic reduction can be attributed to a multiplicity of factors that include dismal economic conditions; the effects of the National Origins Immigration Act of 1924, an immigration act that was primarily designed to shut out Asian and Eastern European immigration; and the growing anti-Japanese American sentiment during that time. The West End of Sacramento's downtown district, an area close to Japantown, began to deteriorate, like other urban centers, because of neglected investment and construction. The Depression slowed and, in many cases, reversed migration

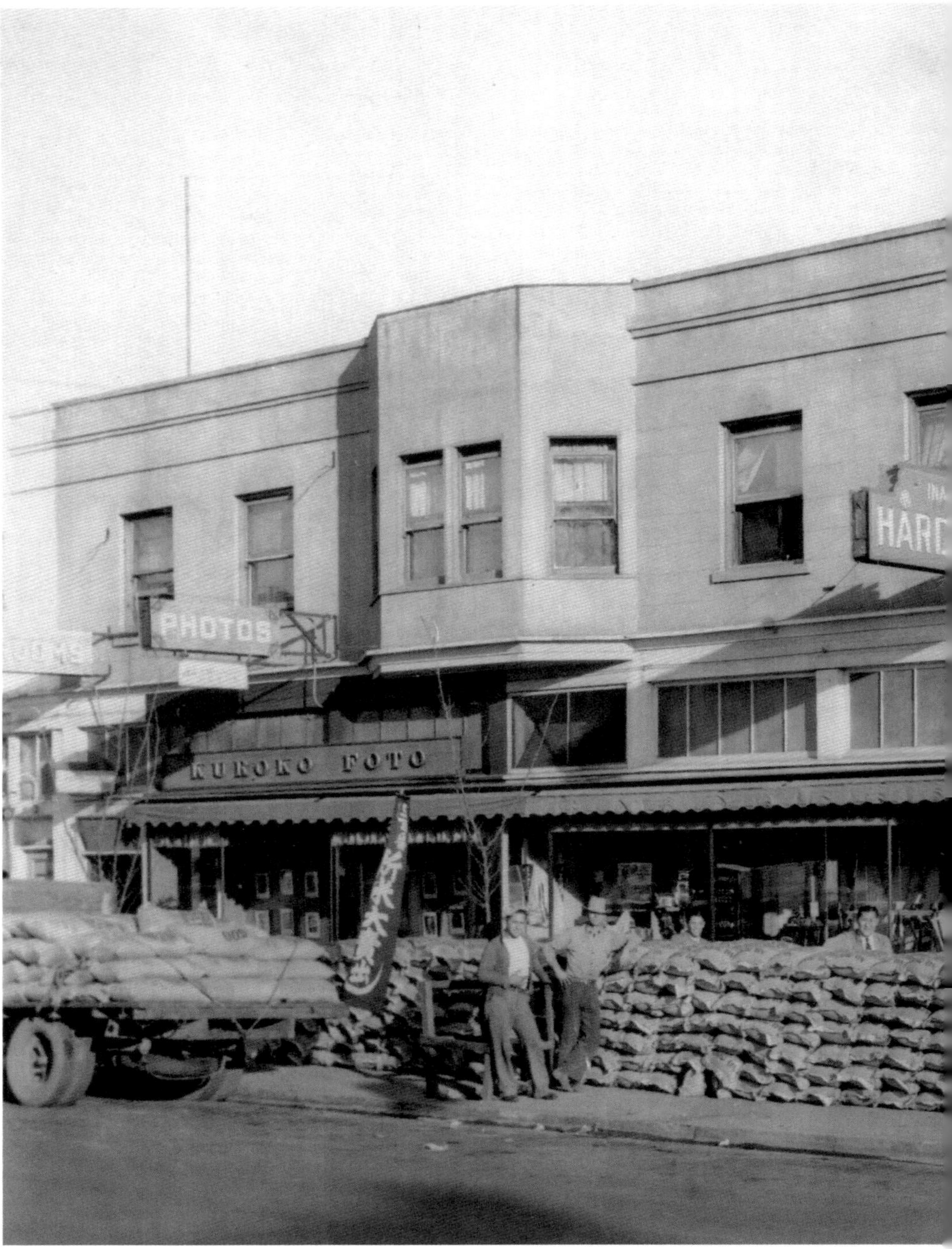

Bags of rice stacked in front of Inaka Hardware and Groceries, New Year's Eve. *Courtesy Center for Sacramento History, Sacramento Community Ethnic Survey Collection, 1983/146/1861.*

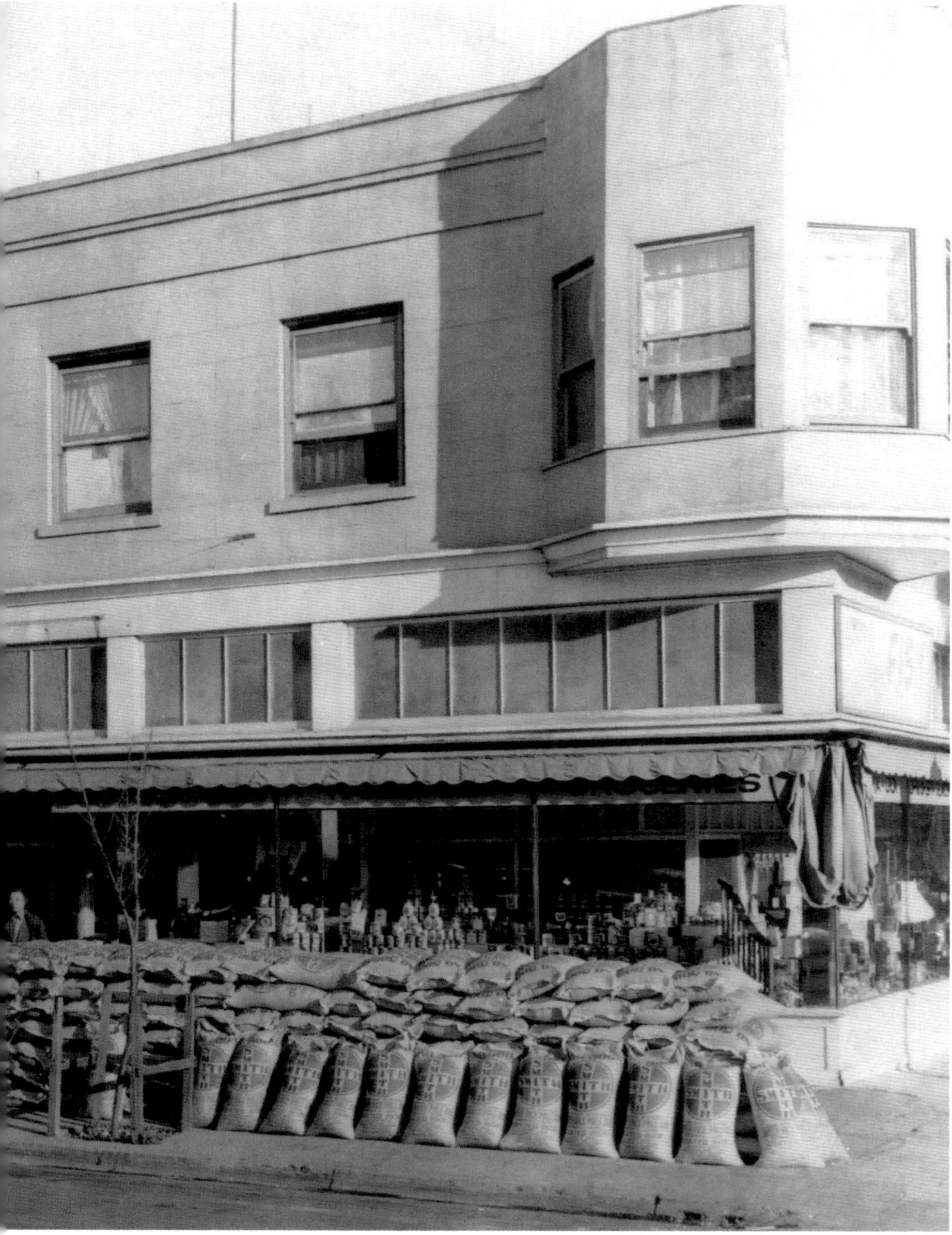
SMITH

to cities, causing urban areas to become pits of unemployment rather than centers of opportunity. By 1935, the West End held little resemblance to the once promising Labor Market area it had been at the turn of the century. For example, in that year, approximately 355 Japanese American businesses and families occupied the six-block vicinity of Japantown. By early 1942, the number of businesses or families was down to 220—a 37 percent decrease in seven years.[123] Merchants in Japantown were not the only ones affected by the Depression. Residents in Sacramento at that time recall how the Depression reshaped the habits of everyday life. "I was staying at the Nippon Hotel in Sacramento one night when we were in town for business," said Shig Miyaki.

> *I noticed a Japanese man carrying a bag early in the morning and was told that he was making the rounds of restaurants and homes looking for food in the garbage cans. Across the M Street Bridge* [now Capitol Avenue Bridge] *in West Sacramento, there was a community called "Hoover Village." Even though the cost of boarding was only 25 cents to 35 cents, they could not afford it. They went out looking for burned boards or...iron sheets after a fire to make shelters for themselves. There were some that were sleeping under the bridge.*[124]

Toshiko Igarashi's family was devastated by the economic meltdown:

> *When the depression came, those small and self-employed people survived but the big ones that were handling groceries and such things had to send* [all the fruit and vegetables] *back to the countryside. But even* [in the countryside] *people couldn't pay for them, and the banks were all closed. They eventually went bankrupt, not being able to do anything about it.*
>
> *We already had our children before we went bankrupt, during the Depression. I certainly did go through hardship then! City gas was turned off, the electricity was stopped also. The city gas was turned off three times or so. We built fires with wood in a stove to keep ourselves warm. The Sacramento River was nearby, and our neighbor across the street who was also from Tokyo...I went to pick up some wood there, built a fire, and gave milk to our children. When food was scarce, I managed to feed my children somehow, though I might have had nothing to eat myself.*
>
> *All of us Japanese in general had a hard time one way or another at that time. Our store was closed down. We couldn't take anything out of our store savings from the bank.*[125]

Entertainment

Despite the early 1920s agricultural recession and the 1930s Great Depression, Japantown's social life not only survived but burgeoned, offering a variety of cultural activities in which many in the community enthusiastically participated. During the summer, Buddhists and others in the community gathered on O Street, bound between Fourth and Fifth Street, for the annual Buddhist Bon Odori Festival.[126] Rooted in a traditional dance to honor the dead, Bon Odori, or simply Obon, transformed Sacramento's O Street into a scene of festivities filled with vibrant colors and rhythmic dancing and singing to the music of flutes and drums that continued far into the night. Writer Allen Eaton's vivid description of a traditional Obon festival captures the imagination:

> *Swaying, posturing in unison, they gesture with the arms, clap their hands, and stamp their feet to the rhythm which changes with succeeding numbers. The costumes worn are often gorgeous in color and design—the girls usually carry fans tucked into their sashes, which they use freely during intermissions and after as part of the dance gestures. Although Obon is performed in memory of the dead and no emotion is shown in the faces, the character of the dance is entirely joyful; ever comic and rustic elements are brought into some of the numbers.*[127]

Although Obon is a Buddhist holiday, everyone in the community joyfully took part in the celebrations. Michiko Takahashi's family attended the First Japanese Baptist Church but joined their Buddhist friends in attending the events. "I wasn't Buddhist but I had Japanese clothes, so my sister and I would dress up. It would start just after dinnertime, and then we would go and take our clothes to the *kaikan* (gymnasium). There were a lot of ladies there to help us get dressed in the *yukata*. We would go out there on the street in front of the church and dance to all the music until about ten or eleven o'clock. It took up the whole block. Everyone looked so nice."[128] Amy (Kamikawa) Wong fondly remembers parading through the streets before the evening dancing began: "Before the war, Obon celebrations would last two days. During the day before the dancing would start, we would have a parade and march up and down Fourth Street or O Street in our *yukata*. They had drums and flutes." For many, half of the excitement was wearing the *yukata*. "Getting dressed in the *yukata* was like an art," Wong continued. "I remember standing for an hour while my mom tried to get it right."[129] Marian Uchida recalled how important

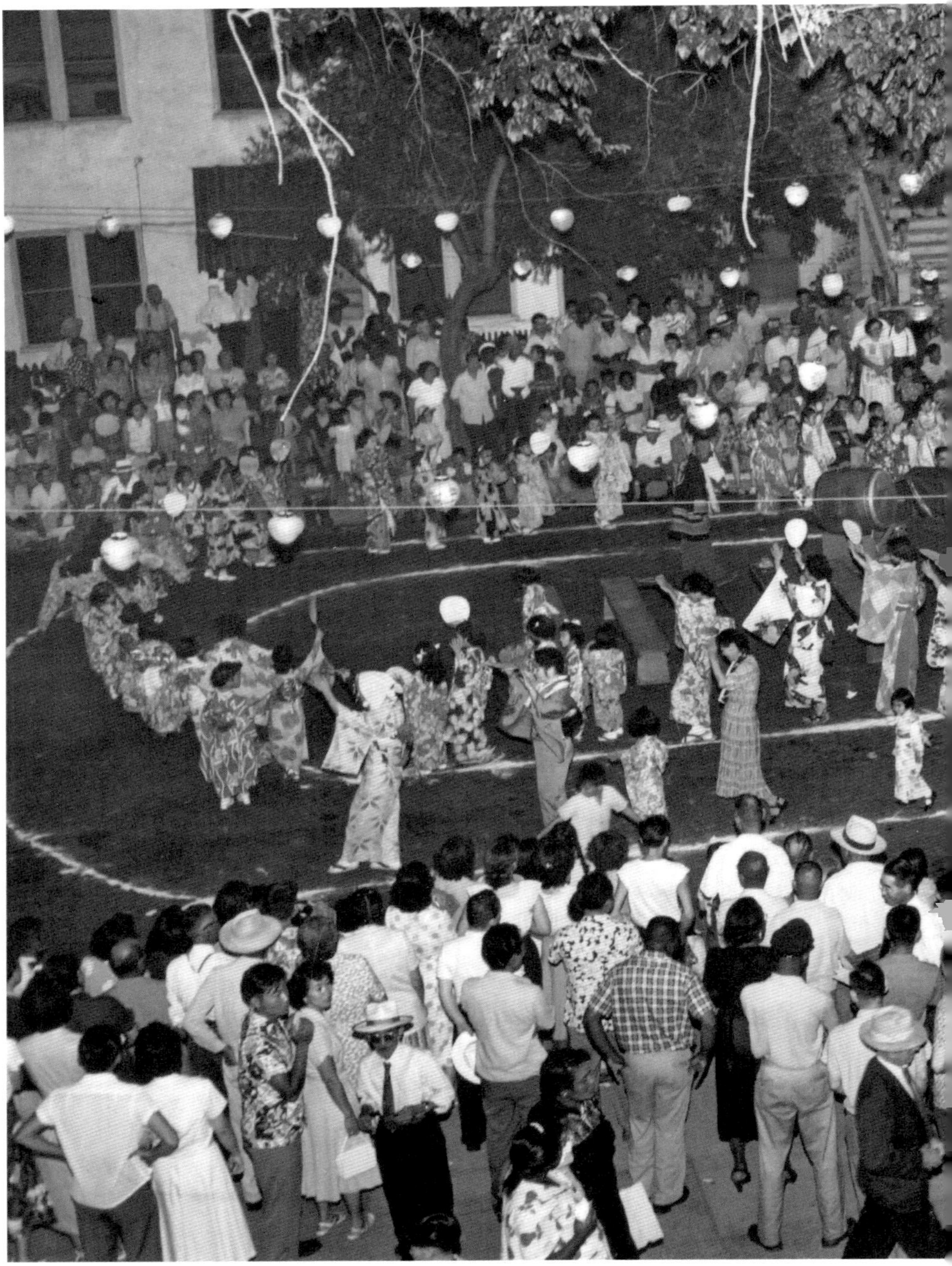

Obon festival in front of the Buddhist Church on O Street between Fourth and Fifth Streets. *Courtesy Keiko Komura.*

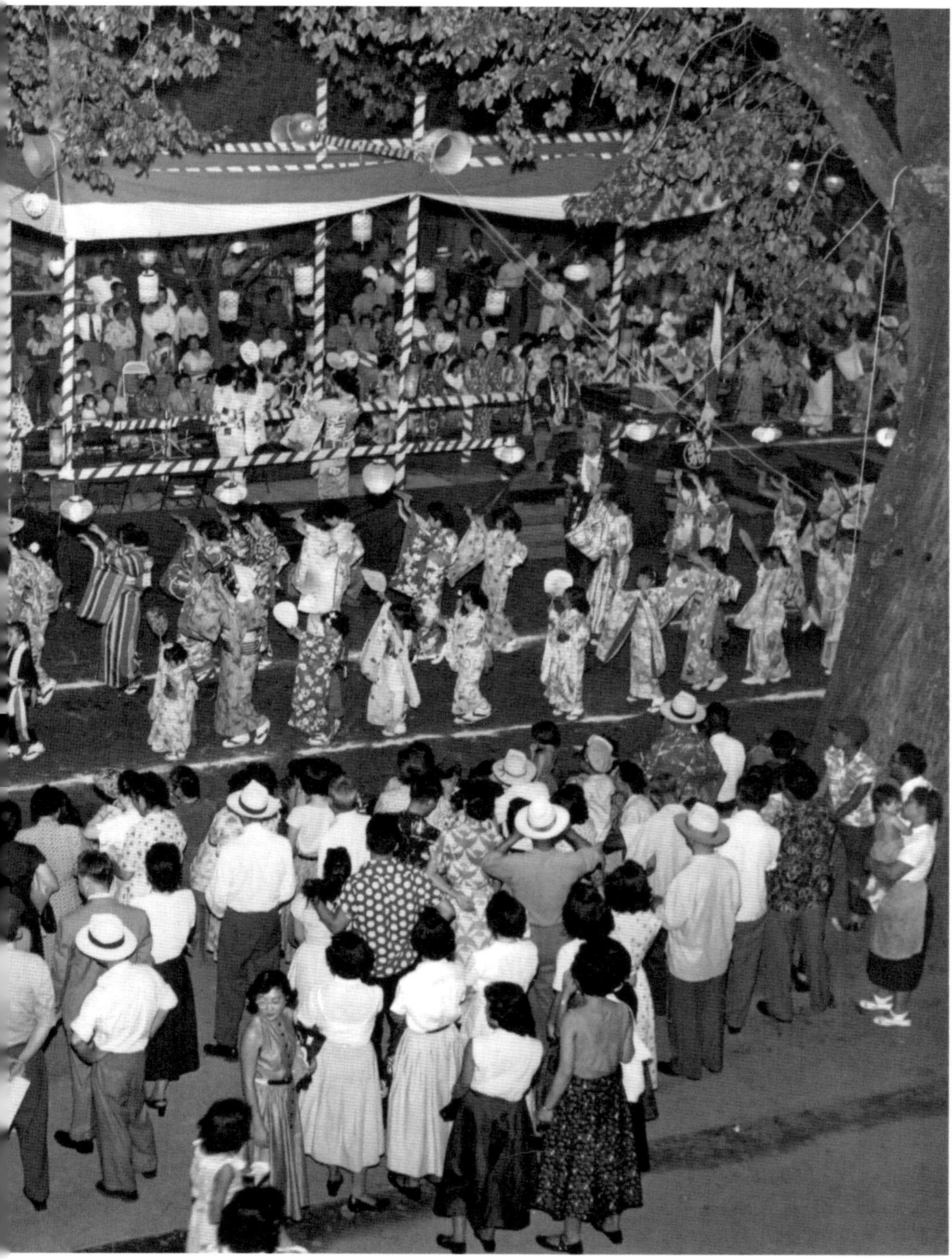

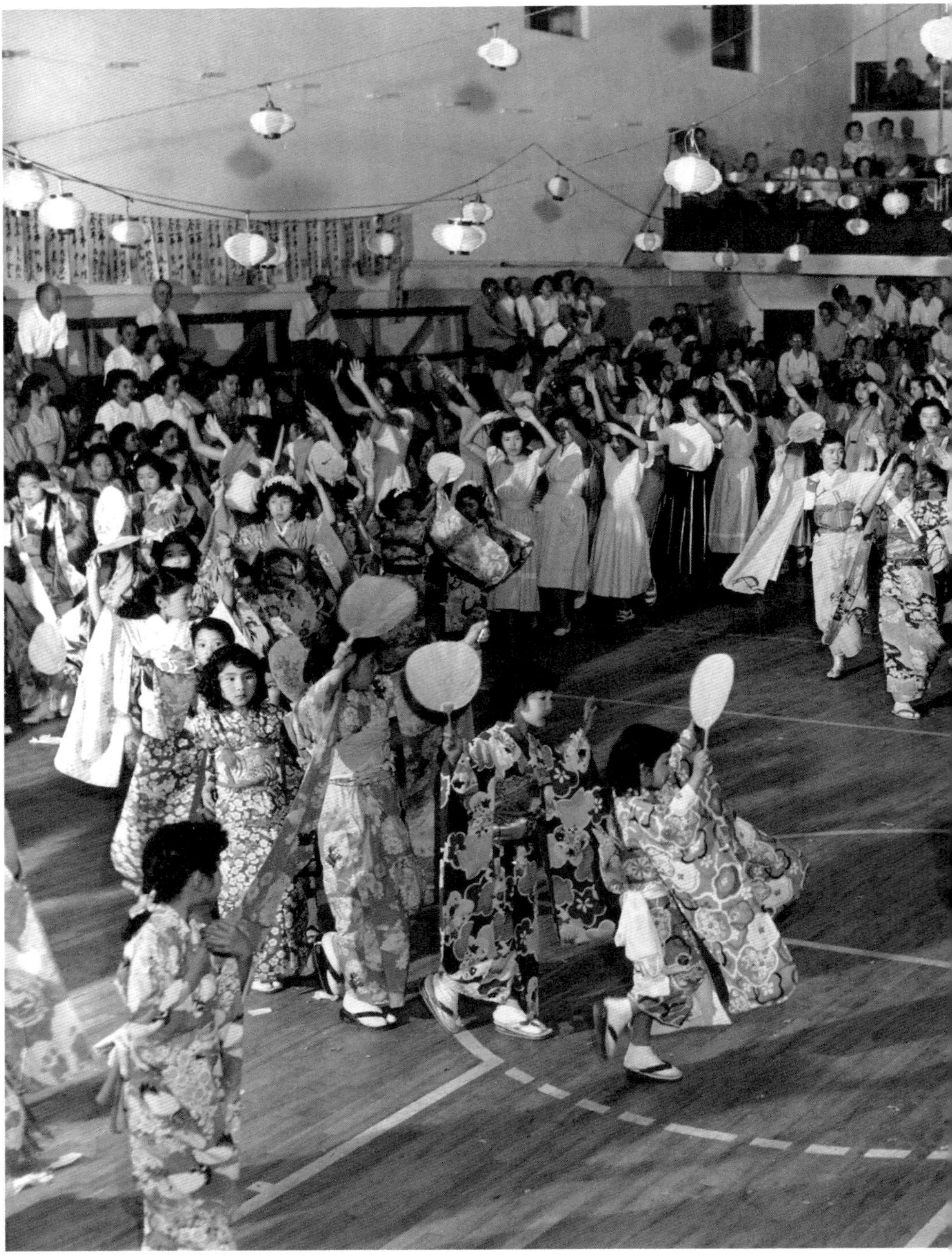

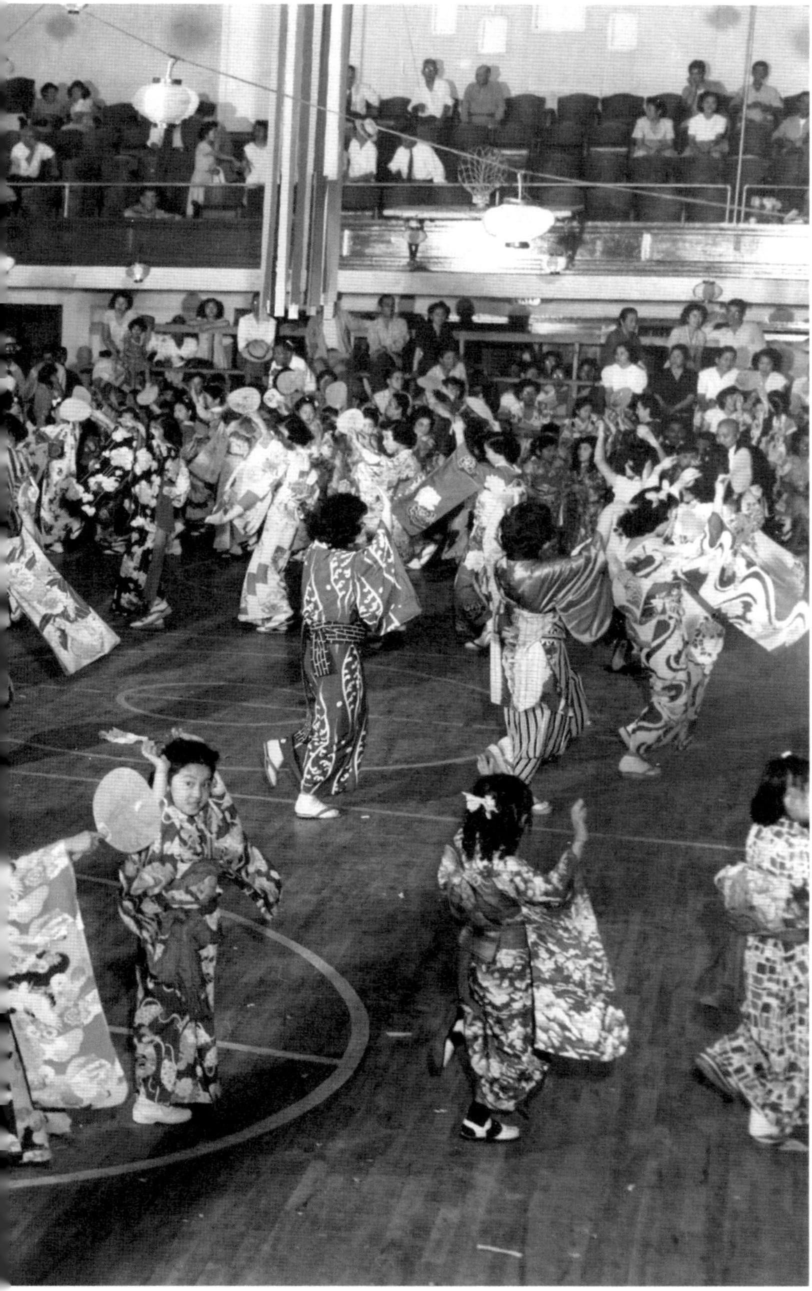

Obon festival in the Buddhist *kaikan* (gymnasium). *Courtesy Mike Sawamura, estates manager for Eugene Okada.*

yukata etiquette was to her mother: "I would walk in my *yukata* to the dance, and my mom would get angry at me because I walked in big strides and the *yukata* would go all over the place. You were supposed to walk in small steps, like shuffle your feet, be more dainty."[130]

Community fundraisers were another source of neighborhood entertainment. Soichi Nakatani, owner of the Nippon Theater at 328 L Street, near Fourth and L Streets, sometimes used his establishment as a community social hall. While most of the movies in the Nippon Theater were American, Japanese films made their appearance usually as fundraisers, an activity in which many happily participated.[131] Every few months, the community congregated in either the Boxing Hall, a gym at 223 L Street, or in the Buddhist *kaikan* at 410 O Street to socialize with friends and watch movies. Toko Fujii remembers the community spirit that accompanied these fundraisers:

> *Only once in a great while would they play Japanese films there because they used to have these independent contractors that brought films from Japan. They would rent the auditorium in the Buddhist Church or something. What they did is make a contract with these people to show the films two nights, like Saturday and Sunday nights…If the Buddhist Church sponsored the film, then we would donate five dollars or something and take the whole family. They would put down on a big donation board how much you donated for all to see. People would be recognized for what they donate. If you donate enough, it would make other people donate more next time. Probably 70 or 90 percent of the Japanese films that were shown in that way were sponsored by organizations. That's why they did not show Japanese films at the regular theaters.*[132]

The streets and establishments of Japantown became landmarks of youthful entertainment for the children growing up in the neighborhood. "I remember when we would play hide and seek on L," said Michiko Takahashi. "I would run into the Ouye pharmacy and hide behind the counter. One day they just finished mopping, and I slipped and fell. They just laughed, but that was one of my favorite places to go. They had an ice machine, and you could get shaved ice and syrup for five cents." Amy Wong recalls many evenings playing in the streets: "We used to play marbles and jacks. We would play hide-and-seek in the alleys and on the street at nighttime when the stores were all closed. Many of the stores, like the Funahashi's, had a screen door and behind that there was another door. We used to hide there in between the doors when we played hide-and-seek." Another popular

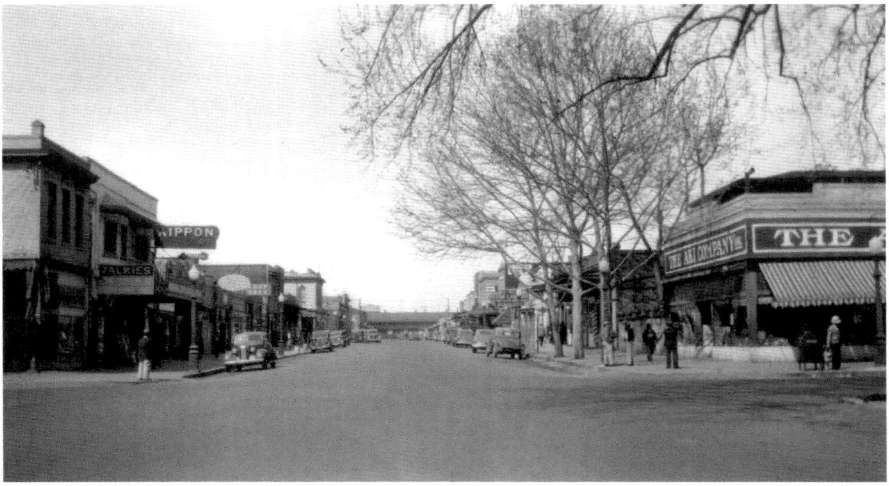

L Street between Third and Fourth Streets, 1935. *On the right*: Aki Company, Okashimo barber, Toyo Laundry, L Street Laundry, Ido cleaners and Nippon (Ouye) Drugs. *On the left*: Nippon Theater, Horimoto Candies, Yumikura Chop Suey, Wakimoto bakery, Kaihara restaurant, Matsumoto Billiards. *Courtesy California History Room. California State Library, 1989/1402.*

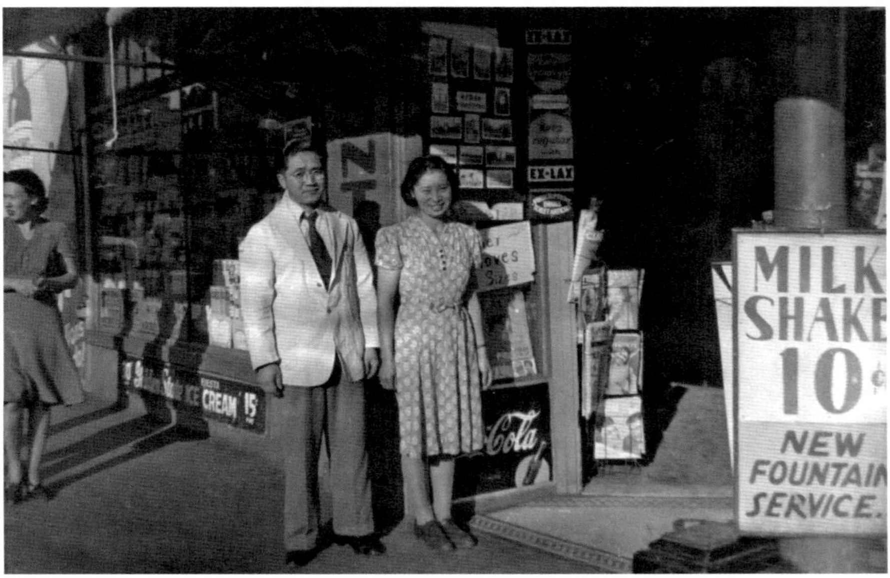

Harold and Grace Ouye standing in front of Nippon (Ouye) Drugs on the corner of Third and L Streets. *Courtesy Lloyd Ouye.*

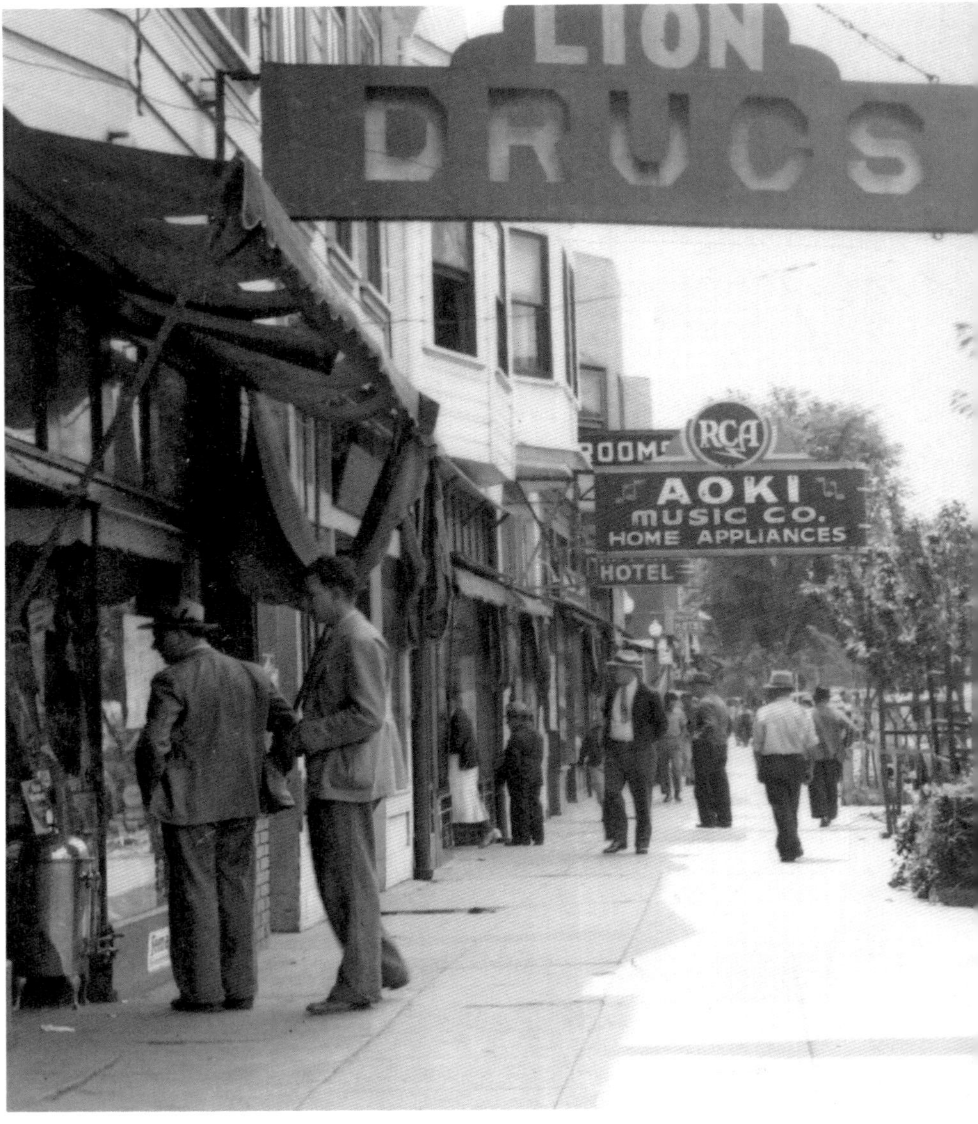

Japantown's Fourth Street business district. *Courtesy Center for Sacramento History, Sacramento Community Ethnic Survey Collection, 1985/024/1872.*

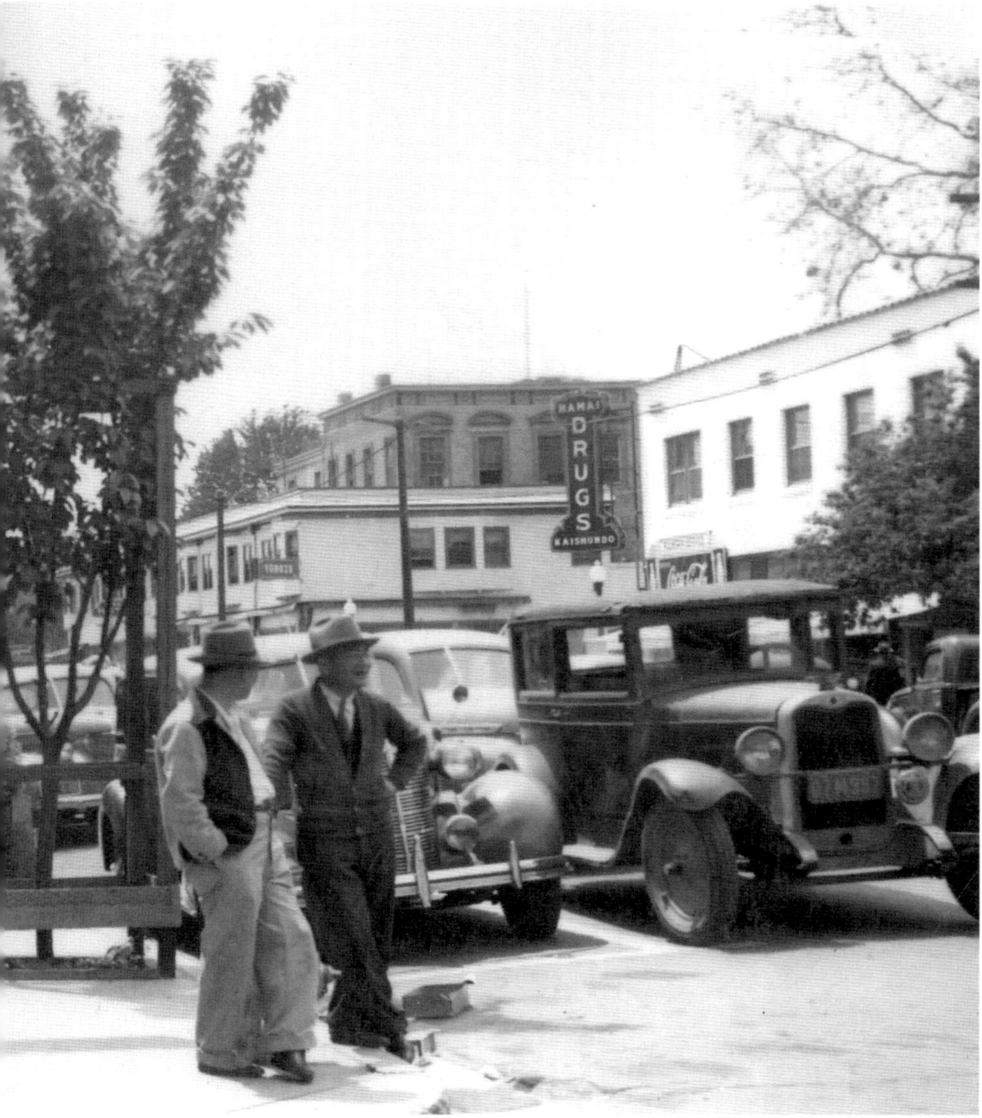
HAMAI
DRUGS
KAISHUNDO

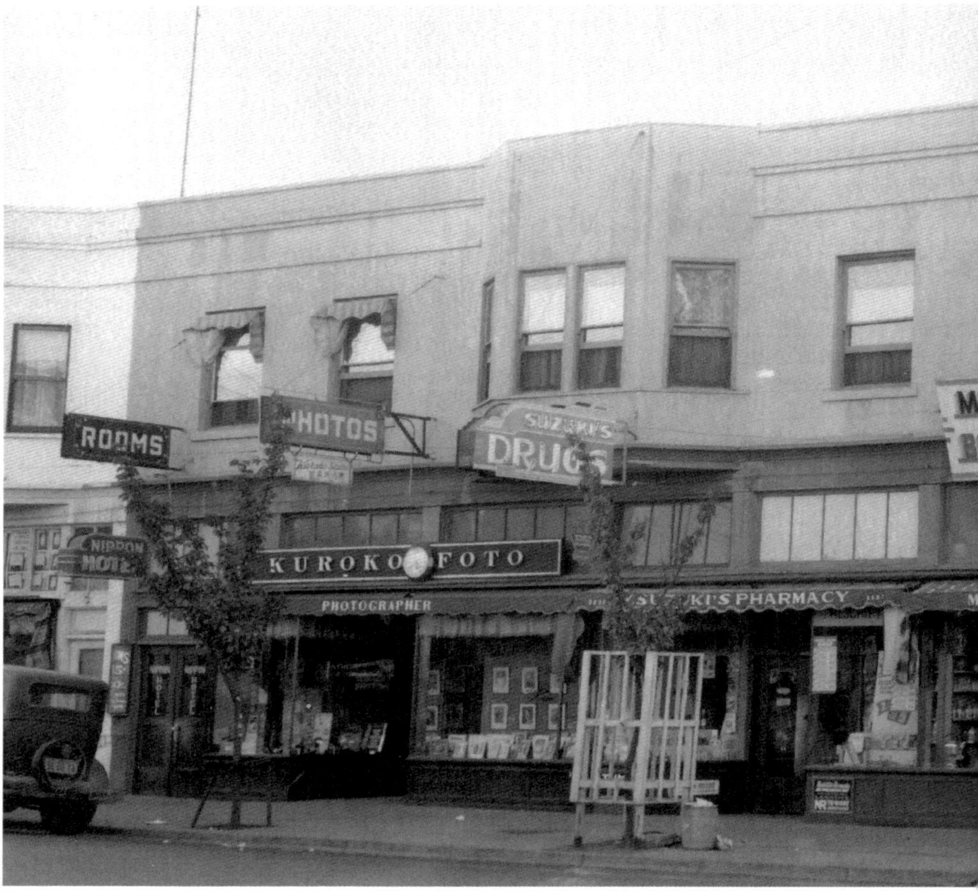

Fourth Street near Capitol Avenue. *Left to right*: Nippon Hotel, Kuroko Photography, Suzuki's Drugs, Mitsu Hardware, Matsuda Brothers Grocery. *Courtesy Christine Umeda.*

Japantown establishment for the younger crowd was Aoki Music store on Fourth Street. "The owner would tell me that if I danced in front of the store to Obon music they would give me a record," Michiko Takahashi fondly remembered. "Even though I was in regular clothes, you know, not in *yukata*, I would dance. It was around dinnertime, so many people would gather around and go into the store. It was funny because I would get a record but I didn't have a record player." Fred Matsuda spent much of his weekends and summer months at the Nippon Theater: "I would go to my grandfather and get a quarter. That was big money then. I would go buy some candy from

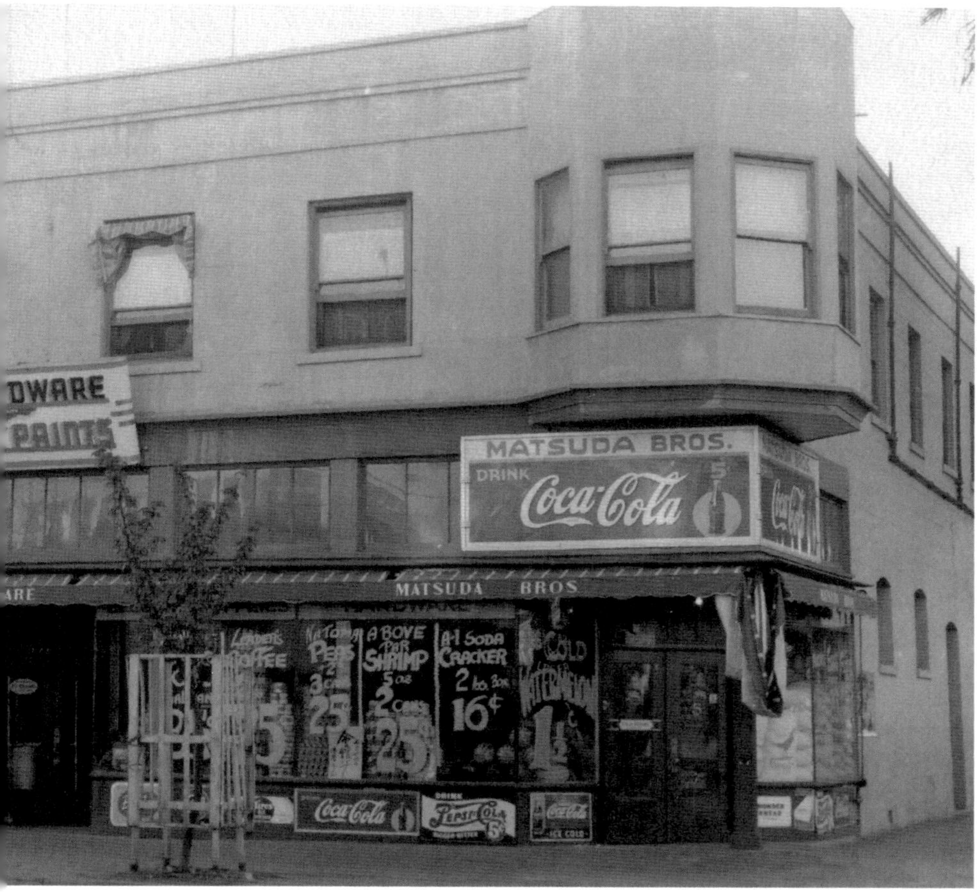

the candy store and go in the back side of the theater. We would go in and out of the candy store all day, say '*matakuryo*' and go back into the theater to watch another movie. It's where all the kids would hang out."[133]

Adults had their favored locations as well. Like other cities during this era, Sacramento had many gambling establishments. Many of them were located in the city's West End, particularly in or near Chinatown around Third and I Streets. Japantown also had some smaller gambling houses sponsored by the Tokyo Club that were frequented before the Depression by Japanese American farmers who came to test their luck and be entertained.[134] In the heart of Japantown, colorful lanterns and flying windmills decorated Japanese Alley in the block bound between L Street and Capitol (M Street) and Third and Fourth Streets.[135] Chikaji Teramoto, who came to Sacramento in the 1920s, described the nightlife found in Japanese Alley: "In the olden days in the evening, twelve or one o'clock, you could walk down Japanese Town Alley and hear the *shamisen* [Japanese stringed instruments] and some ladies and men singing. And that was natural every night. And, of course, we didn't have any geisha, but the waitresses were pretty good entertainers, so I think they sufficed to that extent as part-time entertainers."[136] One of the more popular establishments in the Alley was Ishihara's Bath House. Most of the establishments in the business district of Japantown also served as multifamily dwellings that were not equipped with hot-water plumbing. Therefore, bathhouses became a necessity for those in the area. "When I used to live in L and M Alley, we didn't have a bath in our house," said Michiko Takahashi, "so we used to use the one in the alley, pay five or ten cents. They would give us a towel and they had a ladies' side and a men's side. Across the street from the bathhouse there was a restaurant or club. I could hear the *shamisen* going and people talking and laughing."[137] Even those who lived south of the business district in the residential area of Japantown whose houses were equipped with hot water frequented the bathhouses as a special occasion. "I lived down the block, so we had hot water with a bath and regular bathroom," said Amy Wong. "We had a Japanese bath, but that took a lot of water and you had to heat it, so as a treat we would go to the bathhouse for a nickel."[138]

One block south of Japanese Alley, a variety of small Japanese American grocery stores, fish markets and restaurants surrounded another alley where neighbors combined their backyards to form large vegetable and flower gardens. Among the gardens stood a ten-foot-wide, four-cornered pavilion stage decorated with Chinese and Japanese symbols, vine ornaments and palm tree branches. Neighbors used this platform to practice tai chi, judo and kendo and hold team meets when they would compete with one another and against teams from Japan.[139]

Neighborhood churches would also sponsor elaborate plays and talent shows, usually around *Hanamatsuri* (flower festival) in April, a time that featured dancing, singing and music. One of the more favored entertainers in Sacramento's Japantown was Yuki Shimoda, who would go on to become a famous Japanese American actor.

Sumo wrestling also became a favorite pastime, especially during tournaments. Every Fourth of July, hundreds of cheering Japanese American spectators and teams from San Jose, Alameda, Fresno, Clarksburg, Walnut

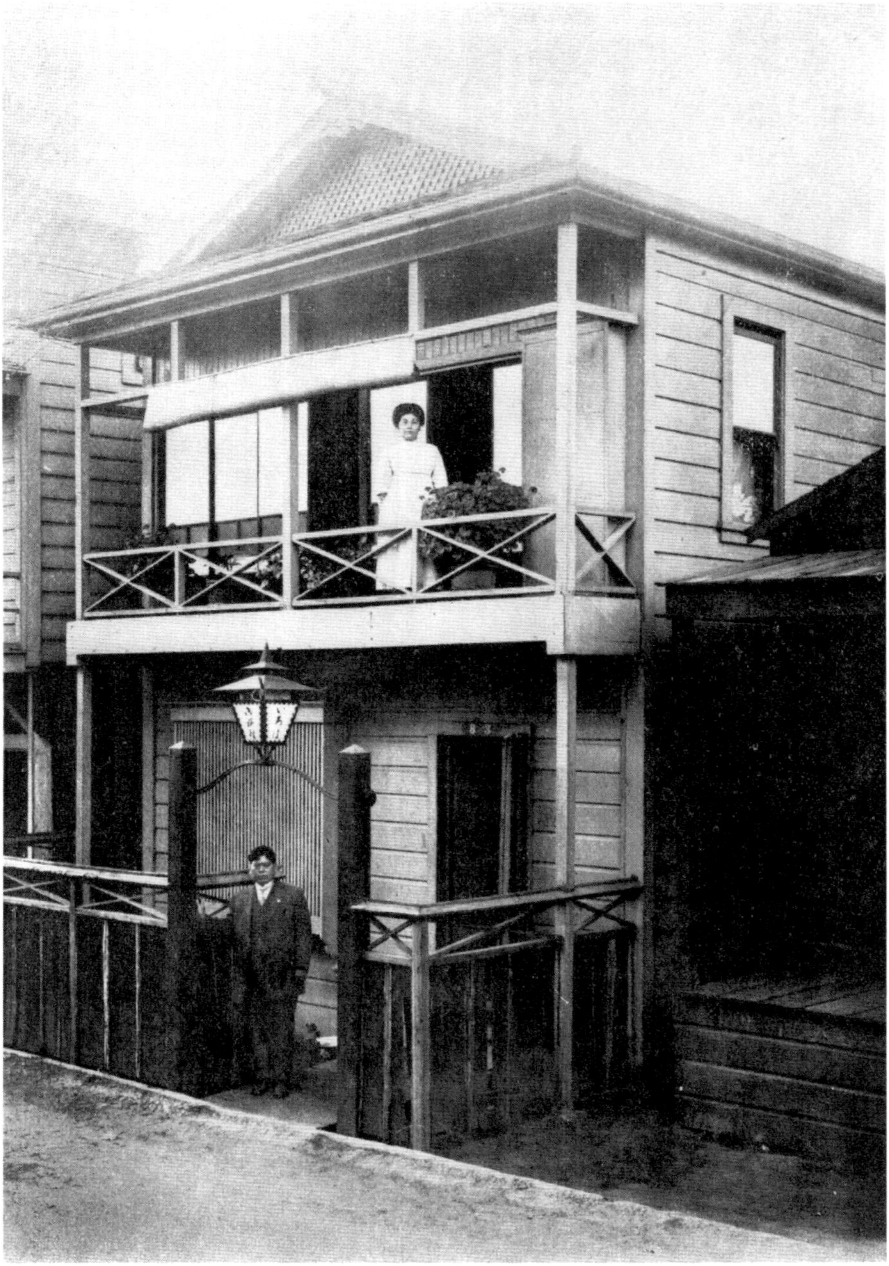

Japan Alley, Iroha and Yoshikawa restaurant, between Third and Fourth, L Street and Capitol Avenue, 1913. *Courtesy Center for Sacramento History, Sacramento Community Ethnic Survey Collection, 1983/146/2270.*

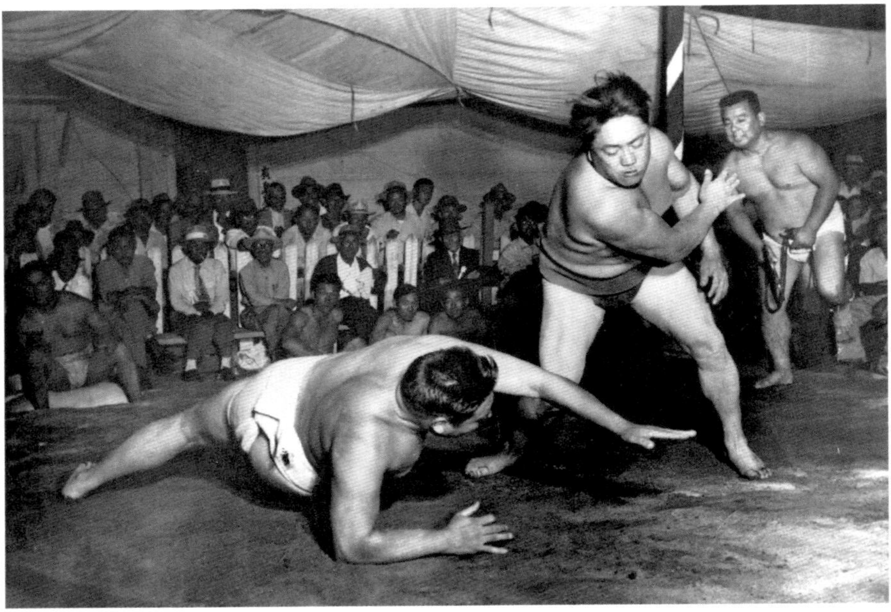

Sumo tournament in Japan Alley behind Tozai Dry Goods. Yoshio Shibata (standing far right) refereed many of these tournaments. *Courtesy Center for Sacramento History, Sacramento Community Ethnic Survey Collection, 1983/146/2273.*

Grove, Courtland, Stockton and San Francisco gathered in an open lot behind Tozai Dry Goods store in Japanese Alley for the competition. Two weeks before the event, participants and volunteers constructed a small arena with a dirt mound at its center. On top of the mound appeared sandbags outlining a ten-foot-diameter circle. Four wood poles encased the stage, supporting the large palm tree branches that overshadowed the mount. Following Japanese tradition, participants placed buckets of salt on opposite corners of the stage. As a spectator, James Kubo witnessed many of these events: "People from all over the area used to come and wrestle. At that time, wrestling was a big honor. You became a big wrestler and you made all kinds of money. The older people would donate, and if you won, they would give you money. There was one man who used to be an official referee in Japan. He used to referee [the fights]. Then we had guys who used to wrestle professionally in Japan and they came over."[140] Fred Matsuda recalled the excitement: "As many as four hundred people or more would gather in the Alley. It was packed. The Issei menfolk would have their share of drinks and put money in an envelope and give it to the good wrestlers."[141]

THE NISEI GENERATION

As already noted, between 1920 and 1940, the Japanese immigrant community in the United States experienced two dramatic changes: first, Japanese immigration shifted from a single-male, migratory-dominated population to a more settled, family-centered life; second, Japanese Americans moved from rural to more urban environments. These two changes fostered the development of many distinct, well-organized Japanese American subcultures throughout the cities and towns of the West Coast and contributed to the birth of the first American-born Nisei generation—consisting of 52 percent of the Japanese American community by 1930. Aside from the larger population's desire to keep social relationships racially segregated and their own inclinations to live among more familiar ethnic surroundings, the Issei insisted that their American-born children not only receive but excel in the educational opportunities found in America that would ensure a brighter future for themselves as a people. Americans by birthright, the Nisei pursued public education and, in the process, were subject to the most powerful assimilating forces in American culture.

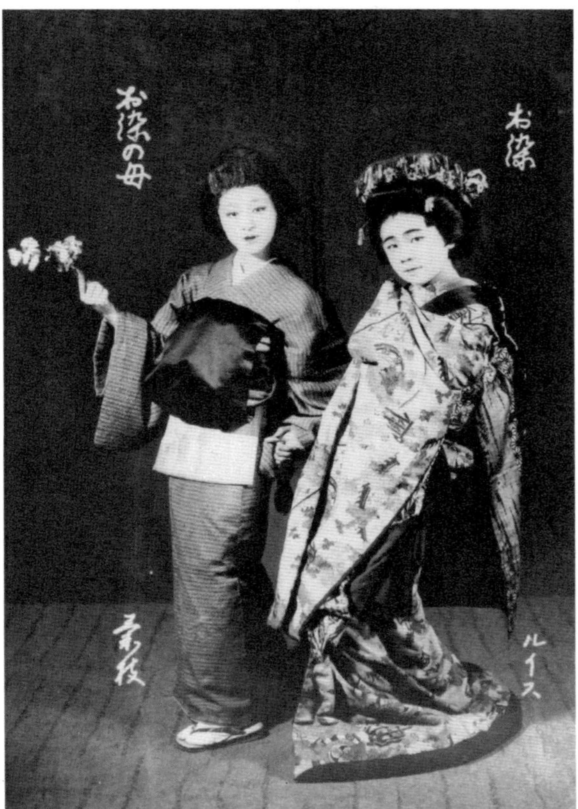

Kodomo Shibai (children's drama group). These students performed *Osome Hisamatsu*, a famous Japanese love story. *Translation courtesy of Yoshimitsu Yajima. Courtesy Japanese American Archival Collection. Department of Special Collections and University Archives, California State University–Sacramento.*

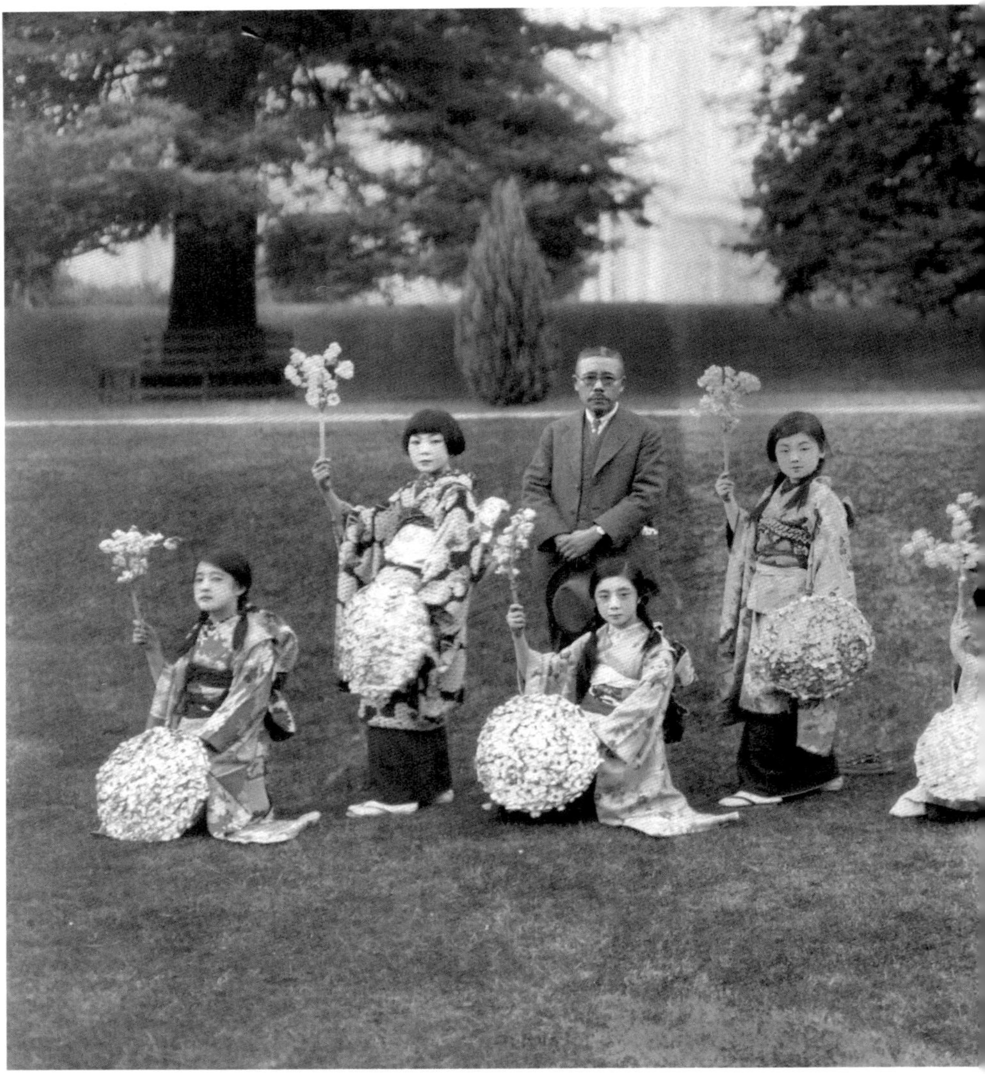

Okada family with children's drama club in front of Capitol building. *Courtesy Mike Sawamura, estates manager for Eugene Okada.*

The Nisei, while influenced by Japanese language, tradition and ways of thinking at home or in Japanese schools, were nonetheless culturally more American than Japanese. The Nisei were native English speakers, associated with a greater diversity of people and were better equipped than their parents

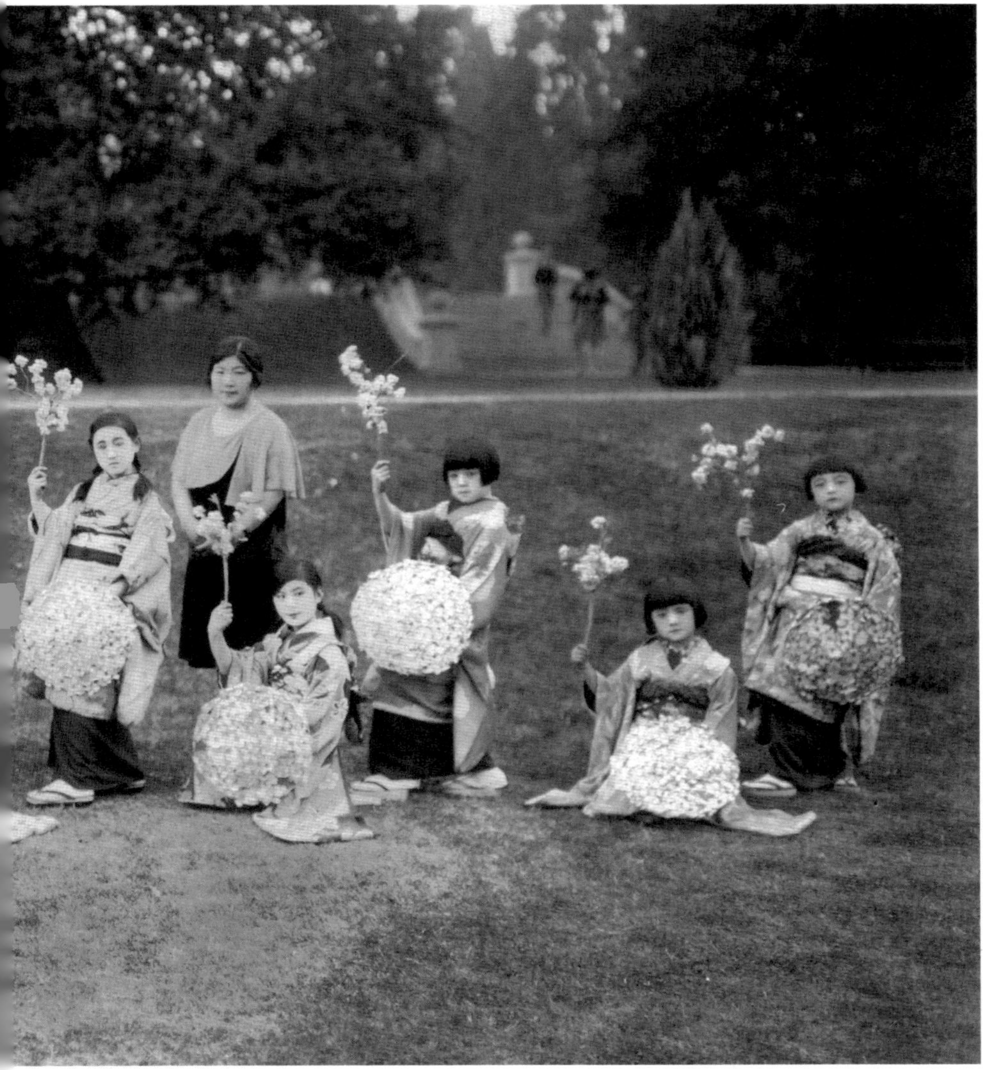

to deal with a wide variety of social situations. They aspired to achieve middle-class American standards and looked for acceptance by American society. Although proud of their parents' success in building new lives in a new, and oftentimes hostile, country, many Nisei rejected their Japanese heritage, with its narrow social vision exclusively limited to neighborhood, church, kin and friends. Therefore, in the years after the 1920s, the Japanese American community gradually moved into two separate spheres: the Issei, largely isolated and primarily Japanese centered; and the Nisei, native and primarily American centered.[142]

Even though the first generation hoped that their American-born children would be more assimilated into American culture and have access to all the opportunities that American society had to offer, they also encouraged the Nisei to never forget Japanese culture and language. In 1924, Toku Yamamura and Yoshiko Koyama began *Kodomo Shibai* (children's acting club), where children could practice the arts of *kabuki* and *odori* dancing. Some of the members were Sachiko Hori, Grace Sakata, Shizuko Inabe, Naoko Takeuchi, Alice Kurotori, Tsugie Takeda, Lillian Takagaki, Lillian Fukunaga and Sayoko Sakumura. Supported by the Tokyo Gambling Club led by Mr. Tomita, the group performed classical dances like "Sakura, Sakura" and "Akino-Yoru" and presented scenes from one of Japan's most famous plays, *Chushingura* (The Treasury of Loyal Retainers). Some of the largest attended presentations were held on New Year's Eve in the Showa hall or the Boxing Hall.[143]

The Japanese American community developed many activities for the Nisei as a result of being denied access into mainstream American activities. Some of these were Boy Scouts, baseball, basketball, golf, kendo and judo. Starting in Sacramento around 1920, kendo, perhaps more than any other activity, became popular among boys and girls. Parents valued the sport for its respect for authority, discipline, Japanese manners, obligation and inner strength.[144] The community also enjoyed a sport that they were familiar with in Japan—baseball. All-Japanese baseball teams appeared also in surrounding areas like Marysville, Walnut Grove, Florin and Penryn. Some areas, such as Walnut Grove, had their own stadiums. Even Nisei girls participated in baseball, putting together their own team in Florin. Competition among these rival teams oftentimes led some prominent Issei from other areas to play for their team.[145]

Opposite, top: Boy Scout Troop 41's summer visit to Japan, 1929. The troop marched to the river and boarded a riverboat for an overnight trip to San Francisco before heading to Japan. *Courtesy Japanese American Archival Collection. Department of Special Collections and University Archives, California State University–Sacramento.*

Opposite, bottom: Sacramento High School Dragons baseball team, 1928. *Bottom, left to right*: George Miyakawa, ___, Yoshio Nakagawa, Frank Sawamura, ___. *Courtesy Japanese American Archival Collection. Department of Special Collection and University Archives, California State University–Sacramento.*

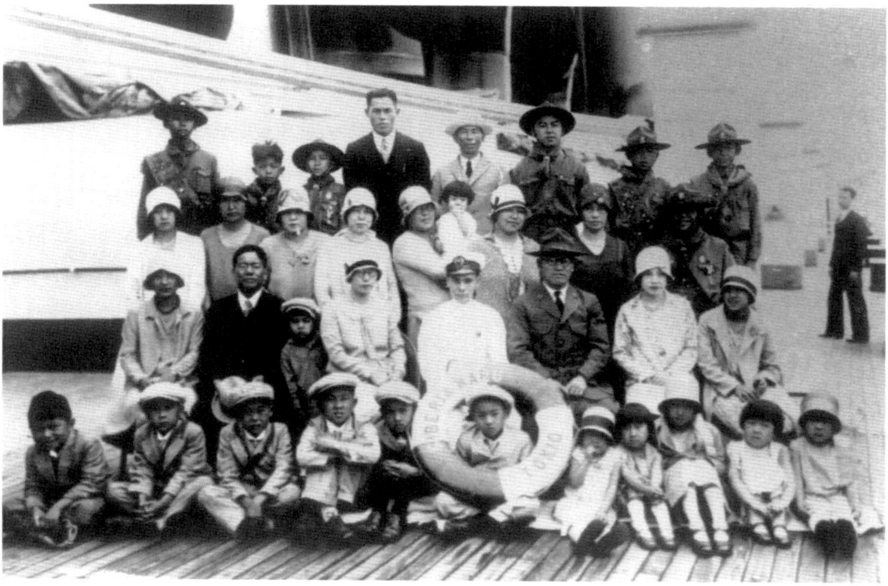

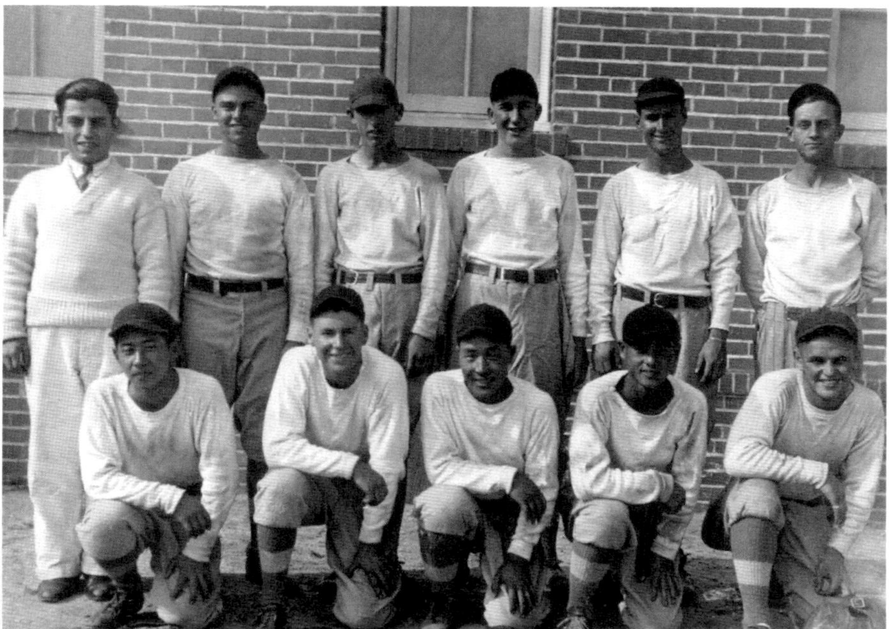

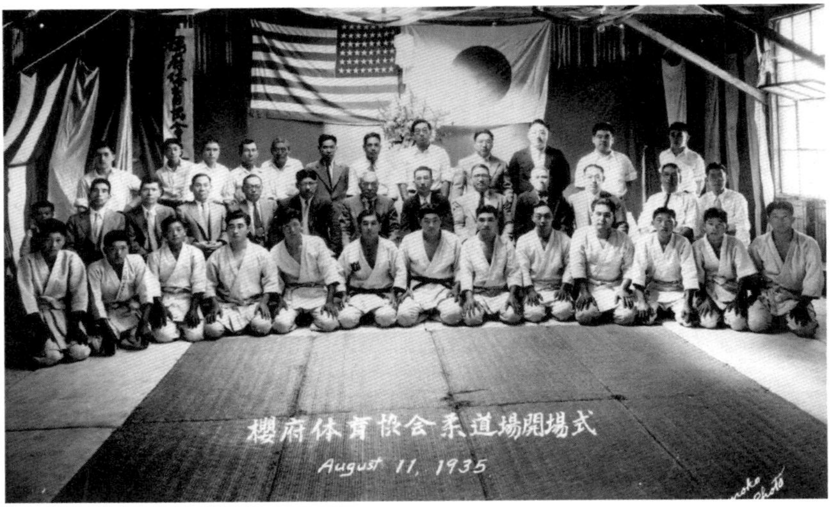

Sakura City Gymnastics, Physical Training and Education Association. Judo opening ceremony. *Translation courtesy Yoshimitsu Yajiima. Image courtesy Center for Sacramento History, Sacramento Community Ethnic Survey Collection, 1983/146/2276.*

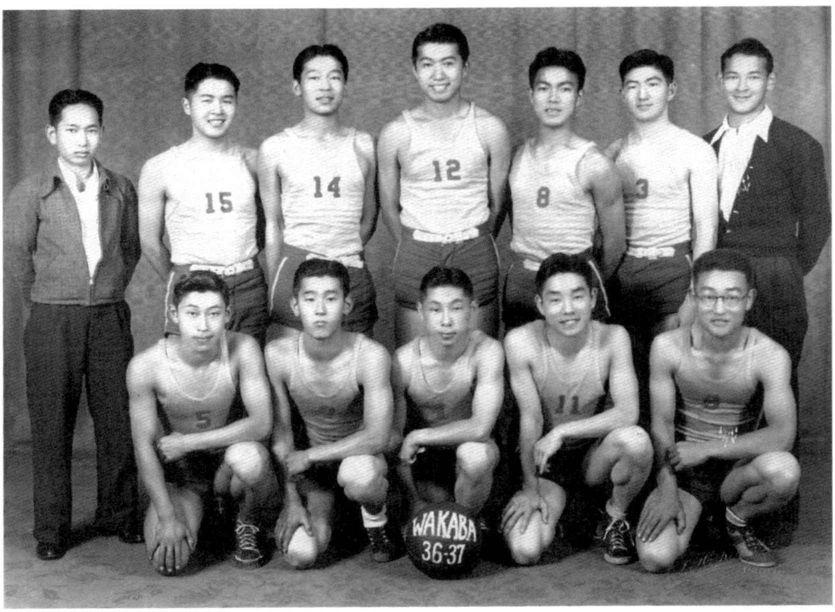

Wakaba basketball team. *Standing, left to right:* Jack Miura, Toko Fujii, Sei Yoshida, Tomo Uyeda, Kuni Nakao, Hatsumi Morimoto, Tom Uchida. *Front, left to right:* Jack Okuda, Cosy Sakumura, Tom Takata, Joe Sasaki, Tosh Yoshimura. *Image courtesy Terry (Fujii) Kornelly. Identification of names courtesy Marian Uchida, April Adachi, C. Hamai, K. Hosokawa, R. Takata.*

But regardless of their American nativity and upbringing in American culture, fluency in the English language and American education, the Nisei faced rejection from the outside world and consequently found it difficult to break out of their ethnic community for greater opportunities. Thrown back into the company of other Japanese, most Nisei had to settle for jobs run by the older generation. Rejecting much of the Issei's social world, the Nisei nonetheless remained locked into the Japanese American economy until the post–World War II era. As historian Kaoru Oguri Kendis states, "Since it was extremely difficult to succeed outside the ethnic community, many [Nisei] had to remain within the community and under the authority of their parents. It was quite common for young men with a college degree to take jobs as salesmen, fruit stand attendants, and vegetable washers."[146]

The Japanese American Citizens League (JACL) served as the Nisei's principal organization. Founded in Seattle in 1930, the JACL evolved out of a coalition of Nisei clubs such as the Loyalty League, located in towns on the Pacific Coast. The league professed as its main goal to Americanize the Nisei by assimilating them into mainstream American culture and developing good citizenship.[147]

In Sacramento on October 31, 1931, six Japanese Americans, led by Walter Tsukamoto, met at the Japanese Student Club to form a Sacramento chapter of the JACL. Prior to this time, Tsukamoto held the office of president for Sacramento's chapter of the Loyalty League from 1922 to 1924, and later in 1938, he served as the JACL's national president. The chapter, mostly composed of those living in the city, held most of its meetings in the Japanese Association Hall, the Buddhist *Kaikan* or the Japanese Presbyterian Church.[148] Although confronted with yearly financial problems, the chapter sponsored a variety of social events for the Nisei, such as the State Fair Dance and JACL conventions. By 1936, the chapter had grown into a larger organization that included Japanese American families from the outlying districts of Woodland, Elk Grove, Yolo-Broderick, Clarksburg, Oak Park, Mills-Perkins and Riverside.[149] Up until the bombing of Pearl Harbor in 1941, when the chapter boasted of its biggest membership of 1,300, the JACL exercised minimal influence on the Japanese American community and less on the larger society.[150]

Between 1890 and 1941, Japanese American settlers in Sacramento established a richly diversified, self-sustaining enclave, firmly imprinting their own unique history on Sacramento's urban mosaic landscape. By 1940, 3,500 persons of Japanese descent were living in Sacramento, most of them in or around Japantown. They ran grocery stores and fish markets, cultivated commercial flower and vegetable gardens and owned labor contracting firms, clothing stores, billiard halls, boardinghouses and hotels, cafes, nurseries and local newspapers. Such vernacular contours cultivated a sense of place for the Issei and provided the seedbed for a unique Japanese American culture.

Other smaller Japanese American communities developed in places like Isleton, Clarksburg, Walnut Grove and Woodland, but Sacramento's Japantown served as the hub that pulled others into a place of connection. Here, doctors, lawyers, Delta fishermen, Wheatland poppy farmers and Florin strawberry ranchers gathered for religious services, judo tournaments, classes in traditional Japanese flower arrangement and authentic Japanese meals. New Year celebrations and Obon ceremonies decorated Sacramento's Fourth Street and O Street with bright, festive colors, Japanese American folk dancing, ethnic foods, music and singing. For many, Japantown cultivated a sense of community solidarity within an unaccepting world and shaped their unique identity not only as Japanese immigrants in America but as Japanese Americans of Sacramento. However, like other Japanese American enclaves on the Pacific Coast, World War II shattered Sacramento's Japantown completely.

CHAPTER 3

SACRAMENTO'S JAPANESE AMERICAN COMMUNITY AND FORCED EVACUATION, 1941–1942

On Sunday morning, December 7, 1941, the nation of Japan destroyed the United States fleet at Pearl Harbor in Hawaii, razing 15 ships and over 150 planes. The United States immediately declared war on Japan. For those of Japanese ancestry in the United States, the bombing was like a nightmare come true, sparking a recrudescence of anti-Japanese hysteria similar to that of the early twentieth century. As soon as news of the attack reached the mainland, local police surrounded Japanese American neighborhoods while FBI agents swept through the Japanese American quarters of every city, town and farm community on the West Coast. Federal authorities, in conjunction with military and naval intelligence, had gathered lists of some 250 to 300 "dangerous" Issei Japanese, although internal security believed only 40 to 50 on each list posed any kind of real "threat." FBI forces quickly seized some 1,500 Issei Japanese. When Germany and Italy declared war, some of their nationals were similarly seized.[151] By the end of December, the FBI had detained almost 2,000 suspected Japanese American sympathizers in the United States. Most notable in this group were leaders of the Japanese Associations, Buddhist priests, newspapermen, Japanese-language school instructors and all Issei suspected of maintaining strong connections with Japan. Although the Department of Justice incarcerated some 16,000 persons of Japanese ancestry barred from citizenship during the war, about two-thirds of these were eventually released, paroled or, in a few cases, repatriated.[152]

The news of the attack launched a shock wave throughout the nation, with a mixture of fear and outrage for those of Japanese ancestry. In

Sacramento, Toko Fujii remembers hearing the dreadful news on the radio in his home: "It was like there was a cloud hanging over the city…I tried to make things as normal as possible…There was a basketball tournament at the Buddhist gym near Fourth and O Streets, so I went to that. But it was kind of eerie. Underlying the whole game atmosphere was this very subdued mood of the people, like they were afraid to go home and face a very unpleasant reality."[153] Michiko Takahashi recalls the bewilderment she and her family felt: "I was at home when my brother came home and said, 'Mom, Japan is in a war with America!' We didn't know what to think, so we just listened to the radio. I was going to Sacramento High School then, and it was a little uncomfortable. You could hear the radio going on about Japan and the war. You're sitting in the class and you are one of the 'Japs' in the class. That's the way it felt. It was very uncomfortable." Florin resident Mary Tsukamoto was just leaving church service when she heard that Japan had attacked Pearl Harbor: "I was shocked, hurt and frightened. I felt like a marionette—dangling, unable to reach the ground…My world had turned upside down. I remember my throat becoming very tight. When we gathered later for our Sunday evening service, I remember the stillness as we bowed to pray, the strong foreboding of eminent darkness. What was going to happen to us now?"[154] Reverend Isamu Nakamura, who at the time was minister of the Church of Christ, later renamed Japanese Presbyterian Church, on the corner of Fifth and Capitol Avenue, also heard the shocking news on his radio at home: "One Sunday morning, on the way home from morning service, I noticed a group of people listening to a radio broadcast in front of a neighborhood corner store. I thought they were listening to some sport event. When I reached home, I learned of the attack on Pearl Harbor by the Japanese…I was simply shocked because I had never given any thought to such an event before that. I expected the general trend and atmosphere of the public's feelings toward the Japanese would not improve but worsen by the attack."[155] That evening, the reverend received a telephone call informing him that a member of his congregation had been murdered. Reverend Nakamura vividly recalled the moment:

> *So I rushed to his place, a hotel on K Street near Fourth Street, and found him sitting in a chair and hunched over in a dim light. I said to myself, "Oh, God, how awful" and called his name believing he was dead. What surprised me the most was that he heard me and looked up at me. I believe that he was just napping when I got there. I couldn't tell him what I had heard about him and the reason for my presence, so I just mentioned to him*

> *that it might be wise to be careful and close up early under the circumstances. After a short prayer, I went back home.*[156]

That Sunday evening, federal agents and Sacramento policemen patrolled the streets of Japantown and the Japanese American farming communities throughout the Sacramento area, stopping Japanese Americans in their automobiles to search their cars for explosives. The United States Treasury Department shut down the businesses of all Japanese Americans under surveillance while federal authorities ordered all Japanese Americans ineligible for citizenship to surrender their firearms, radio transmitters, short-wave receivers and cameras. Government agents also restricted the travel of all Issei beyond the limits of their home communities.[157] These orders applied to all first-generation Germans and Italians as well. Within the first few hours after the bombing of Pearl Harbor, a number of Sacramento's Japanese Americans were arrested on suspicion of being "enemy aliens." These included Riichi Satow, secretary of the Sacramento Valley Japanese Association at 1309 Fourth Street and local correspondent for the *New World Sun*, a Japanese newspaper located on the corner of Fourth and N Streets; F.J. Miyagawa, correspondent for the *Japanese-American Newspaper* at 1414 Fourth Street; and Giichi Aoki, proprietor of the Aoki Music Company at 1223 Fourth Street.[158] Others were also picked up that evening for FBI interrogation. Reverend Nakamura recalls, "That night, the FBI picked up Mr. Aoki, Mr. Ishizaki, and Mr. Itano, who were the backbone of the local Japanese community and our church. The following morning, Monday, when I went to the church, I noticed a large inscription 'Down with Japs,' on the front wall. I felt quite uneasy."[159] Federal agents arrested many Issei who were attending Sunday evening service at the Buddhist temple on O Street. Kanji Nishijima, born in Sacramento in 1922, whose father, Shuzo, opened up L and M Appliance in 1926 on Fourth Street in the heart of Japantown's business district, was one of those individuals. Nishijima recalled: "My father was picked up by the FBI when the war broke out because he was active in the Japanese community. He was at church in the Buddhist temple. All the first generation, like the teachers and ministers, especially the Buddhist Church ministers, they were picked up by the dozens."[160] These FBI roundups oftentimes caused disarray within families and left abandoned wives to carry on family-operated businesses on their own. It was not uncommon for some of the older children whose families remained intact to be sent to assist others in the community. Michiko Takahashi had just started her freshman year at Sacramento High School when her father sent her to live with a family friend:

> *Mr. Funahashi, one of the dignitaries of our town who owned a good-size grocery store, was taken away with other dignitaries of our Japanese town. Mrs. Funahashi was left alone, so I was sent by my father to stay with Funahashi bachan to help her, eat with her and go to school from there. I was like a daughter to help her. I missed most of the things that went on at that time with my own family. We didn't know what was going to happen to all of us.*[161]

Treasury Department officials, escorted by Sacramento police, seized "lock, stock and barrel" the Sumitomo Bank of California on the corner of Fourth and L Streets, in effect shutting down all Japanese American banking activity. Trepidation spread among the Japanese American community, especially those engaged in business. Without access to their commercial accounts, Japanese Americans feared that their checks would bounce and that Japantown's business district would eventually collapse. Optometrist James Kubo, who held his business account in the Sumitomo Bank, vividly remembers the financial disarray in which he found himself the morning after Pearl Harbor:

> *I wrote all my checks for my bills and sent them out on Saturday. Monday morning I go into the office and I get all kinds of phone calls saying, "Your check is no good. We want the cash." PG&E called me. The phone company said, "If you don't get the cash, we'll cut off your phone." The beauty of the whole thing was that one guy, an optometry wholesaler where I got my supplies, called me. He said, "I know your checks are bouncing because I heard about this. I tell you what; if there is anyone who wants their checks cashed from you, tell them to call me and I'll pay the bill off." He not only took care of me but he took care of the other* [optometry] *guys.*[162]

Except for a few Issei whose accounts were still held "suspect," Japanese American banking transactions resumed normal operations within a few weeks. Officials continued to freeze the assets of Japantown merchants, such as Ichiro Hamatake's Pacific Trading Company at 309 O Street, Dr. Ed Ishii's Eagle Drug Company at 1401 Fourth Street, Yasuno and Masao Tambara's Japanese import company at 1021 Front Street and Frank Sakata's Highland

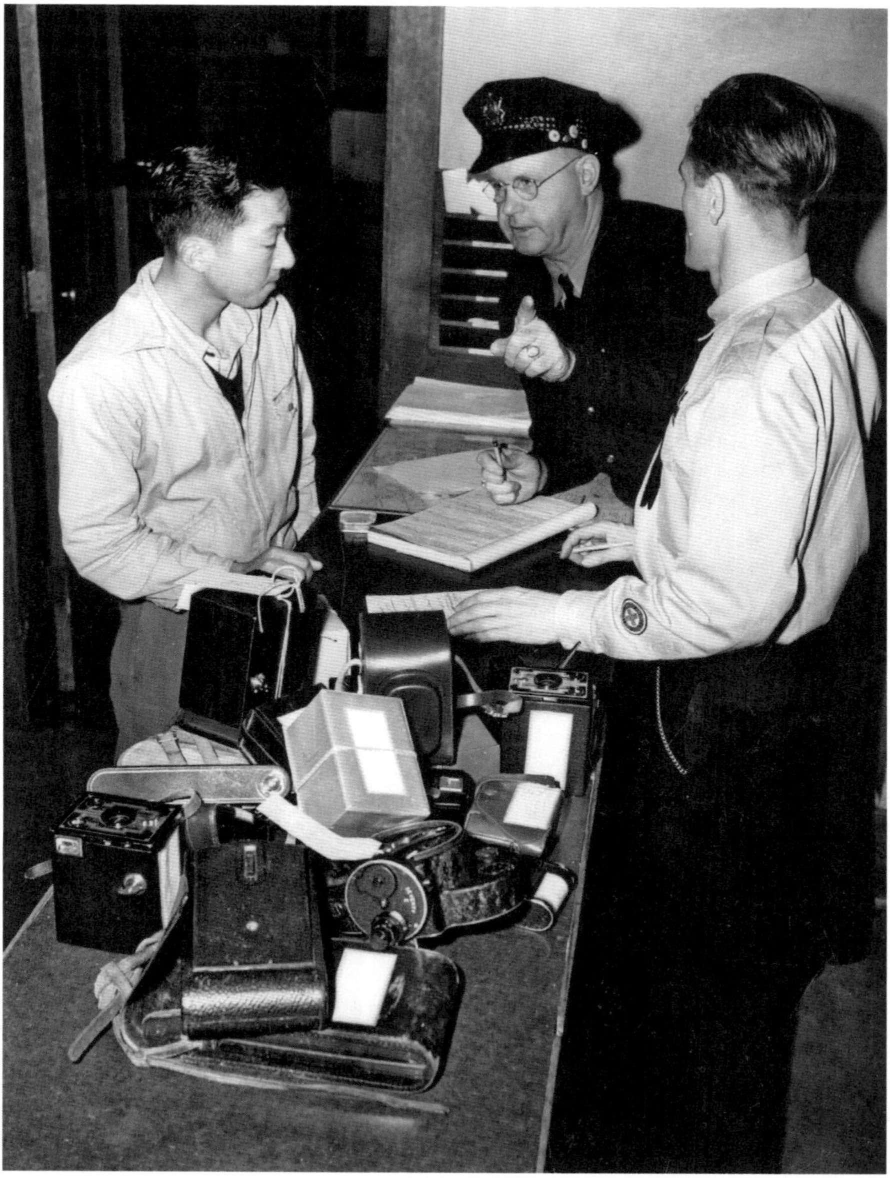

All persons of Japanese ancestry were required to turn in all personal cameras and films to the Sacramento police station. *Courtesy Center for Sacramento History, Sacramento Bee Collection, 1983/001/13,134b.*

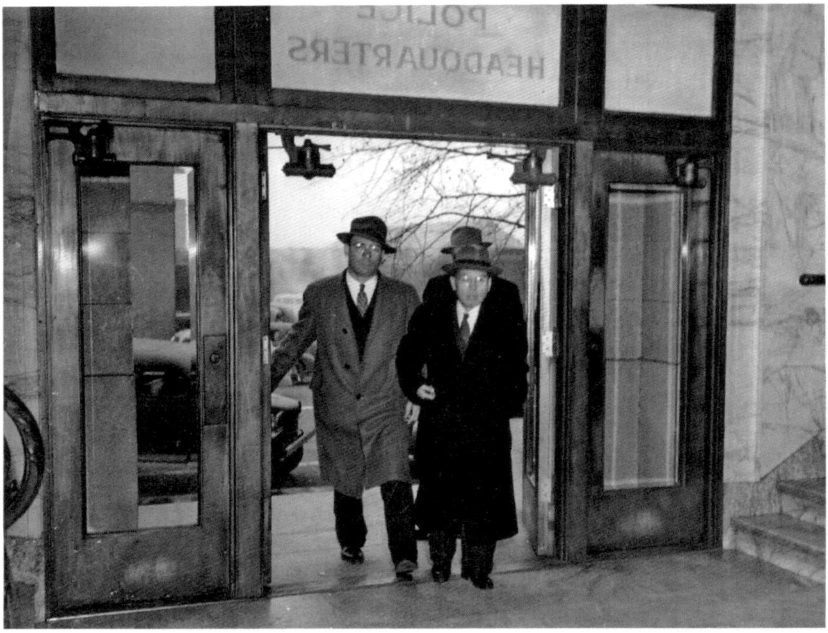

Giichi Aoki, owner of Aoki Music, interrogated by Sacramento Police. *Courtesy Center for Sacramento History, Sacramento Bee Collection, 1983/001/13,130.*

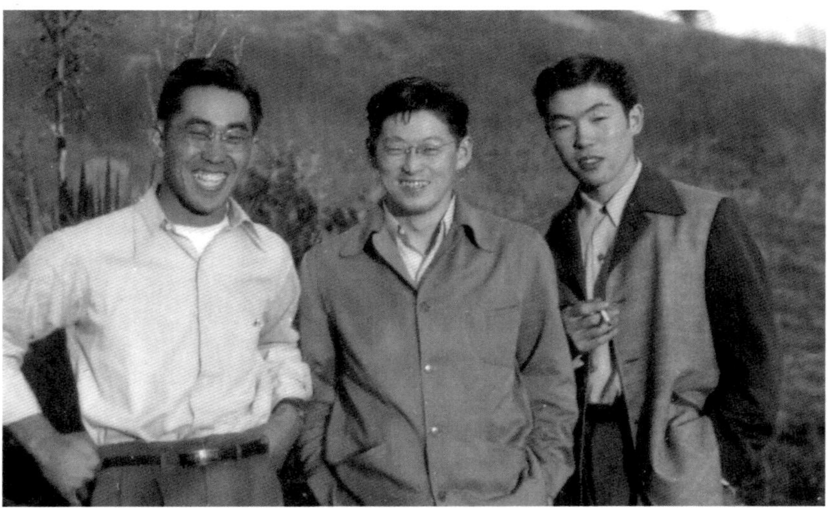

Kanji Nishijima (center) with friends George Makimoto (left) and Hideo Clark Shintaku (right). *Courtesy Jane (Nishijima) Komure and Bonnie (Nishijima) Okamoto.*

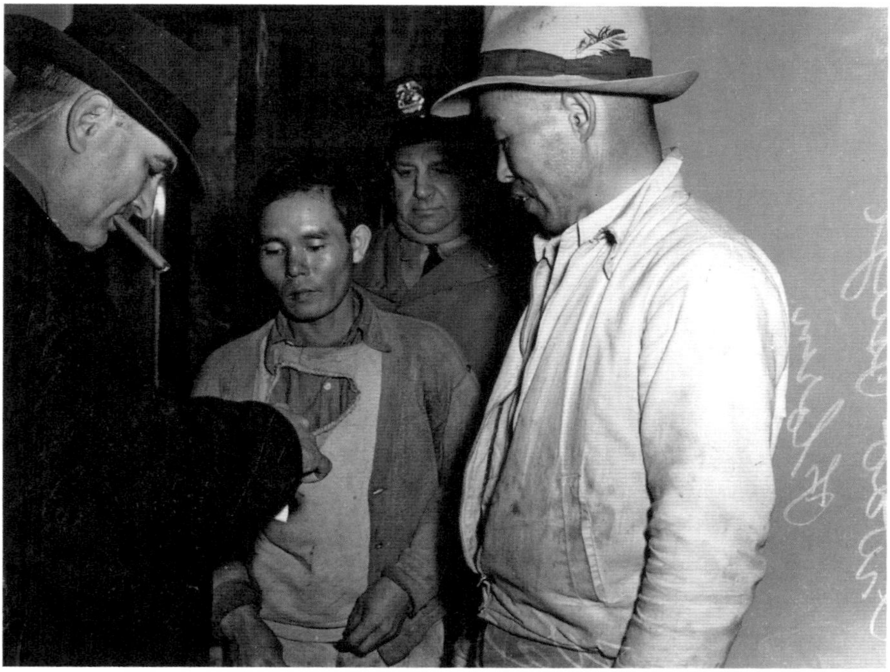

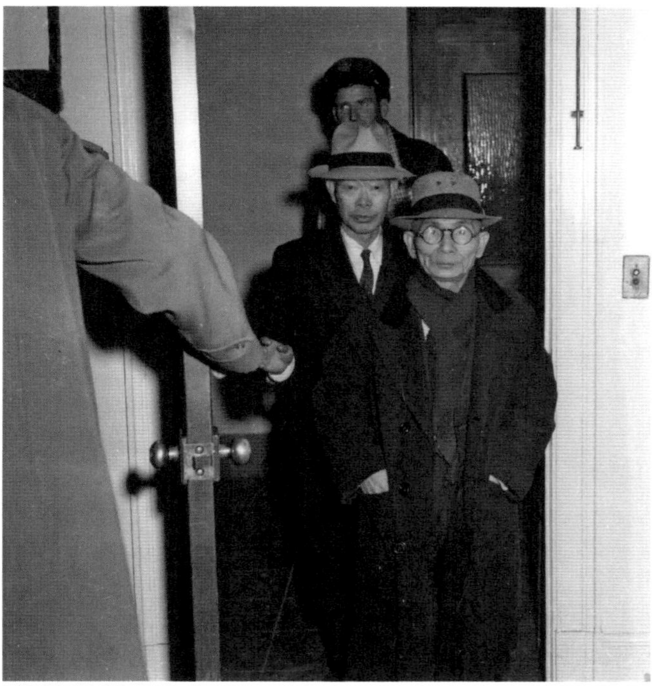

Japanese Americans interrogated by Sacramento police and FBI agents. *Above*: *Courtesy Center for Sacramento History, Sacramento Bee Collection, 1983/001/13,134. Left*: *Courtesy Center for Sacramento History, Sacramento Community Ethnic Survey Collection, 1983/001/13,134d.*

Investment Company. Sakata was one of Sacramento's most successful farmers and a well-respected member of the Japanese American community. At the time the FBI detained him, he held the office of the president of the Sacramento Valley Japanese Association.[163] The FBI also interrogated those who had previously collected and sent aluminum foil from chewing gum wrappers and cigarette boxes and scraps of iron to Japan to help fight the war in China, a gesture that was never intended to be against the United States. As Reverend Nakamura stated, "No one ever suspected that Japan and America would engage in actual warfare and all those patriotic gestures [toward Japan] were not meant to be against this country."[164]

The police also investigated the Nakatani family's Nippon Theater at 328 L Street, seizing film reels worth over $50,000 belonging to Shigezu Matsui. Although the films were only documentaries about the war between China and Japan, Matsui, out of fear of being labeled by authorities a Japanese propagandist and sympathizer, tried to burn the films in his backyard at 512 N Street before police arrived. After an investigation, Sacramento Police classified the reels as "not dangerous." Still, within two days after the attack in Hawaii, Sacramento police and FBI agents had taken over one-fifth of Japanese-owned businesses in Sacramento and had detained twenty people for interrogation. All would be found innocent of espionage.[165]

Despite the presence of FBI agents and the increased police patrols around Sacramento, the Japanese American neighborhood appeared to remain calm. Fortunately, the city experienced relatively few racially motivated disturbances the week following the attack on Pearl Harbor. One reporter for the *Sacramento Union* wrote that according to a police report, there was "little outward change of routine in business and social activity in the local Japanese quarter." Despite increased patrol forces in the area, the police reported an "intense quiet that had descended over the various sections occupied by Japanese businesses and residence."[166] Another reporter from the *Sacramento Bee* testified to the pervasive cloud of silence that had crept over Sacramento's Japanese American neighborhood: "There was little outward evidence of the disturbance in the Japanese quarter of the city this morning. The most noticeable phenomenon was the unusual quiet." The reporter went on to describe the ambiance in Japantown five days after the bombing:

> *Few Japanese men were to be seen on the streets. On one corner three Japanese women were talking together, their faces impassive and unsmiling. From time to time they darted quick looks to one side. Japanese children,*

> *carrying their books and pencils, were on their way to school, playing, and pausing to look into store windows.*
>
> *Practically all of the stores in the quarter were open as usual with their doors swung wide. Two or three had their doors closed but signs, freshly painted for the occasion, hung on the latches and bore the word "Open." In the stores themselves the clerks were behind the counters but few customers were in evidence.*
>
> *The vegetable trucks from the Japanese farms around Sacramento were delivering their usual loads of carrots, lettuce, and other produce, but the drivers did not pause to gossip in front of the stores. They unloaded the carrots and hurried on to the next store or back to their farms.*[167]

Throughout the West Coast states, FBI raids and incarceration of community leaders paralyzed entire Japanese American neighborhoods, leaving the once stable enclaves leaderless. Issei organizations folded, businesses closed their doors or remained open at a loss and churches continued to hold services without many of their elders. Under heavy police patrol, the Japanese American communities' institutional and organizational infrastructure teetered on virtual collapse. The Nisei-dominated JACL, which had just recently established an office at 1205 Fourth Street, appeared as the most stable organization to deal with the pending crisis. Throughout the winter of 1941–42, Nisei leaders achieved recognition among government officials and civic leaders and established the JACL as the principal spokesman for the Japanese American community in the United States. The league sought to improve the image of all Japanese Americans with public statements denouncing the nation of Japan and by establishing cordial relations with various levels of government in an attempt to discourage plans of mass forced removal and incarceration of persons of Japanese ancestry from the West Coast.[168]

In Sacramento, the local chapter of the JACL immediately sprang into action. On the day of the bombing, Dr. George S. Muramoto, president of the Sacramento chapter and representative for three hundred second- and third-generation Japanese Americans in and around Sacramento, held an emergency meeting in his home at 1900 Seventh Street with other prominent members. That evening, they pledged to aid the United States government "in every way possible." Their formal statement of loyalty, signed by Walter T. Tsukamoto, Dr. Jiro Muramoto, Dr. George Muramoto, Henry Taketa and Dr. George S. Iki, was given to City Manager James S. Dean on December 8, 1941.[169] Other Japanese Americans followed the JACL's lead, working

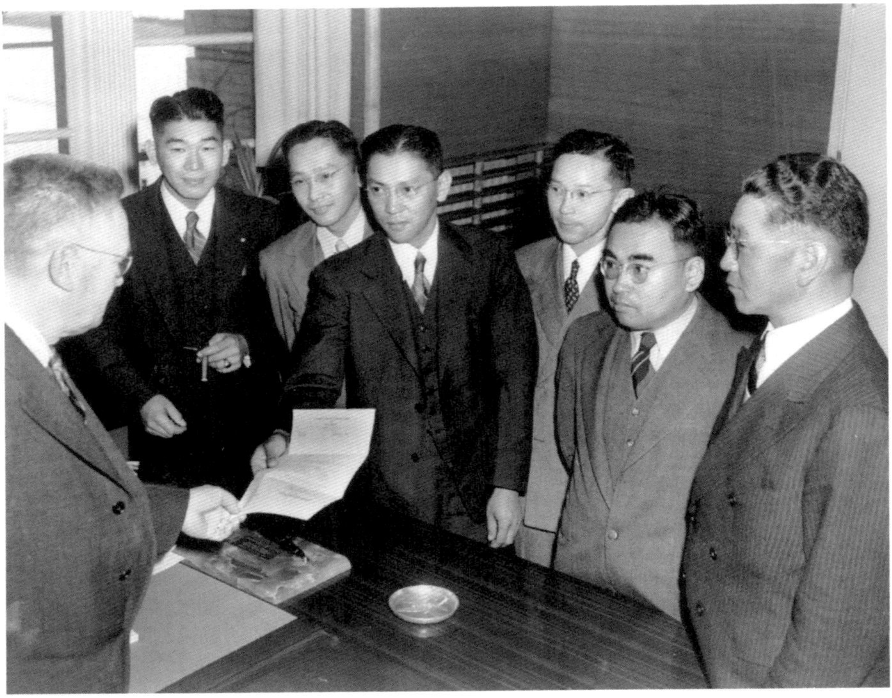

Representatives of the Japanese American Citizens League issuing a statement of loyalty to City Manager James S. Dean the day after the bombing of Pearl Harbor. *Courtesy Center for Sacramento History, Sacramento Bee Collection, 1983/001/13,134a.*

diligently to prove their unwavering commitment and loyalty to the United States. The day after Japan attacked Pearl Harbor, a Japanese American girl, Fumiko Yabe, led the audience in the Sacramento City College Auditorium in the singing of "The Star-Spangled Banner" at the opening of the junior college symphony orchestra's annual concert. One report stated:

> *For a few minutes yesterday afternoon, Sacramento musical folk brushed aside the grim realities to attend the annual concert...and were rewarded with a beautiful program which symbolized the ideals of Christianity and of racial tolerance for which America stands. An American girl of Japanese parentage led the audience in the singing of the "Star Spangled Banner."* [As] *she stood there beside the flag, she seemed to symbolize the thousands of other "Americans with Japanese faces" whose only allegiance is to the land of their birth.*[170]

A few days later, more than fifty Japanese American women, led by Jean Nagata, volunteered at local American Red Cross outlets. One story in a Sacramento newspaper entitled "Picture Brides Roll Bandages" reported that "Japanese women who came to America years ago as 'picture brides' were now volunteering at women's cadet corps to make surgical dressings and roll bandages."[171] The national organization of the JACL, representing sixty local chapters, including Sacramento, closed most of its language schools so as to avoid any misunderstanding about its allegiance to the United States. Prefecture clubs also closed. Many Japanese Americans participated in the selling of defense bonds and stamps.[172] On two occasions, thirty-four Sacramento Japanese American businessmen signed a full-page ad in the *Sacramento Union* that said, "YES, WE ARE AMERICANS." The ad continued:

> *As long-time residents, we fully realize our responsibilities and pledge our fullest support and cooperation toward this, our country! We join with all Americans of Japanese descent in condemning the treacherous actions that have forced this peaceful country into the war. We hope to continue our normal business activity here in order to support our families and do our part toward keeping America a free leading democracy!*[173]

Similar statements soon appeared from other area Japanese American organizations, such as the Delta Japanese American Citizens League and the JACL chapters in Florin, Marysville and Yolo. All expressed unreserved loyalty, firm unity and a "burning desire to assist" in the prosecution of the war.[174]

However, their actions to assure the rest of the community that they were loyal Americans did not always guard them from incriminating and embarrassing situations, such as in the case of six Japanese American Sacramento High School ROTC students who were asked by school authorities to turn in their uniforms and remain out of the graduation picture so as to "remove possible causes of embarrassment to themselves."[175] Some people even lashed out in ways reminiscent of times earlier in the century. One sign in a Yuba City store window stated, "A Merry Christmas and a Happy New Year to you, but DAMN those Japs."[176] Letters to the editor appeared in Sacramento newspapers calling for the mass incarceration of all persons of Japanese ancestry. One person wrote in the *Sacramento Bee*, "I say intern all the alien Japanese in defense areas and use them under supervision to care for and harvest the crops. They are monopolizing the agricultural

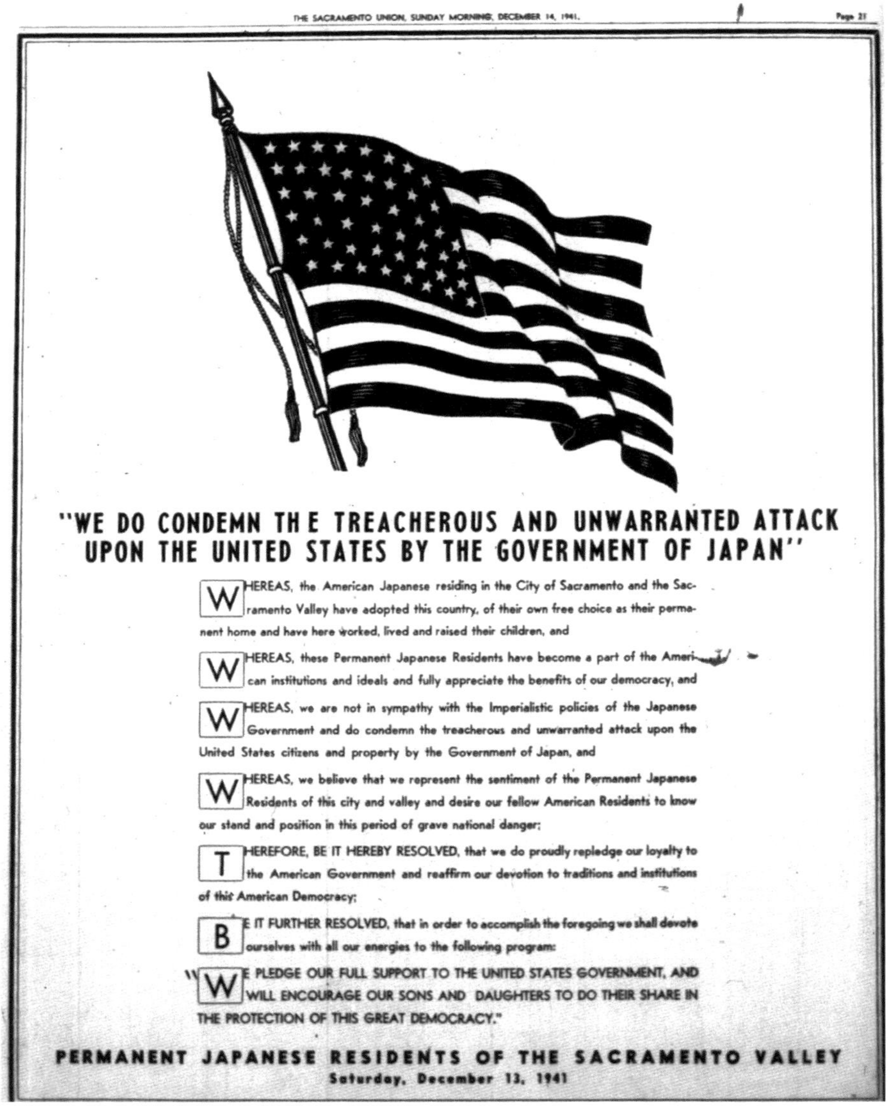

THE SACRAMENTO UNION, SUNDAY MORNING, DECEMBER 14, 1941. Page 21

"WE DO CONDEMN THE TREACHEROUS AND UNWARRANTED ATTACK UPON THE UNITED STATES BY THE GOVERNMENT OF JAPAN"

WHEREAS, the American Japanese residing in the City of Sacramento and the Sacramento Valley have adopted this country, of their own free choice as their permanent home and have here worked, lived and raised their children, and

WHEREAS, these Permanent Japanese Residents have become a part of the American institutions and ideals and fully appreciate the benefits of our democracy, and

WHEREAS, we are not in sympathy with the Imperialistic policies of the Japanese Government and do condemn the treacherous and unwarranted attack upon the United States citizens and property by the Government of Japan, and

WHEREAS, we believe that we represent the sentiment of the Permanent Japanese Residents of this city and valley and desire our fellow American Residents to know our stand and position in this period of grave national danger;

THEREFORE, BE IT HEREBY RESOLVED, that we do proudly repledge our loyalty to the American Government and reaffirm our devotion to traditions and institutions of this American Democracy;

BE IT FURTHER RESOLVED, that in order to accomplish the foregoing we shall devote ourselves with all our energies to the following program:

"WE PLEDGE OUR FULL SUPPORT TO THE UNITED STATES GOVERNMENT, AND WILL ENCOURAGE OUR SONS AND DAUGHTERS TO DO THEIR SHARE IN THE PROTECTION OF THIS GREAT DEMOCRACY."

PERMANENT JAPANESE RESIDENTS OF THE SACRAMENTO VALLEY

Saturday, December 13, 1941

Japanese Americans declaring their loyalty to the United States in the *Sacramento Union* newspaper, December 14, 1941. *Courtesy Mike Sawamura, estates manager for Eugene Okada.*

industry and are forcing other races off the land, including Whites from pioneer families. I say this is America for Americans."[177]

Fear of race riots prevailed up and down the Pacific Coast, particularly among Japanese and Filipino Americans. Outraged by Japan's war on the Philippine Islands, Filipinos in Stockton, California, shattered the windows of businesses, slaying one Japanese American man. Three other Filipinos attacked two Japanese American residents of Walnut Grove who were fishing along the Sacramento Delta, slashing one with a knife and striking the other with a blunt instrument.[178] April Adachi, whose father owned the Tozai store on Fourth Street, was nine years old at the time of the bombing and remembers the palpable anger and tension: "The next morning, I walked out of my dad's store, and a Filipino man just came right up and hit me on the head. I didn't know what was going on."[179] In Sacramento, one Filipino man tried to take the life of Yoshiro Sakatachi, a hotel manager in Japantown. Although the man fired three shots, only one hit Sakatachi in the shoulder, causing a mild injury. Fortunately, such violent and tragic events were few and the number of those attacked or beaten negligible.[180] Other Filipinos disassociated themselves from the Japanese. Speaking at a mass rally in the Manila Pool Hall at 309 L Street, an establishment surrounded by Japanese American businesses, president of the Philippine Commission of the Pacific, Manuel Isigne, urged his three hundred listeners to quit working for Japanese American managers, to move out of Japanese-operated hotels and to avoid Japanese Americans altogether.[181]

After almost three months of activity, the JACL's loyalty campaign failed to block the decision for mass incarceration. On February 19, 1942, President Roosevelt issued Executive Order 9066, which permitted the War Relocation Authority (WRA) to uproot all 120,000 persons of Japanese ancestry residing on the West Coast and incarcerate them behind barbed wire without due process of law. By the end of the first week of May, Lieutenant General John L. DeWitt had ordered 63,000 Japanese Americans to leave selected Pacific Coast areas. Restricted to only what they could carry during their forced evacuation, most Japanese Americans had anywhere between forty-eight hours and one week with which to sell, lease or store their property in vacant stores, churches, houses, garages or other buildings on their vacated land.[182] Some posted "evacuation sale" signs in front of their houses and store windows, while others placed ads in newspapers, frantically selling their belongings at deflated prices.[183]

On May 7, 1942, the Fourth Army Command in San Francisco issued a series of orders for the forced evacuation and incarceration of 8,600

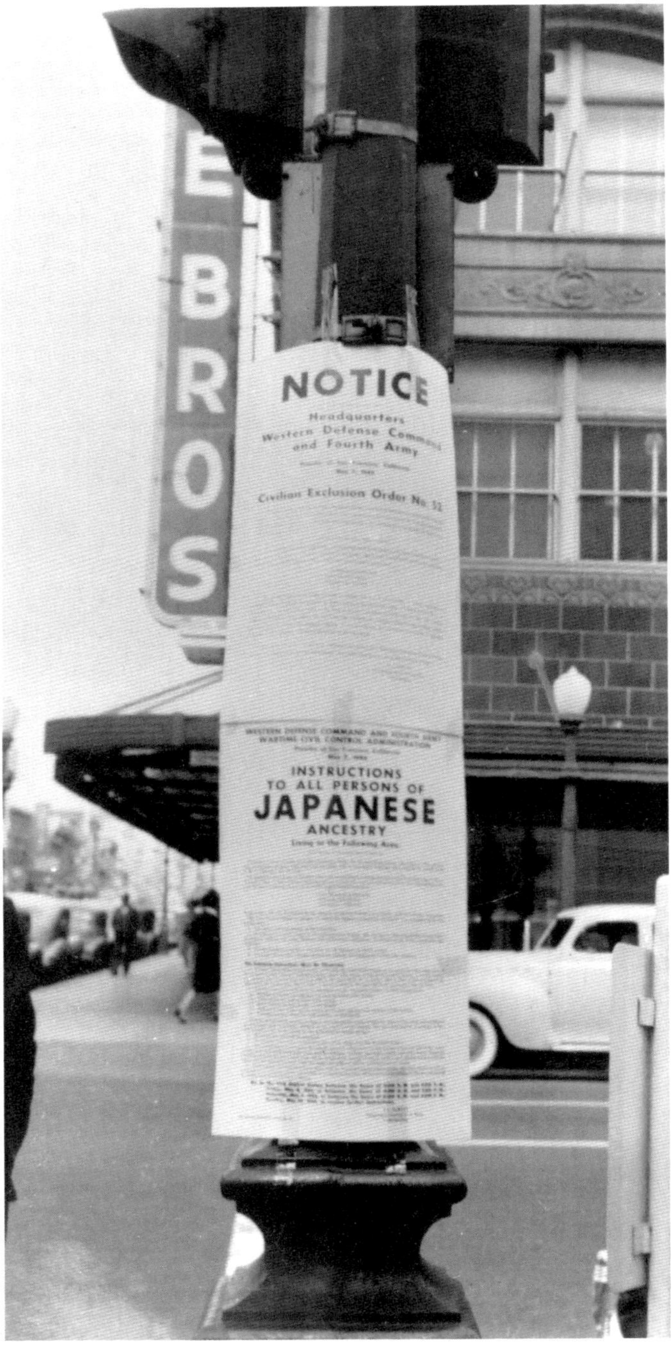

Left: Incarceration order on corner of K and Fourth Streets. *Courtesy Center for Sacramento History, Eugene Hepting Collection, 1985/024/1864.*

Opposite, top: Incarceration order posted near Buddhist Church on corner of Fifth and O Streets, May 11, 1942. *Courtesy War Relocation Authority Photographs Collection, 1967.014, Series 14, Bancroft Library, University of California–Berkeley.*

Opposite, bottom: Mayor Tom B. Monk, City Manager James S. Dean and City Council representatives preparing the city for emergency evacuations. *Courtesy Center for Sacramento History, Sacramento Bee Collection, 1983/001/13,134i.*

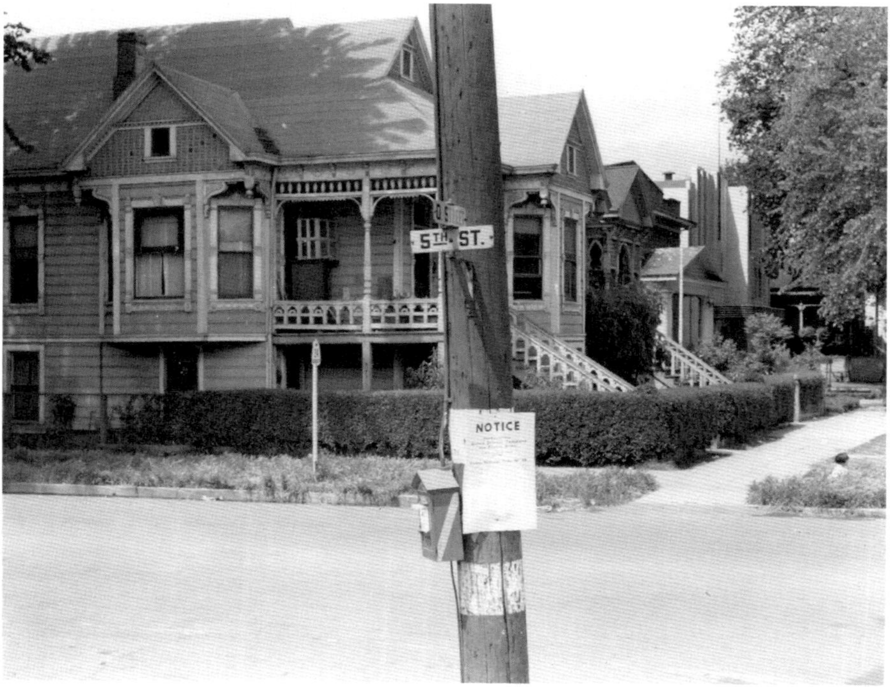
5TH ST.
NOTICE

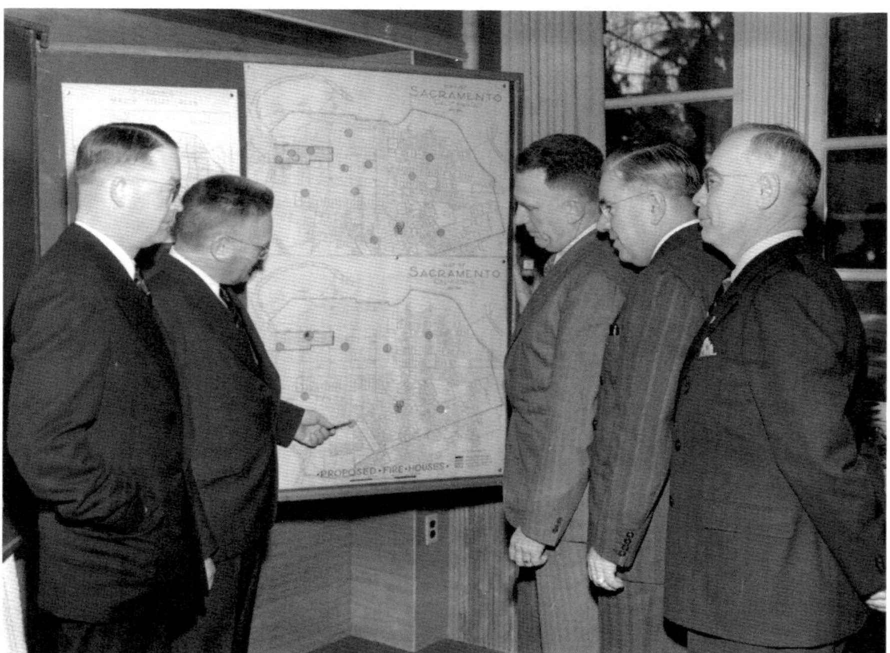
SACRAMENTO
SACRAMENTO
PROPOSED · FIRE · HOUSES

Japanese Americans from within the entire city limits of Sacramento and Stockton and other smaller sections in the Central Valley of California. That evening, headlines in the *Sacramento Bee* announced, "All Japanese Must Get Out of Sacramento." City authorities posted incarceration orders in front of the Capitol and on light posts scattered throughout the downtown district. All persons of Japanese ancestry were ordered to report to the Sacramento Memorial Auditorium within five days for removal to Walerga detention center, a temporary incarceration compound fourteen miles northeast of the city, until much larger incarceration centers were ready.[184] Japanese Americans worked with city officials and the WRA to help them clean up their homes and ranch problems and find storage shelters for their furniture, automobiles and other personal belongings. Reverend Kenzaburo Igarashi and his wife, Toshiko Igarashi, of the First Japanese Baptist Church near Fifth and P Streets, opened their church doors to members and nonmembers alike to be used as a storehouse for personal property:

> *We helped people haul their belongings...They piled up everything like a mountain in front of our church. We left all of our belongings in the church. The Baptist Church also took charge of keeping non-members' belongings. You see, it was three-story. We put them in the back corner of the third floor. Later, we learned through a white church by letter that it was broken into at a time when the director wasn't there. We reported it to the main office in California, and I believe they assigned someone to be there from then on. The Christian Center was originally called Japanese Christian Center, but no sooner had the war broke out, then it was ordered to drop the word "Japanese." Next to our church was Lincoln School, the grammar school, you know. So we changed it to the Lincoln Christian Center.*[185]

Many Japanese American merchants wrote cordial letters to their customers in Sacramento newspapers. Unosuke Kurotori, for example, owner of L Street Laundry in Japantown, wrote two letters in the *Sacramento Union*: "To Our Dear Patrons: We will close our plant temporarily on May 10 so that we can prepare for evacuation. We thank you sincerely for your past patronage and wish you to continue your favor upon our return."[186] In an attempt to sell the property they could not store or take with them to camp, some used classified ads. One such ad in the *Sacramento Union* read, "Evacuation Sale—36 Studebaker... Sedan, radio, $200. 37 Ford pickup, $325. Complete parts for Rockne 32 model. 1 Mule and harness. 8 varieties of tomato plants, pepper plants.

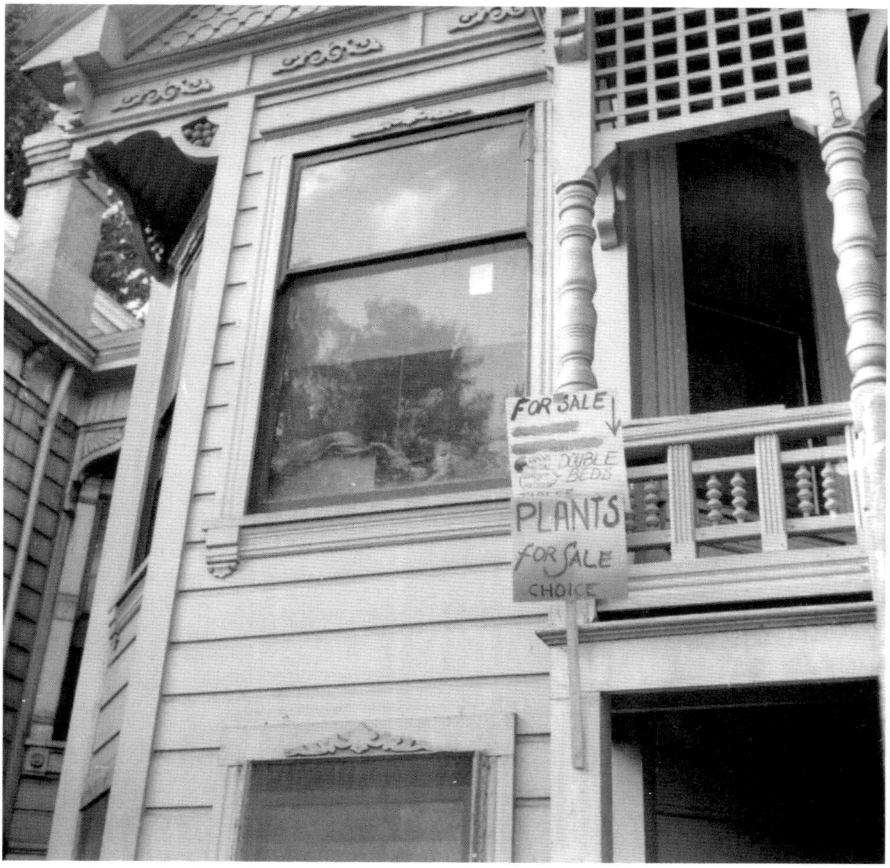

Courtesy War Relocation Authority Photographs Collection, 1967/014, Bancroft Library, University of California–Berkeley.

Lease Ranch 40 acres, 3 acres bush berries, vegetables, plenty water. 5 room house, barn, chicken house."[187]

Because automobiles were not allowed in the incarceration centers, many Japanese Americans hastily placed them on the market at reduced prices. One advertisement stated, "Sacrifice—1938 Chevrolet $495, Evacuating." Owners of cleaners placed ads for customers: "Evacuating! Come claim clothes by May 15th."[188] Signs advertising "Good Metal Beds, Plants for Sale" or "Must Evacuate, 50% off, Everything Must Go!" appeared in house windows up and down the streets of Japantown. "When the evacuation notice came out," said Reverend Nakamura of the Japanese Presbyterian

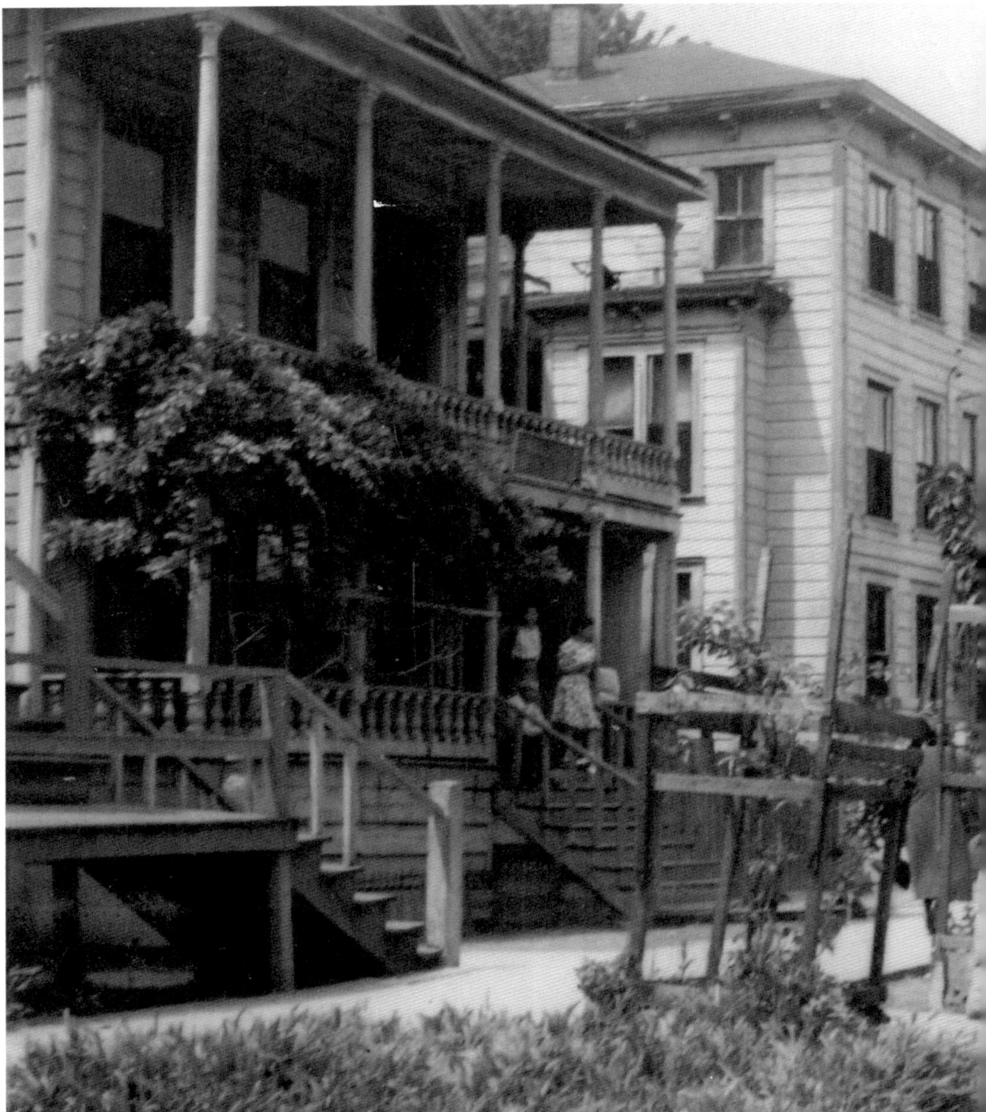

A Japanese American family prepares for incarceration. *Courtesy Center for Sacramento History, Eugene Hepting Collection, 1985/024/1864.*

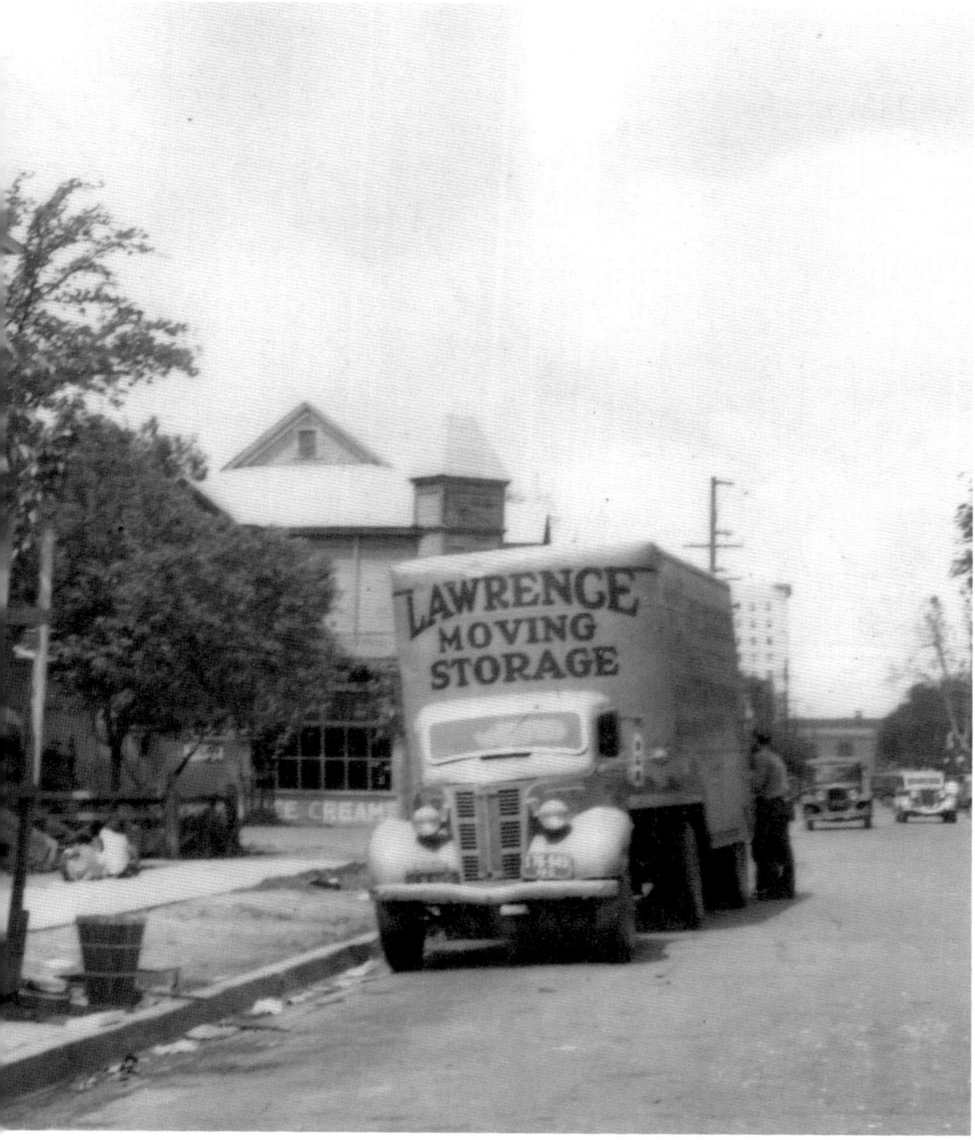
LAWRENCE
MOVING
STORAGE

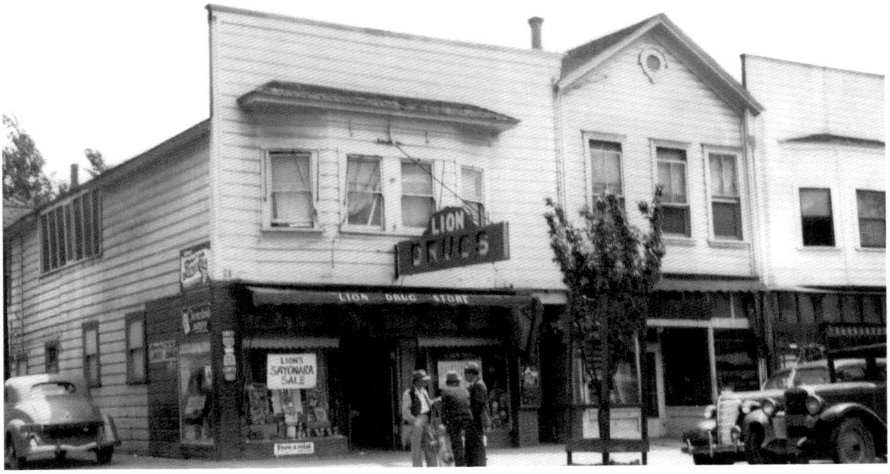

Lion Drug Store's "Sayonara" sale preparing for incarceration. *Courtesy Center for Sacramento History, Eugene Hepting Collection, 1985/024/1871.*

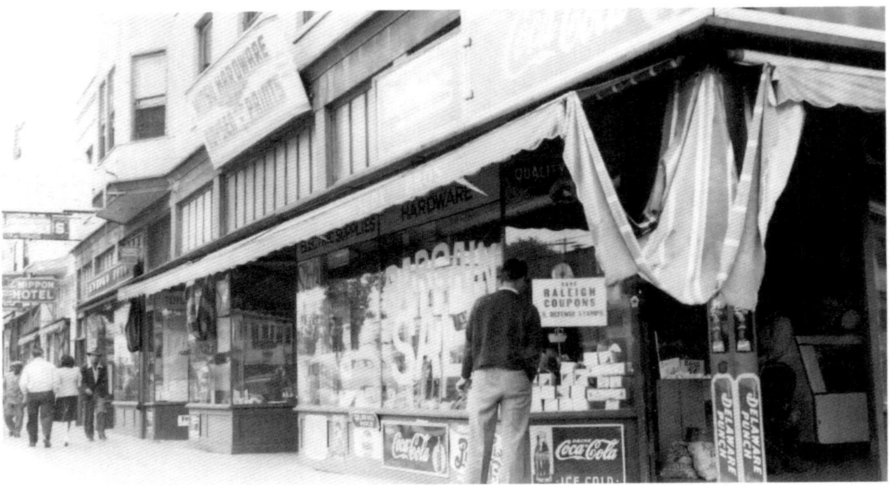

Matsuda Brothers "bargain sale" preparing for incarceration. *Courtesy Center for Sacramento History, Eugene Hepting Collection, 1985/024/1869.*

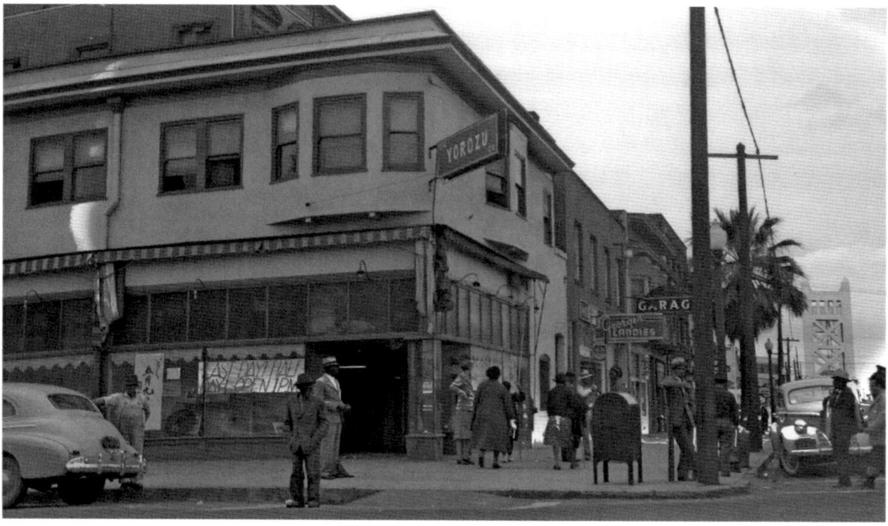

Yorozu closing sale preparing for incarceration, corner of Fourth Street and Capitol Avenue. *Courtesy Center for Sacramento History, Eugene Hepting Collection, 1985/024/1877.*

Church, "merchants were buying up properties, furniture, and anything of value from the evacuees for cheap prices." He continued:

> *The local Church Federation promised the owners of the hotels (there were fourteen or fifteen Japanese owners) that the Federation would look after the business, but the day before we were evacuated,* [the Federation] *changed its mind and could not take care of the hotels as they promised previously. Subsequently, the hotel owners had only one day to find buyers for furniture, bedding, and supplies. This was a buyer's market and they probably bought all the things dirt cheap.*[189]

A farmer in Broderick, just outside Sacramento, sold his $200 stove for $15 and sold his radio, washing machine, tools and appliances at similarly reduced prices. As he said, "We had to sell everything so cheaply that it was just like throwing things away."[190] Such flurry of commercial activity by the Japanese American community caused one local reporter to write:

> *One of the complaints of the evacuation is the throwing on the market at low prices the household effects, automobiles, and other belongings of these sons of Nippon, whether alien or American born. The disruption locally*

has been widespread and some weeks will pass before adjustments can be made and the changes be absorbed.

We hear stories of Sacramentans buying up the belongings of the Japanese and profiting rich thereby. We hear other stories of markets for certain goods being gutted during the changeover and trade in them virtually brought to a standstill. [However,] *the evacuation is a military necessity. Through no choice of its own, California has been made combat area and for the safety of its citizens the people of Japanese origin must be moved away.*[191]

Uncertainty about what the future might bring caused a few young Japanese American couples to rush into marriage. Activity in the Sacramento County Marriage License Bureau was almost exclusively Japanese American the day after the evacuation orders appeared. And the animal control center became overwhelmed with pets previously owned by Japanese Americans families.[192]

Some evacuees were able to receive help from others who were sympathetic to their situation. Jerry Miyamoto, a Nisei native of Sacramento whose father, Sumio, owned the Miyamoto Insurance and Travel Agency near Fourth and N Streets, recalls his father's fortunate situation at that time: "During the evacuation, he found some white people to rent the house who took really good care of it. He considered himself fortunate."[193] "Lucky" is how optometrist James Kubo described his situation after he received notification that he had a week to vacate his home and office: "When we had to leave, I had all my optometry equipment and I did not know what to do with it. The guy who I bought all my equipment from said, 'Give it all to me, and I'll take care of it for you.' So I sent it all to him, and when I was at camp, he sent me a check with all my stuff broken down, showing the value of each thing."[194] Friends from neighboring churches also lent helping hands to those in need. Reverend Nakamura remembers:

A few days before evacuation, Dr. Kircher and members of the Westminster Church came to our church to bid us farewell by singing hymns and offering their prayers. During these hard times, people were somewhat hesitant to help the Japanese, but Mr. Frank Muench, a worker at the Lincoln Christian Center of the Baptist Church, helped not only the members of the Baptist Church but everyone who needed assistance in preparation for evacuation. When we went into Walerga Assembly Center near McClellan Air Force Base, he was just about the only White who transported our luggage on his truck for us.[195]

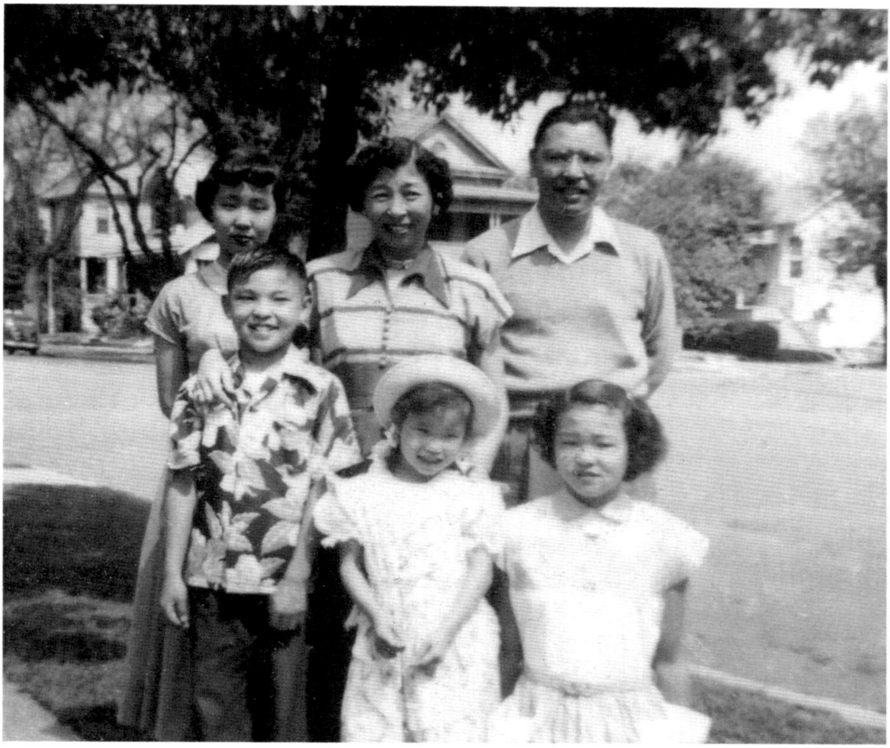

Miyamoto family. *Back row, left to right*: Terry, Emma, Sumio. *Front row, left to right*: Jerry, Patty, Kiyo. *Courtesy Jerry Miyamoto.*

Not all were as fortunate. Under such pressing conditions, substantial hardship ensued. Alice Hayashi could only carry baby supplies for her two children while on her way to the Memorial Auditorium. "When evacuation came, they told us we had to go and take only what we could carry. All I could carry was diapers because I still had two in diapers at that time. We put some things in storage, but jewelry and clothes—I lost everything. I never found that stuff again."[196] Many Japanese Americans ended up losing their homes. For example, the total number of Japanese-owned or -leased farm properties in the evacuated areas of the West Coast states dropped from nearly seven thousand tabulated just before mass incarceration to a little over two thousand after the war. Although Japanese Americans in the western states owned $400 million worth of farm property in 1942, the federal government only paid $38 million in property claims to them after the war.[197]

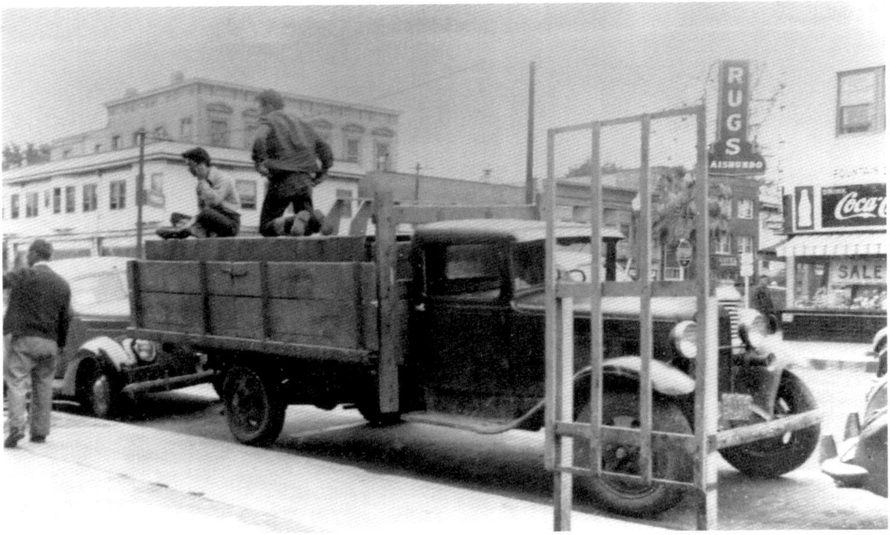

The Matsuda brothers preparing for incarceration, corner of Fourth Street and Capitol Avenue. *Courtesy Center for Sacramento History, Eugene Hepting Collection, 1985/024/1866.*

Material sacrifices were not the only price of mass incarceration. Fear of racial hatred; the trauma of possible separation from family, friends and community; and the tremendous psychological pressure inflicted by the dominant culture to feel guilty about one's ancestry added to the confusion and sense of uncertainty shared by most Japanese Americans at this time. One Japanese American man in Los Angeles ended his life by swallowing poison. In Sacramento, a Japanese American farmer took his own life by hanging himself with an electric cord. Confronted with the trauma of evacuation, a thirty-five-year-old man in Southern California committed suicide by hanging himself in a public park. A note pinned to his coat read, "My country goes greatly wrong. I cannot face my good friend Americans. So I have to die. Please bury quietly."[198] Fortunately, such tragic events remained few.

Japanese Americans in Sacramento were not the only ones affected by the mass incarceration. A large portion of the downtown area was denuded of population, the schools were deprived of 1,006 pupils, many white ranches were stripped of their Japanese American workers and many Sacramento businesses were weakened. Lincoln Elementary School at 416 P Street experienced a 33 percent drop in its student body population. The Hancock Branch library at Lincoln Junior High School on the corner of

Fourth and Q Streets was forced to close since its average book circulation figure of over 3,500 plunged to a meager 200 almost overnight.[199] Because Japanese American farmers cultivated the greater part of the 1,600 acres of strawberries and grapes in the Sacramento area, their incarceration devastated one of the nation's largest strawberry- and grape-producing sectors, which was located south of Sacramento in the Florin district. One week after forced evacuation, 342 farms out of the 735 Japanese-owned farms in the area still awaited new operators. The combination of a late spring and mass incarceration left thousands of crates of strawberries to rot on the ground. In an effort to hastily recruit farm laborers and cushion the agricultural crunch, the agricultural division of the Civil Wartime Central Administration converted the Buddhist church in Florin into a regional farm bureau. In the words of one reporter, "Sacramento is experiencing an economic upheaval. In the channels of trade there is profiting and suffering of losses from the evacuation."[200]

On May 13, 1942, the first of 3,800 persons of Japanese ancestry from Sacramento carrying only their suitcases or bundles of clothes and personal belongings tied with string gathered in the Memorial Auditorium and waited for buses to take them to Walerga detension center just outside Sacramento's city limits. The detention center held two hundred frame buildings, each divided into five family units, erected in the center of a large oak grove on a 160-acre tract. Some 600 Japanese Americans who were the first to be confined at Walerga made preparations for the other 4,000 detainees. Among the more prominent Sacramento Japanese Americans was Dr. George Iki who had previously practiced medicine in the Taketa Building located on Fourth Street in central Japantown. With other Japanese Americans, Dr. Iki prepared a 150-bed hospital in the detention center.[201]

For many, Walerga provided comfort, security and a sense of social solidarity from the uncertainties of the outside world. "I felt that we were being protected in the camp," said Issei Riyo Orite. "The reason I felt so is that I had been treated terribly before I moved to the camp. People threw rocks at me and did all kinds of bad things to me."[202] Riichi Satow agreed: "When the news came that we were going to be put into camp, it in fact eased my mind, because in it I saw the possibility of getting our life stabilized."[203] Dr. George Iki, after settling in Walerga, felt as if a "ton of bricks had been lifted" from his shoulders. As he explained, his problem and that of other prominent Japanese Americans had been to calm the worries of those in his community.[204] Now, for the first time in months, the community as a whole began to regain the feeling of solidarity it had before Pearl Harbor. Reverend

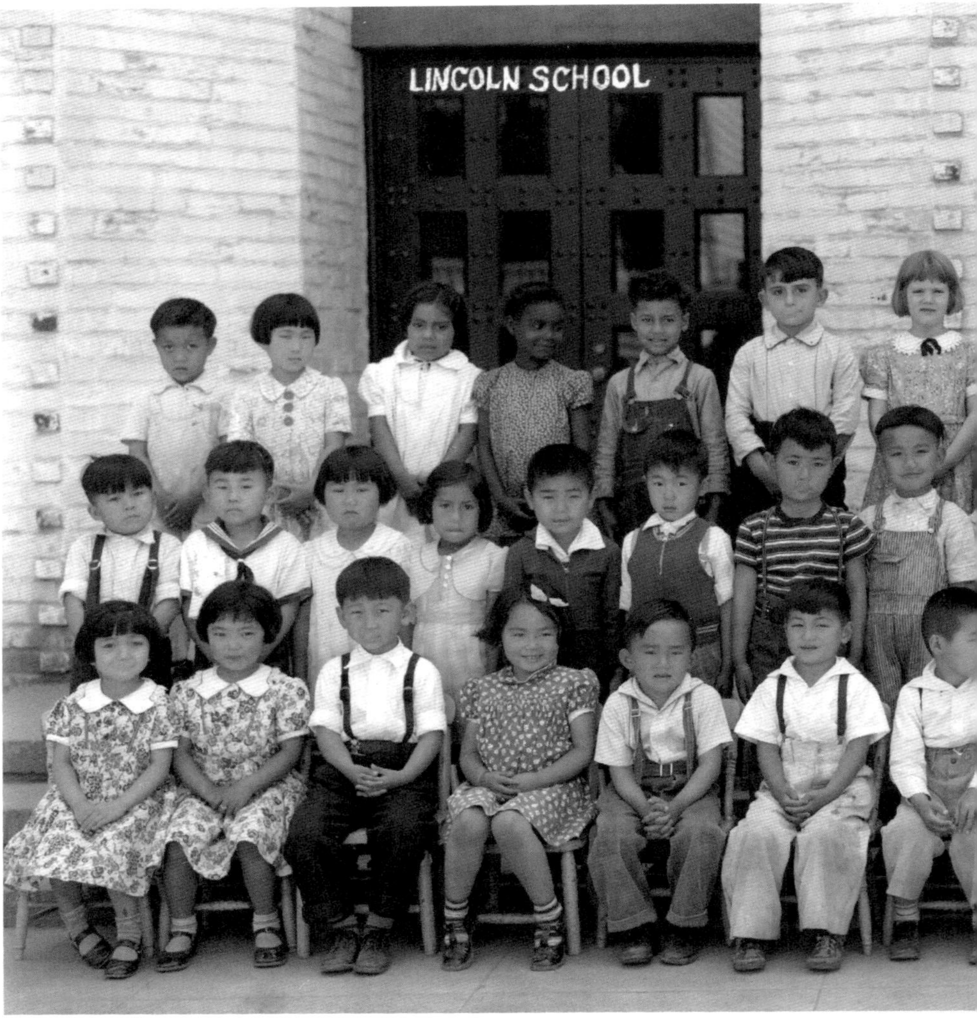

Lincoln Elementary School, 1938. *Top row*: Henry Wong, Masaka Tsuruda, Angelina ___, ___, ___, John Kakavas, ___, ___, Peter Osuga, ___, Antoinette ___, ___, Pauline Gee, Norman Hue, Jane Fong. *Middle row*: Gordon Fong, ___, ___, ___, Freddy Shirasago, ___, Bobby Tanaka, Arthur Lee, ___, ___, ___, ___, Violet Yoshizuka, Irene Fong, ___, Jonny Lai, William Fong, Victor Gorre. *Bottom row*: Helen Dairiki, Sally Kikumoto, Bobby Eto, Marian Uchida, George ___, John Nishimi, Akira ___, Thomas Toyama, April Adachi, Tommy Yamamoto, Kathryn Neri, Fusako ___, Tomoko ___, Jean Kawano. *Courtesy Fred and Katie Shirasago and Marian Uchida.*

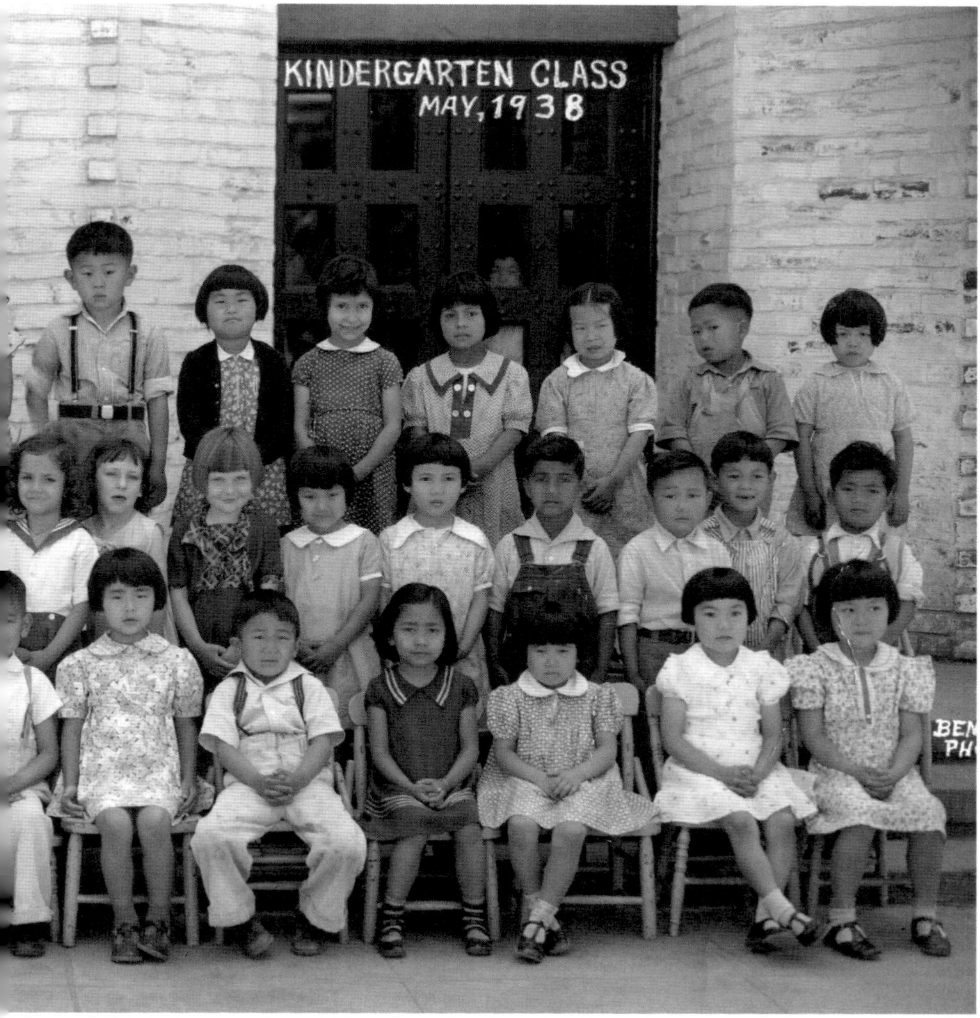
KINDERGARTEN CLASS
MAY, 1938

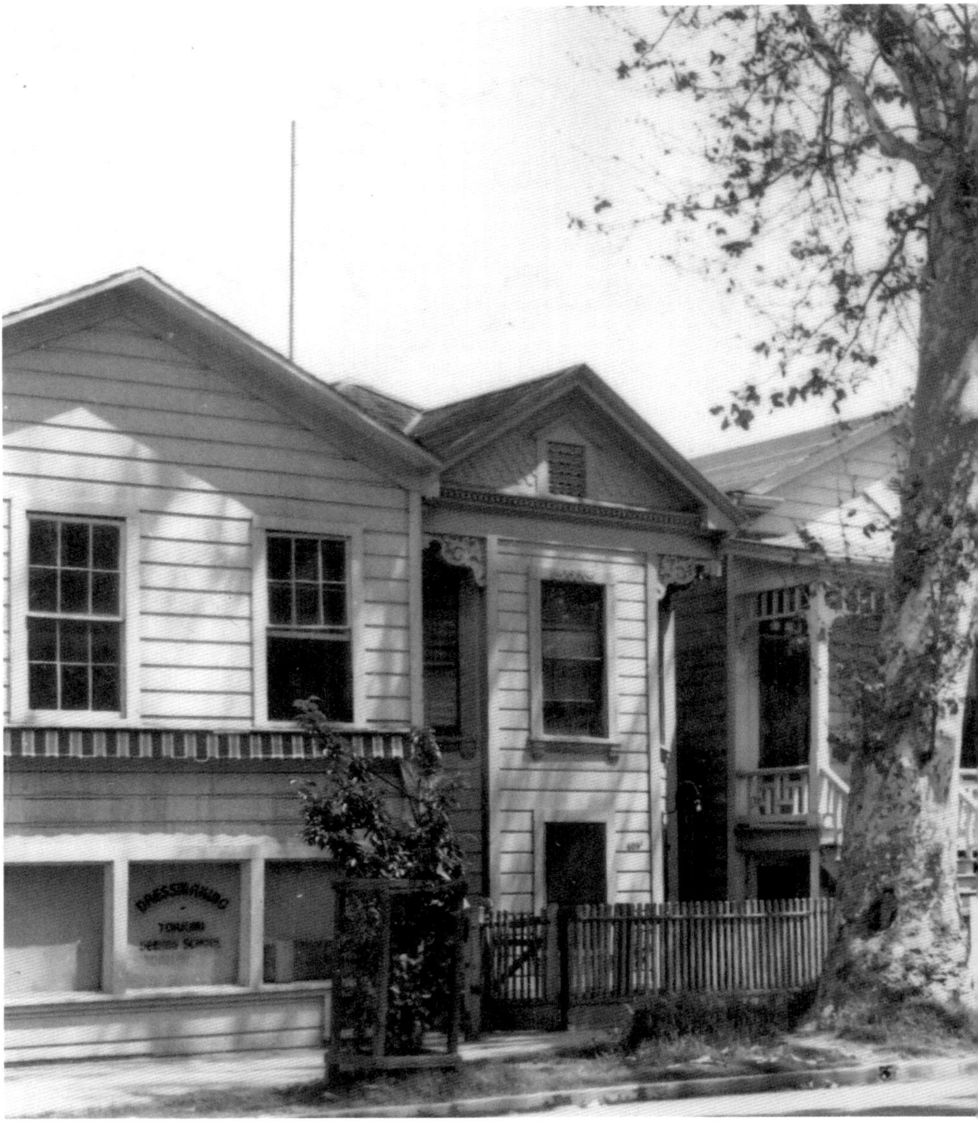

Empty homes in Japantown's residential district on N Street, between Fourth and Fifth Streets, the day after the incarceration of all persons of Japanese ancestry. Michiko Takahashi's home is second from last. *Courtesy Center for Sacramento History, Eugene Hepting Collection, 1985/024/1888.*

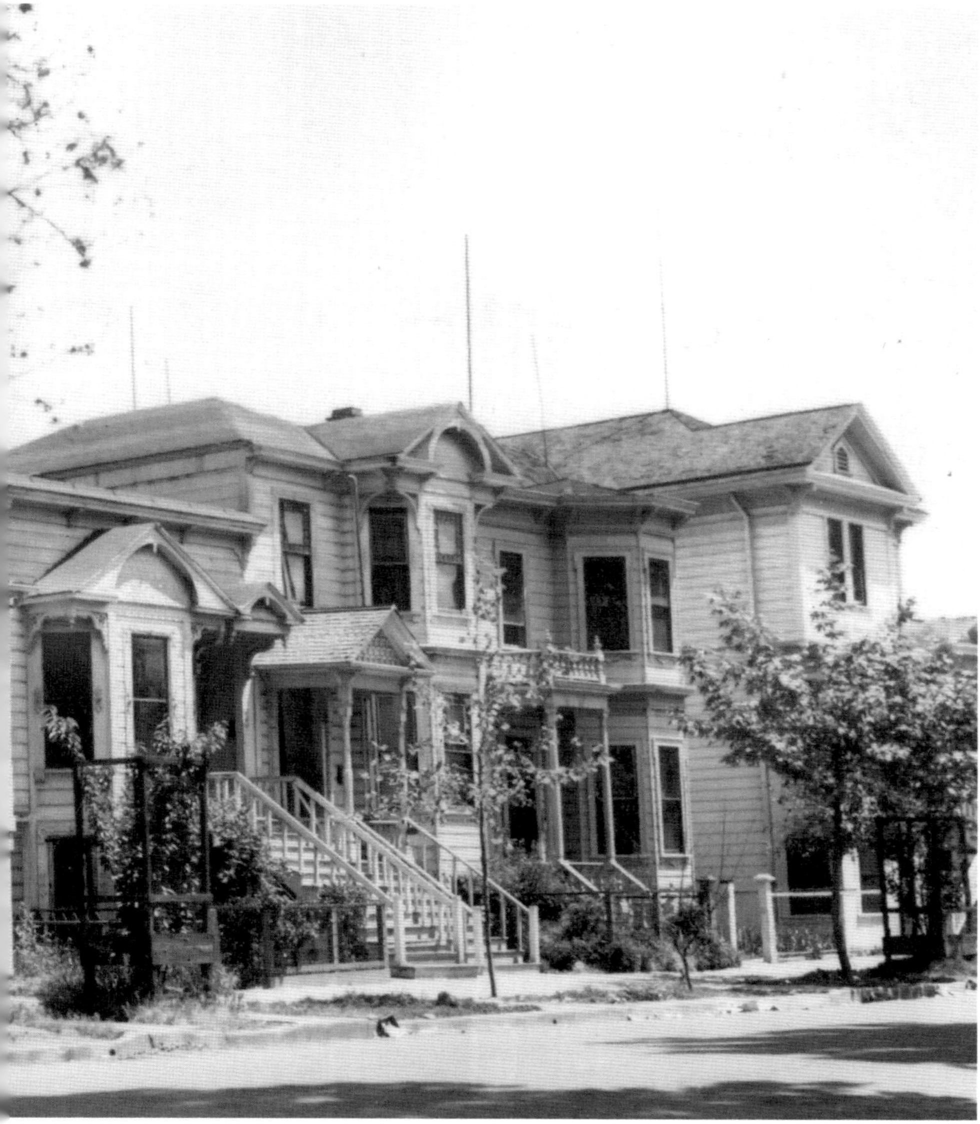

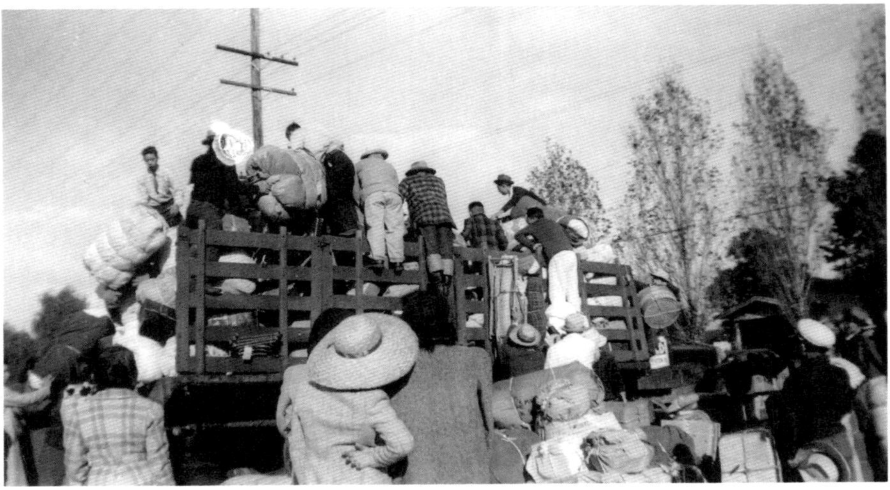

Japanese Americans preparing to go to Walerga detention center. *Courtesy Japanese American Archival Collection. Department of Special Collections and University Archives, California State University–Sacramento.*

Nakamura noticed that although the general feeling in the detention center seemed to be "tense and alert," not knowing what to expect, the Japanese Americans had cultivated a "feeling of unity" because so many of them were concentrated in one place.[205] As one reporter wrote, "The scene among the oaks at Walerga…does not resemble either a place of confinement or a picnic ground. But to the Japanese Americans of Sacramento it does represent the closest approach to a normal living that has been possible for them since Pearl Harbor."[206] In an effort to ease the community's traumatic upheaval and create a more "livable atmosphere" among a chaotic forced evacuation and mass incarceration, community leaders quickly set up a detention center council that consisted of Walter Tsukamoto, George Takahashi, Henry Taketa, Dr. Goro Muramoto and Sumio Miyamoto. Others quickly worked together to establish barbershops, a general store, a garden and a library that was organized through the efforts of Nori Shiba and Florence Hayashi, while Howard Imazaki, Jobo Nakamura and Art Morimitsu managed a new Walerga detention center newspaper, *The Wasp*.[207]

Walerga detention center was open for fifty-two days, detaining some 4,770 persons of Japanese ancestry. After a few months, most of those incarcerated from Sacramento, Yuba City and Marysville ended up at Tule Lake, California incarceration center. Most from Florin were taken to other incarceration centers, either to Manzanar in California, Poston in Arizona or Jerome in Arkansas. California's Japanese Americans were joined in the incarceration centers by others throughout the Pacific Coast.[208]

At the time of the attack on Pearl Harbor, 127,000 persons of Japanese ancestry, more than 60 percent of them native-born American citizens, lived in the continental United States. Of this number, 90 percent lived in the three coastal states of Washington, Oregon and California and the border state of Arizona. Despite naval and FBI reports that found no evidence of Japanese American espionage or sabotage, and therefore declared mass incarceration unnecessary, the United States government forcefully uprooted and incarcerated 120,000 persons of Japanese ancestry from their homes, placing them in ten incarceration centers in seven different states all located west of the Mississippi River.[209] Passage of Executive Order 9066 was a culmination of a complex combination of factors that included a long legacy of anti-Asian racism, the success of Japanese American farmers, their geographic concentration along the West Coast and the supposed "internal threat" of Japanese nationalism. Mass incarceration profoundly altered the Japanese American community, shattering Japanese American farm villages and Japanese American neighborhoods along the western seaboard.

Not unlike other cities, Sacramento's Japantown had been destroyed, uprooted by the Relocation Authority. Except for perhaps a few signs left in empty shop windows, the churches, social halls and stores that had provided a source of livelihood and a sense of place for two generations of Japanese Americans now stood as desolate monuments to Sacramento's once resilient ethnic community. For the dominant culture, mass incarceration appeared to have permanently sapped the life out of the Japanese American community, erasing Japantown from Sacramento's landscape forever. As one reporter derogatorily put it, "We know of many houses, stores, hotels, and other buildings left vacant by the removal of their occupants, and wonder, as do many others, what new residents will move into these abandoned structures in what was formerly referred to as 'Jap Town.'"[210]

However, the most dismal yet telling description of the effect of mass incarceration on Japantown appears from a writer for the *Sacramento Union*: "[Japantown] has been blitzed. A few days ago, lower Capitol Avenue and N Street were chock full of Japanese grocery stores, furniture marts, bait shops, restaurants, rooming houses, and other businesses. But last night that district was full of 'for lease' signs on homes, 'new management' placards in stores, and heaps of receipts and other commercial papers piled on the sidewalks."[211] At the time of their forced evacuation, Japanese Americans had owned approximately one out of every three business establishments in the eight-block area of Japantown. Despite their large numbers, few Japanese Americans could be found on the streets at nighttime during this chaotic week. Most Japanese Americans were in their homes, and those who were not were in their place of business, packing their remaining merchandise or tallying up their records. The *Sacramento Union* reporter went on to describe the scene:

> *Practically* [no Japanese] *are in the streets, except the only discordant note—a troop of Japanese Boy Scouts practicing for drum and bugle corps as though they were living in a piping time of peace and not when Japanese ancestry makes one suspect.*
>
> *Office buildings, where Japanese dentists and doctors kept their offices open after dark, were lightless, except for some who were busy checking over their final records…A large number of stores formerly owned by Japanese have been taken over by whites and bearing signs "Under New Management," or "Will Be Open Again Soon."*
>
> *…In a barbershop, the aged proprietor sat alone in a room denuded of barber chairs, razors, brushes, hair oil, and the other appurtenances of his craft, and played solitaire…In another shop, once a laundry, the erstwhile proprietor sat by himself at a small table amid a disordered pile of shirt wrappings and collar stiffeners, writing.*[212]

Like all Japanese American neighborhoods on the West Coast, Sacramento's Japantown had been "blitzed." A way of life for a people who had been living in Sacramento for over fifty years quickly vanished. Now, within the cauldron of incarceration centers, Japanese Americans confronted the greatest injustice ever set before them as a people, and one of the most atrocious violations of Constitutional rights in U.S. history, a challenge that strained but did not shatter their spirit of community.

CHAPTER 4

POSTWAR RESETTLEMENT, URBAN REDEVELOPMENT AND THE END OF JAPANTOWN, 1945–1960

In December 1944, the United States military announced the closing of America's concentration camps and mass incarceration of persons of Japanese ancestry. Yet when the war ended in August 1945, some 30 percent of the incarcerated remained in the camps. Fear of rejection and possible violence, coupled with the lack of guaranteed employment, housing or financial assistance, persuaded some to stay in the centers, where at least bare necessities were available. With the closing of all the centers in the winter of 1946, the remaining incarcerated were eventually handed train fare to return to their cities or towns. With the end of mass incarceration loomed the journey back home and the arduous task of piecing together the lives they had left behind. It was the beginning of a new struggle, the search to find their place in postwar American society.[213]

Like all Japanese Americans returning from on the West Coast, Japanese Americans in Sacramento confronted a vigilant racial intolerance that hoped to prevent their return to their old neighborhoods. The Sacramento Home Front Commandos led an effort to prevent Japanese Americans from returning to the city and declared that "Nisei were unfit for the human race" and that "no Jap is now fit to associate with human beings." They called for all Issei to be deported and vowed to prevent American citizens of Japanese ancestry from establishing businesses or securing employment before "pacifists, religious cliques and the brotherly love gang frustrate anything that may be attempted when peace comes."[214] City leaders wasted no time siding with the Home Front Commandos in declaring their opposition

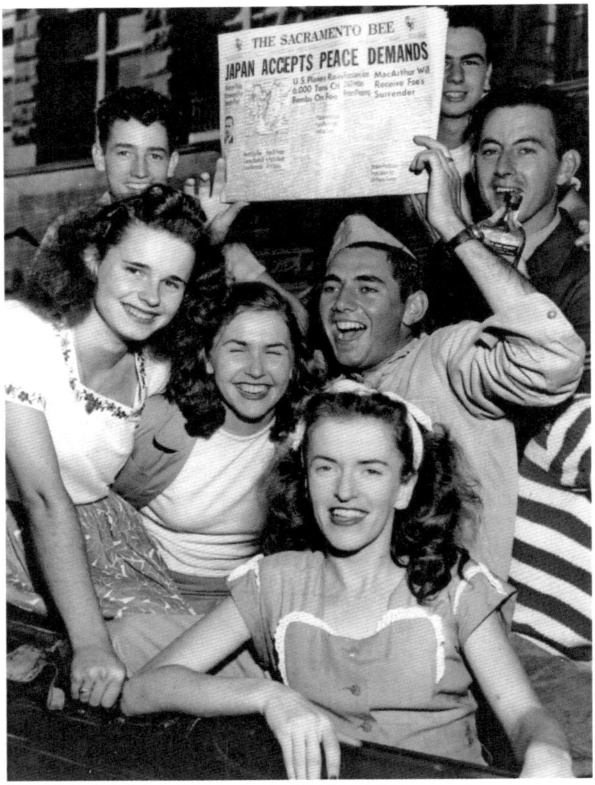

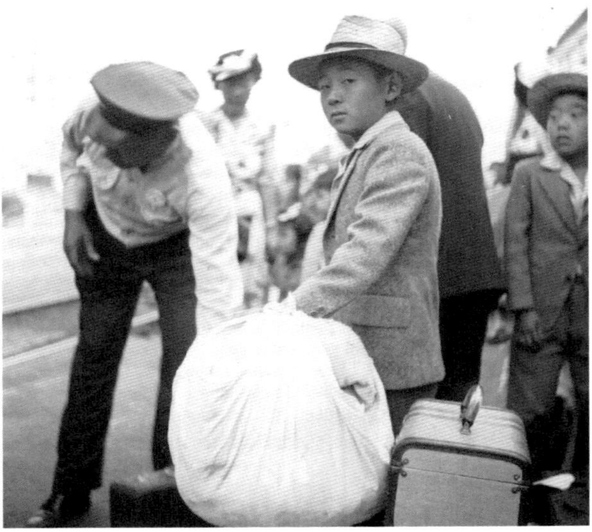

Top: Sacramento residents celebrating the end of the war. *Courtesy Center for Sacramento History, Sacramento Bee Collection, 1983/001/13,134j.*

Left and opposite: Japanese Americans returning from incarceration, July 30, 1945, at the Sacramento train station on the corner of Nineteenth and J Streets. *Courtesy War Relocation Authority Photographs Collection, 1967.014, Series 16, Bancroft Library, University of California–Berkeley.*

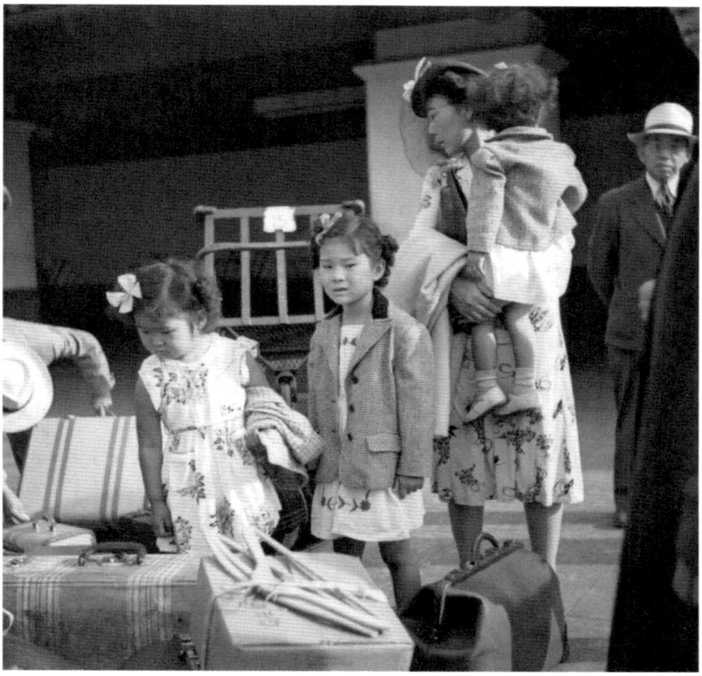

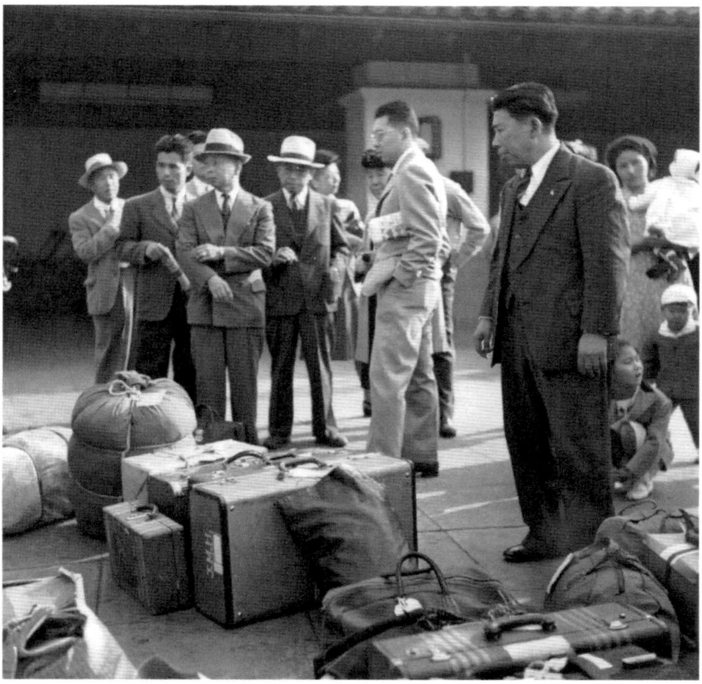

to resettling Japanese Americans in the city. While the city's Japanese American population was incarcerated behind barbed wire, the Sacramento City Council and the mayor of Sacramento, Tom B. Monk, had joined in solidarity with the Home Front Commandos to unanimously pass Resolution 207. Authored by Councilman M.B. Kunz, the resolution declared:

> *Whereas, the atrocious conduct of the Japanese at Pearl Harbor and the murder of the aviators recently acknowledged...has brought sharply to the attention of the American people the treachery, faithlessness and untrustworthiness of the pagan Japanese, and the Sacramento people being thoroughly conversant with the conduct of these undesirable people, be it resolved by the city council of Sacramento, that we are opposed to the return of any Japanese from concentration camps to their former locations, and we endorse the orders made by Gen. John L. DeWitt of the western defense command that all Japanese be confined in concentration camps and that they be not returned to any Pacific coast state.*[215]

The Sacramento, Auburn, Winters and Vacaville chapters of the California Preservation Association (formerly named the Anti-Japanese Association) sent members to Sacramento to organize a statewide campaign to block returnees. One of the delegates urged members to "treat them rough" if they do return. Other organizations, such as the American Legion, the Native Sons of the Golden West and the Sacramento Farm Bureau (which called for immediate confiscation and sale of all farming equipment owned by Japanese), joined the movement to restrict Japanese Americans from returning to their old neighborhoods.[216] Although Japanese Americans in Sacramento did confront a barrage of racist sentiments and opposition to their return, returnees did find support from other parts of the city. Among the most vocal supporter was the Sacramento Council of Churches, whose members assisted in facilitating their return.[217]

Housing became the most immediate problem for returning Japanese Americans.[218] Those who did come back early found that the ethnic composition of their old neighborhood had transformed into a mosaic of white, Latino, Chinese, Muslim and, most prominent of all, African American. This change was common in other cities along the West Coast, particularly Los Angeles. One headline in a Japanese American newspaper declared, "Little Tokyo in Los Angeles Is Now Negro Community." The article continued, "Spurred by the critical housing shortage in the Los Angeles area, particularly in relation to the housing needs of non-white groups who are discriminated against in other city districts, the 'Little Tokyo' area…is now a center of Negro population. On the buildings and store windows throughout the district there are signs today that read 'This is Bronzville. Watch Us Grow!'"[219] Japanese Americans returning to Sacramento confronted the same issue. One unfortunate side effect of their returning was the displacement of many of these other minority individuals and families, forcing them to find housing in other lower-income areas either closer to the river or in places like Oak Park, Del Paso Heights and Elder Creek.[220] Jobo Nakamura commented on this transformation of his old neighborhood: "When the Japanese Americans left Sacramento in 1942, the Nihonmachi was quickly populated in turn by Mexican and Negroes. Today there are some honky-tonks and tortilla houses firmly entrenched in the 'Japanesetown' to which the Japanese react with patient resignation."[221]

Japanese Americans who were able to find housing or who were able to hold on to their property during the war opened their houses to other families, hanging sheets in rooms to divide them into smaller units that often held up to four or five families at once. Others were forced to take shelter in basements or leaky barns or sleep on haystacks.[222] Churches also served as hostels, among them the Buddhist Church and the Methodist Church. Peter Osuga was one of the first to orchestrate housing relief, utilizing the facilities at Parkview Presbyterian Church on the corner of Eighth and T Streets, which at one point held thirty people.[223] The Baptist Church used its social hall, the Lincoln Christian Center, to house up to one hundred people.[224] Michiko Takahashi recalled her family's housing situation: "When my parents came back they lived with the Funahashis upstairs of their poultry shop on Fourth Street, but when I came home there was no place for me to stay. Across the street, Mr. Hosokawa had a soda fountain [Mary's fountain]. Upstairs they had a big old room with an old double bed. Mr. Hosokawa said, 'If you come and work here, I'll give you one room for you to stay.' He was very nice about it, so I lived there and started working at Mary's fountain."[225] By the end of 1946, some 150 families had returned to the Japantown district, some of them fortunate enough to reopen their old businesses.[226]

One of the first people to come back to Sacramento was Henry Taketa, a young Nisei lawyer who would soon become known as the "mayor" of Sacramento's Japantown. As a teenager, he, along with Walter Tsukamoto, helped establish the Sacramento chapter of the Japanese American Citizens League in 1931. While under incarceration, the chapter appointed Taketa,

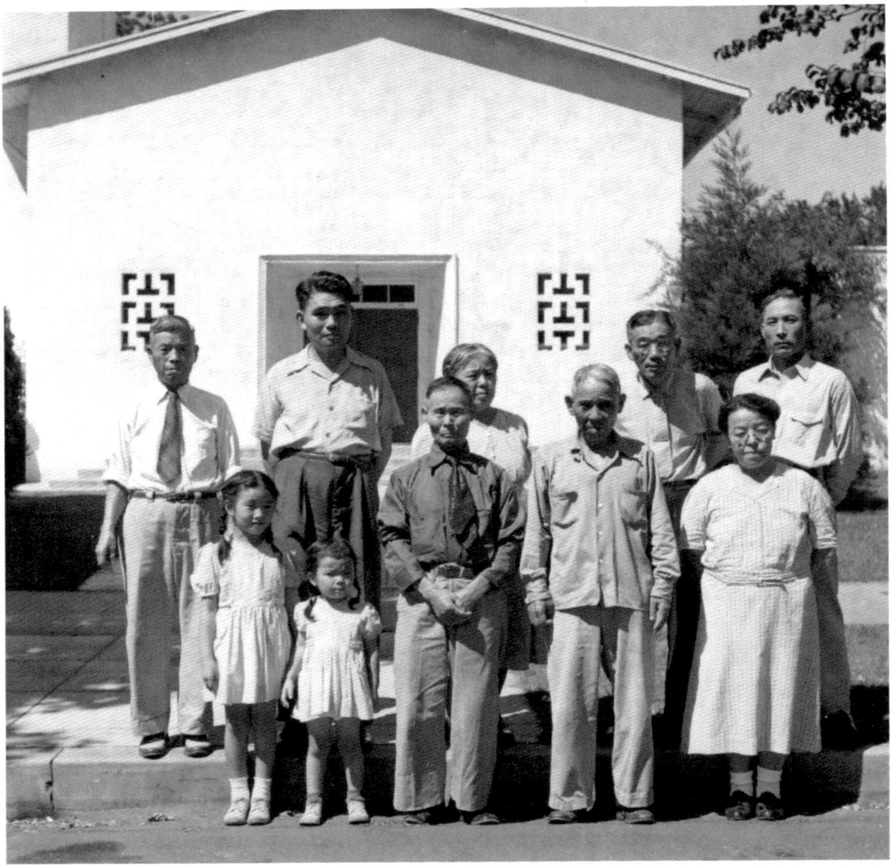

Japanese Americans released from incarceration in front of Parkview Presbyterian Church. The church was used as temporary living quarters. *Back row, left to right*: Takejiro Shimatsuko, Reverend Isamu Nakamura, Mrs. K. Oshima, Reverend Igarashi, William Otani. *Front row, left to right*: Etsu and Miye Nakamura, Mr. K. Oshima, Mr. Y. Hirotsu, Mrs. Shimatsuko. *Courtesy War Relocation Authority Photographs Collection, 1967.014, Series 13, Bancroft Library, University of California–Berkeley.*

along with George Takahashi and Goro Muramoto, trustees of the chapter's funds for the duration of the war. When Taketa returned to Sacramento in 1945, hastily setting up his law practice in an automobile, he used $4,000 of the fund to establish hostels, help others returning from the camps to find work and reinstitute the local JACL chapter. Henry Taketa, perhaps more than any other individual, became a Nisei spearhead for Sacramento's Japanese American community affairs in the postwar era.[227]

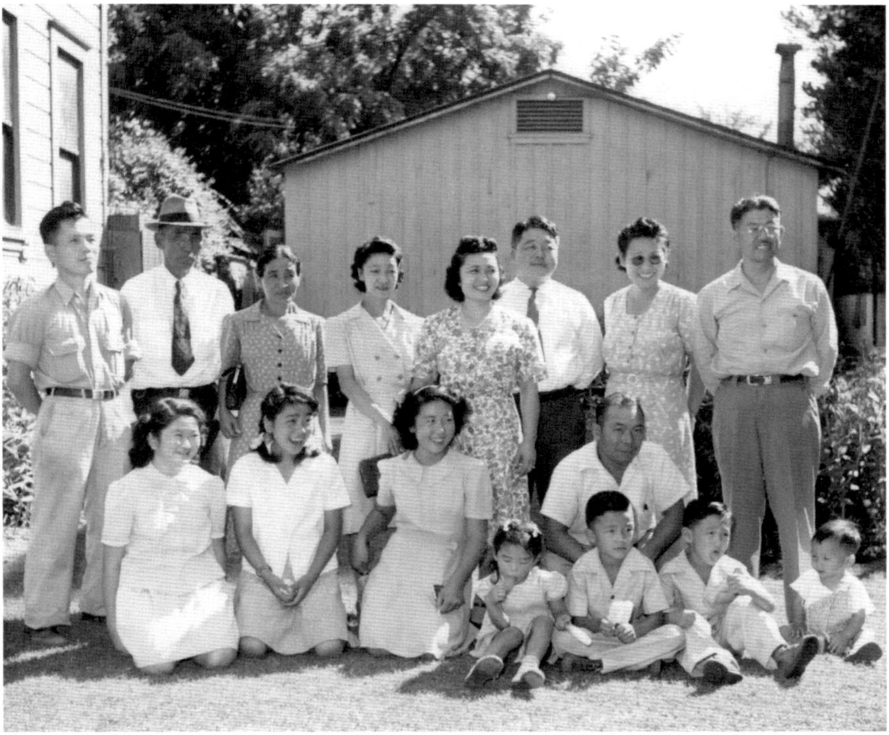

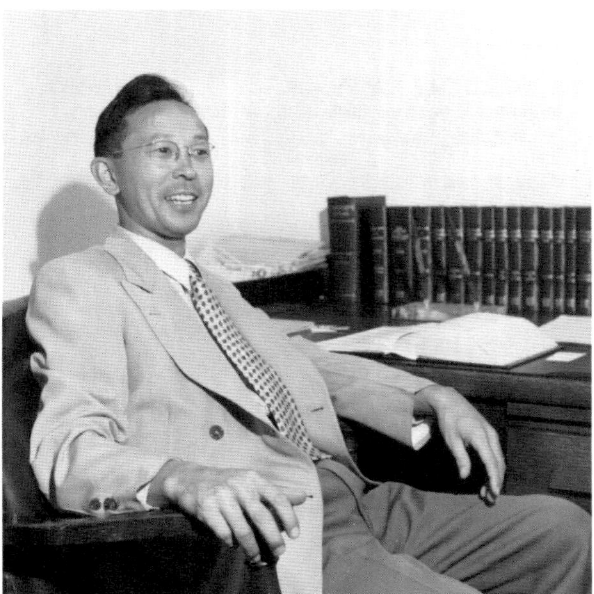

Above: Picture taken at 522 N Street, Peter Osuga and others released from incarceration. *Adults, left to right*: Mitsu Hara, H. Matamura, Y. Matamura, Akio Hayashi, Su Harada, Hiroshi Takemoto, Grace Sigami, M. Niyashi, Peter Osuga. *Courtesy War Relocation Authority Photographs Collection, 1967.014, Series 13, Bancroft Library, University of California–Berkeley.*

Left: Henry Taketa in his law office, August 16, 1945. *Courtesy War Relocation Authority Photographs Collection, 1967.014, Series 16, Bancroft Library, University of California–Berkeley.*

Using his parents' house on the corner of Fifth Street and Capitol Avenue to house people for a few nights until they could find their own living quarters, Taketa, with other lawyers, gathered blankets and cots from the Relocation Authority and renovated three buildings downtown that housed hundreds of people. He also found employment for the many older Issei who before the war were in farming, buying hand tools and placing ads in newspapers advertising their gardening services. For the first six months after his return, he provided legal services from his parents' house, mostly dealing with legal restitution of lost property. By 1947, he was back in his office building in Japantown, a building that had housed military police during the war.[228]

In part, the housing problem for those previously incarcerated stemmed from the anti-Japanese feelings that were still lingering after the war. Many, including the more assimilated Nisei generation, found it difficult to find suitable housing in other areas outside the West End. Kanji Nishijima remembers trying to buy a house in the Fair Oaks area of Sacramento County a few years after coming back from Tule Lake incarceration center. The real estate agent told him it was a "restricted area." "They just did not want to sell to Asians," said Nishijima.[229] Frank Hiyama vividly recalls the animosity he encountered after the war when he tried to purchase property outside Japantown near McKinley Park:

> *I had visions of building my own home on my own property. I had a deposit down on the house when the real estate agent asked if he could be released from the company because the neighborhood put so much pressure on him for selling to an Asian. The neighbors said that if he sold it to an Asian, he must be a communist and would press charges that he was a communist sympathizer. Here I lived in Sacramento and went to a Baptist church, I was a Boy Scout. I saluted the flag. I went to public schools. Still they were going to say that he was a communist...because he was going to sell the property to me.*[230]

Although some were able to find residences outside Japantown, most Japanese Americans returned to their old neighborhood.

Many returning Japanese Americans were dismayed that their stored property had been stolen or destroyed. April Adachi's family experience was not uncommon: "Some of our stuff we had stored in Mayeda's soda factory in Japan Alley. I remember my mother putting the *koto* [stringed instrument] in there. But when we returned, it was all vandalized. My father lost a lot."

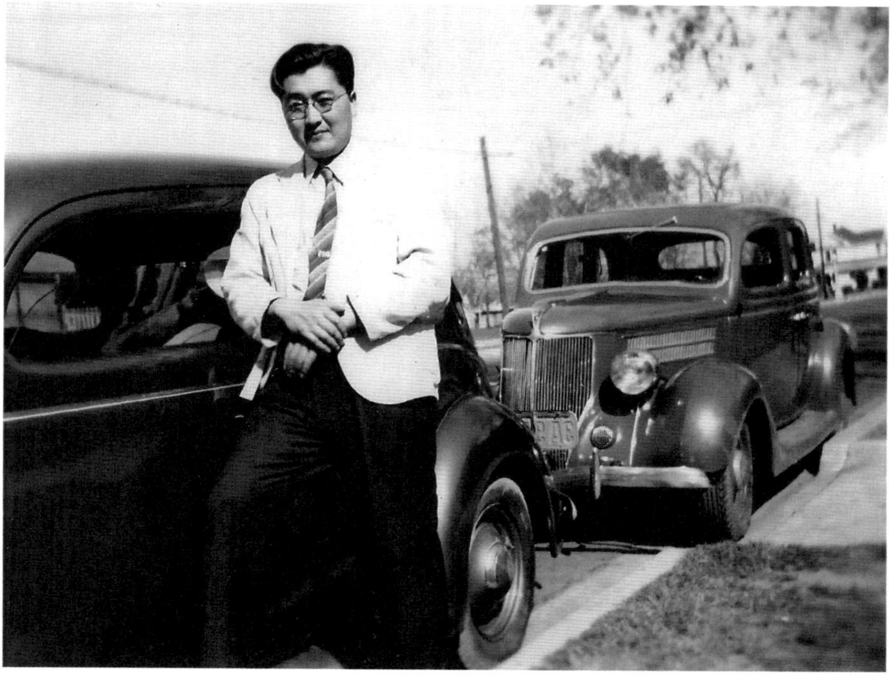

Fred Ouye. *Courtesy George Hisatomi.*

Fred Matsuda's family lost much of their Manju bakery equipment: "My father went to West Sacramento because my cousins [the Yamamotos] had a farm there, three acres of land in Yolo and put much of his property from the store, like the mochi machines and supplies, in the barn…When we returned, much of the stuff was destroyed." Although devastating loss of property and personal items was common, some were more fortunate. Marian Uchida's family owned their house at 1616 P Street and was able to store property in their basement. During their incarceration, their neighborhood friends, the Mantis family, watched over their property.[231]

Japanese Americans not only faced a substantial loss of livelihood but also had to contend with severe anti-Japanese agitation. In 1946, Fred Ouye returned to Sacramento, where he joined his brother, Harold, in reestablishing his pharmacy in 1946 in the old Sumitomo Bank on the corner of Fourth and L Streets. "It was hard to start businesses in Sacramento after the war because of the anti-Japanese feeling," said Ouye. "My brother had a hard time. Even many other Asians were anti-Japanese."[232]

Postwar Japantown hardly compared in size or diversity to its prewar composition. For example, in 1941, Sacramento had 471 Japanese American businesses, primarily located in the Japantown vicinity. But by 1954, the number had declined to some 300.[233] Most Japanese, particularly the older first generation, lost a substantial amount of money during incarceration and could not afford to reestablish their businesses upon their return. As Riichi Satow of Sacramento said, "We were economically destroyed, completely uprooted. We were all busy trying to recover from our losses [from incarceration]."[234] Because the price of farmland had increased during the war, independent farming ceased to be the primary occupation for the greater Sacramento Japanese American population. Japantown's business district had traditionally depended on the success of Japanese American farmers in the surrounding area. The absence of a strong, independent farming population further weakened the business sector. Also, the more assimilated second (Nisei) and third (Sansei) generations no longer bought exclusively from Japanese American stores. Therefore, success in business was not as promising as it was in the prewar era, when Japanese American businesses could rely on a large Japanese American clientele.

Despite its complete devastation during World War II, historic Japantown regained its position as the heart and soul of Sacramento's Japanese American community by the late 1940s.[235] By 1954, 80 percent of the city's Japanese-owned businesses and homes stood in the eight-block area bound between L and P Streets and Third and Fourth Streets. Because many of these buildings were multifamily dwellings, an accurate count derived from the *City Directories* is impossible. However, based on those listed, some five hundred Japanese Americans lived and occupied over 50 percent of the living quarters.[236] Japanese Americans also owned or managed at least 95 percent of the real estate or insurance businesses, 57 percent of the eating establishments, 40 percent of the grocery stores and 33 percent of the apartments, motels and smaller specialty shops.[237] They also owned more property in the eight-block area than before the war—fifty-one parcels in 1941 compared to seventy in 1954.[238] Similar to most postwar Japanese American businesses, the smaller establishments primarily served a Japanese American clientele, but they also served the other minority and transient populations found in the area. As pharmacist Fred Ouye recalled, "[After the war,] our store was really doing well. We had all kinds of people trading with us—Mexicans, black people, Chinese, Koreans, Hindus and whites."[239]

After the war, a sizable Japanese American professional population appeared in the neighborhood. This fact is indicative of the rise of the Nisei

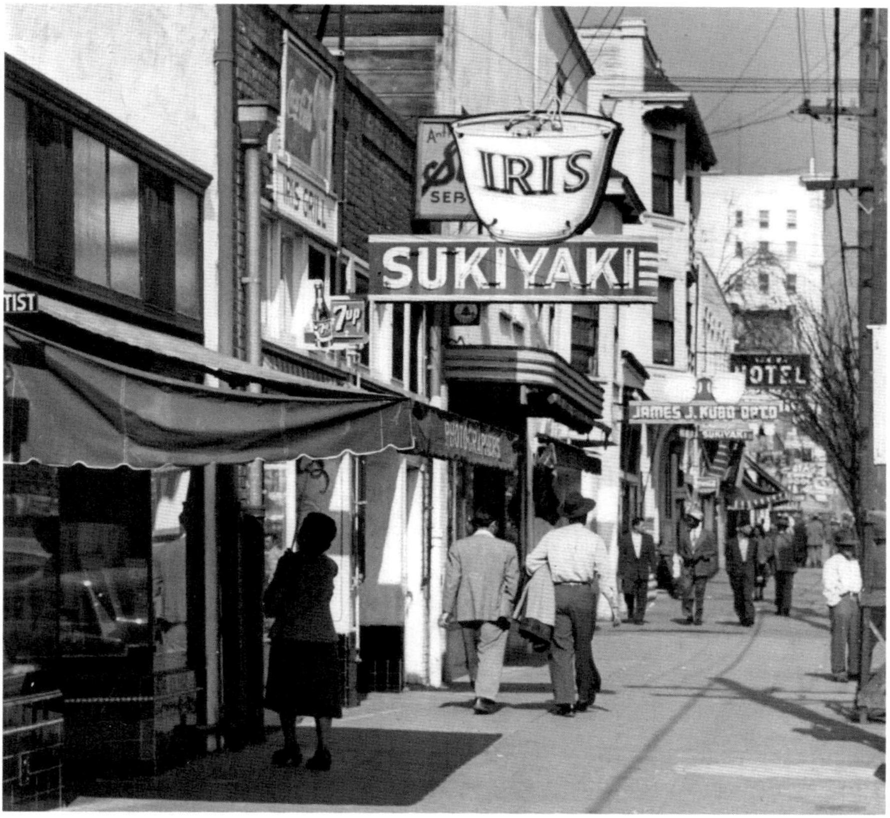

Fourth Street business district after the war. *Courtesy Center for Sacramento History, Frank Christy Collection, 1998/722/2435.*

generation. As noted earlier, the American-born generation was far better educated than their parents, so they were the first generation to enter the professional ranks in large numbers. For example, in 1940, the number of Japanese American professionals was half the number of white professionals in California and Hawaii. By 1950, Japanese Americans in California had narrowed the disparity, and by 1960, they had slightly more in professional occupations than did whites. Japanese Americans, because of the Nisei success in the postwar era, soon began to prosper in American society. Historian Kendis states that by 1960, more than 38 percent of Japanese Americans were in professional, technical and white-collar fields. Also, they had a greater percentage of college graduates than the white population (18 percent Japanese Americans to 10 percent white). They also had more

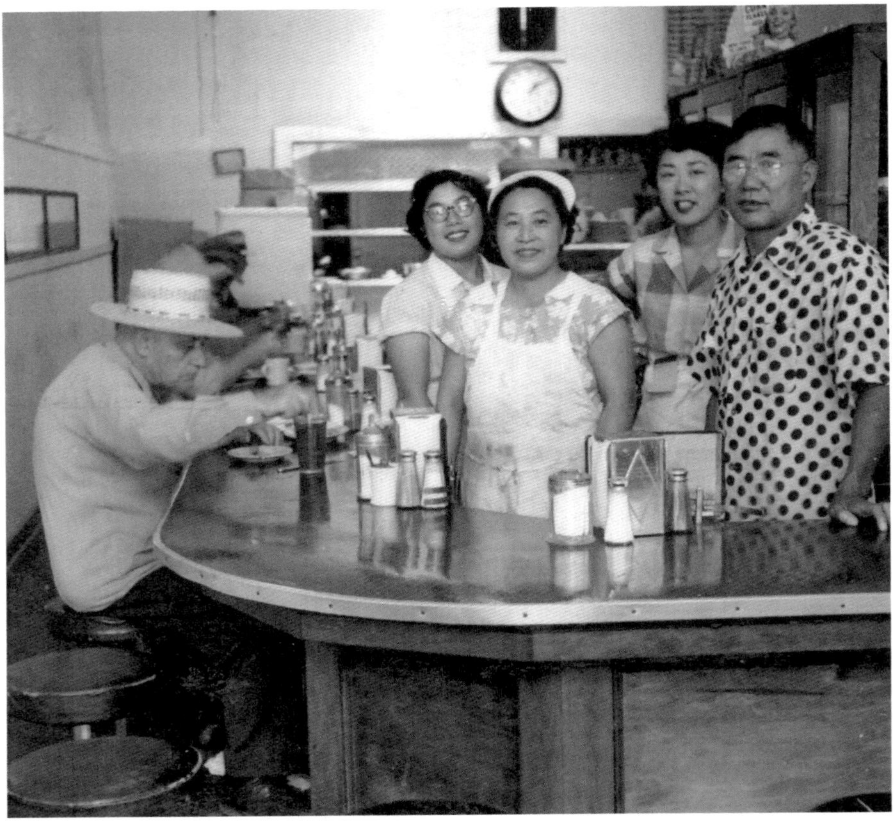

Shimono's Diamond Café. *Left to right*: Setsuko, Kimiyo, Grace, Masuichi. *Courtesy Shimono family.*

people in professional occupations (56 percent Japanese Americans to 42 percent white) and were second only to white males in median income (the median income for Japanese American males was 99 percent of white males). Despite all the harsh anti-Japanese American sentiment and legal obstacles, the Japanese American community persevered, making its place in society through hard work and dedication.[240]

Despite the anti-Japanese American feelings that were prevalent, Nisei assimilation persisted in weakening ethnic social barriers for Japanese Americans after the war. Most discovered that their education provided new opportunities previously unavailable to their parents. Accordingly, many Nisei professionals sought employment outside their community, an activity that served to alleviate the Japanese American stereotypes of "clannish"

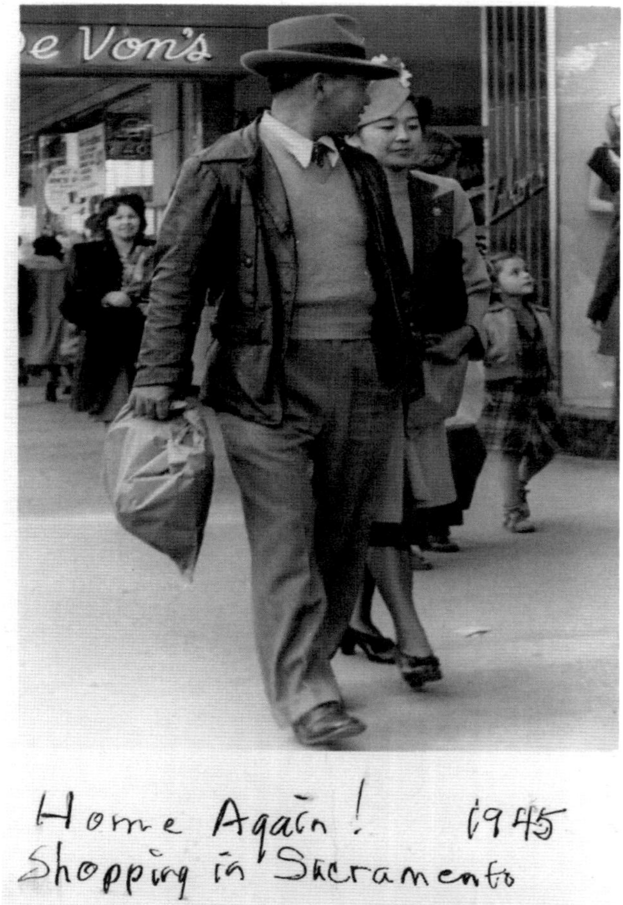

Al and Mary Tsukamoto shopping on K Street after returning from their incarceration. Mary Tsukamoto became a key civil rights activist in the struggle for redress and financial reparations from Japanese American incarceration. *Courtesy Japanese American Archival Collection. Department of Special Collections and University Archives, California State University–Sacramento.*

and "unassailable." Fred Ouye recalls, "Before the war, like in pharmacy, they would not hire Nisei. That's why me and my brother had to open up our own store. Most of the guys had to work for other Japanese American stores. But after the war, we got a little more assimilated." The majority of professionals listed in the area in the 1954 *Sacramento City Directory* are Japanese, including five dentists, four physicians, three lawyers and three optometrists. The Yamasaki building and the Taketa building were office facilities in which many of these professionals provided their services. The only Japanese-owned bank, the Sumitomo Bank of California, also stood in the heart of old Japantown. The fact that the Japanese American Citizens

League and the official Japanese American daily, the *Nichi Bei Times*, were all in the Japantown vicinity illustrates the prominence the Japanese American community regained in its historic neighborhood after the war.[241]

By 1950, the Japanese American community had formed social and economic bonds similar to those that existed before the war, reestablishing the vernacular landscape that had provided a sense of place for the community since the first pioneering generation arrived in Sacramento in the 1890s. Jobo Nakamura, a resident of Sacramento before being evacuated, returned to the city in the summer of 1949. Nakamura shared his homecoming with the *Pacific Citizen* newspaper:

> *Japanese American evacuees have returned to Sacramento to pick up life where they left off. Although the Nihonmachi (Japanese American district) has lost a great deal of the color and the atmosphere that made it distinctive before the war, the basic pattern of community is essentially the same. On Saturday mornings the Japanese truck farmers come into town to shop at Yorozu or at Aoki's and exchange crop news with other farmers, then join their families at Wakanoura chop suey house for cha shu, pakkai, and ham-yu. They weep over a Japanese movie drama at the Kaikan hall next to the Buddhist Church. Nostalgic songs such as "Tsumagoidochu" and "Shino-no-yoru" emanate from Nishijima's P.A. system in loud, lifting melody and compete with the protesting noise of the chickens at Funahashi's poultry market. Old Issei bachelors stand in front of a Fourth Street pool room under the hot sun, staring forlornly at the young gay blades passing by. They look tired and their eyes are beady. I am told that the asparagus crop was not too good this year because of the rain, and the migrant workers loafed into town with not much money to spend in the Nihonmachi. Young high school boys loiter in the soda fountain, discussing plans for summer work.*[242]

Returning evacuees proved wrong the predictions that the city's Japantown community would never recover from the chaos of the war and scars of the concentration camps. It did recover. Within a few years, members of the community reopened old businesses in the same or different locations or established new enterprises; reactivated the Sacramento chapter of the JACL that published a biweekly newspaper edited by Eugene Okada and Stirling Sakamoto; and sponsored the first annual conference of the Northern California Young Buddhist League. In December 1950, the Buddhist Church celebrated a "Golden Jubilee"

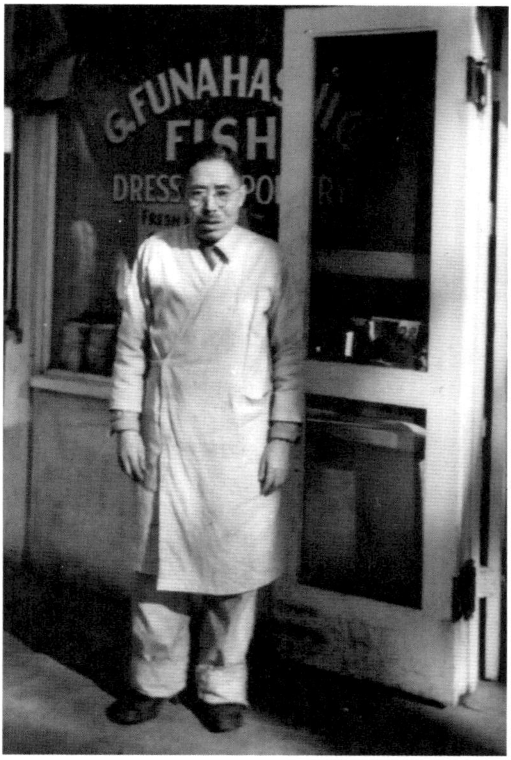

Left: Funahashi Fish and Poultry Shop. *Courtesy Michiko (Takahashi) and Joey Ho.*

Below: Toyo Photography Studio on Fourth Street next to Funahashi's Grocery. Mrs. Komura is in the door window. *Courtesy Keiko Komura.*

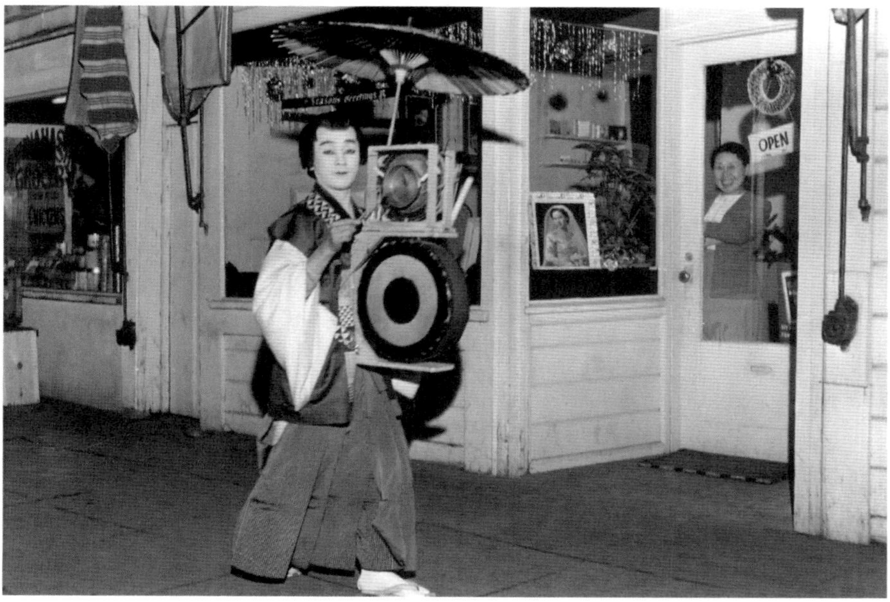

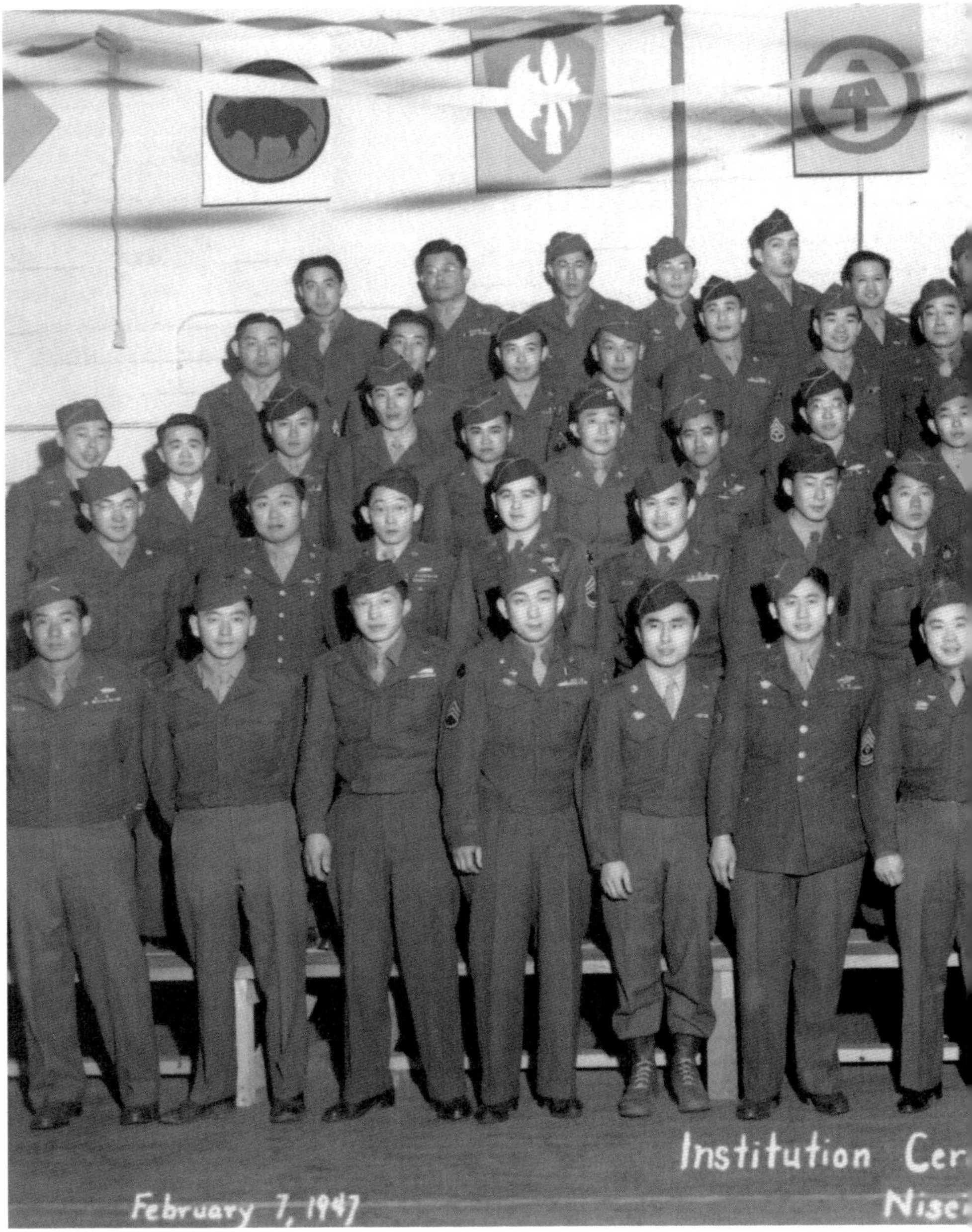

Institutional ceremony and installation of officers, Sacramento Nisei Post 8985, February 7, 1947. *Courtesy Japanese American Archival Collection. Department of Special Collections and University Archives, California State University–Sacramento.*

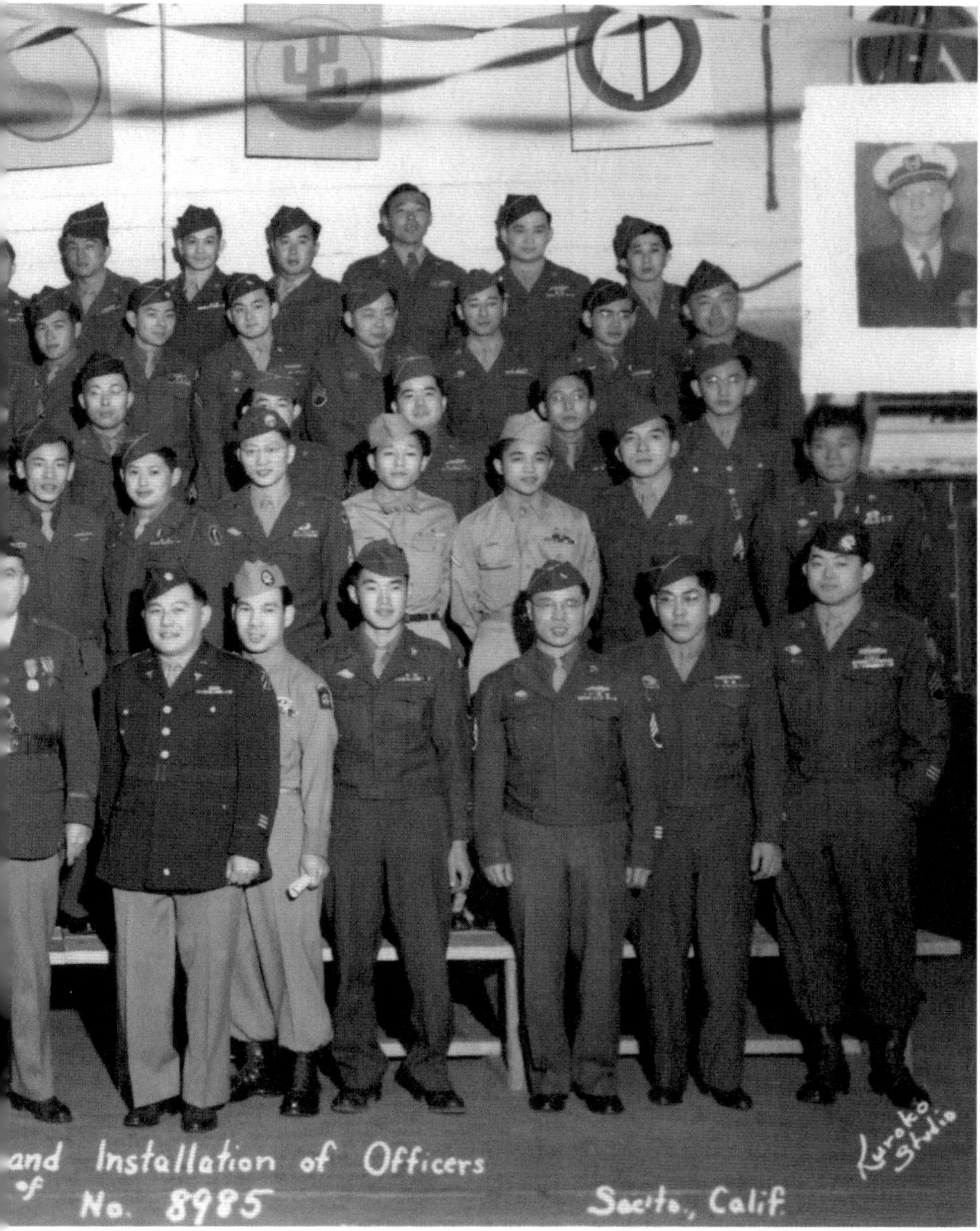
and Installation of Officers
of No. 8985
Sac'to., Calif.
Kuroko Studio

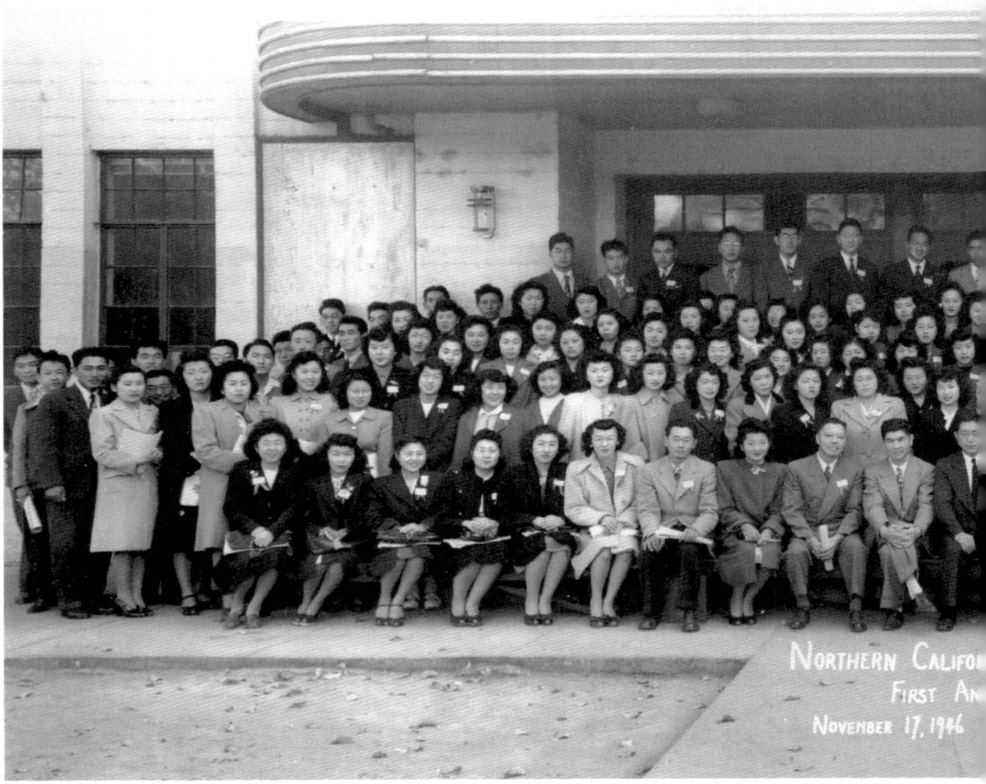

Northern California Young Buddhist League Conference, Sacramento Buddhist Church, November 17, 1946. *Courtesy Mike Sawamura, estates manager of Eugene Okada.*

that marked the fiftieth anniversary of the founding of Sacramento's Buddhist Church, the second largest in the United States. The church also sponsored a popular "Stars of Tomorrow" talent show series usually held in the Buddhist *kaikan*. One year later, a new Japanese Methodist church, pastored by Reverend Waichi Oyanagi, opened at Fourth and O Streets. The JACL and a network of churches worked together to bring back to life the annual Obon festivals that decorated O Street with bright, festive colors, the sounds of traditional Japanese music and spirited parades. Volunteers, spectators and participants rebuilt the sumo mound in Japan Alley that brought excitement to the neighborhood every Fourth of July. Along with baseball and basketball, one of the recreational activities that

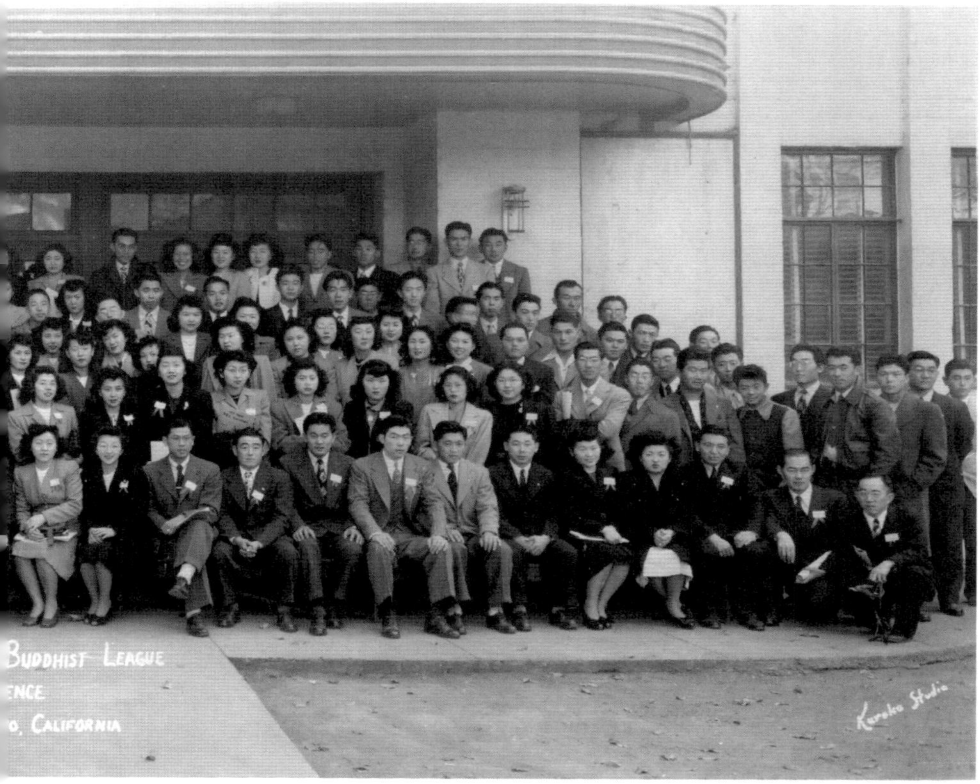

quickly gained momentum among the Nisei was bowling. Neighborhood members organized a new Nisei Bowling League that, by 1951, held 128 members, the largest of its kind in the nation.[243] One of the more vigorous community activists in organizing such social activities for the postwar generation was Toko Fujii. Jobo Nakamura commented on Fujii's public spirit in an article published in the JACL newspaper, the *Pacific Citizen*:

> *The spacious YBA hall, the community center, provides a recreational outlet for more than 500 Nisei youths. During the basketball season, Nisei kids from 12–35 participate in one way or another in league games. A strong manifestation of community spirit is the casaba team known as the*

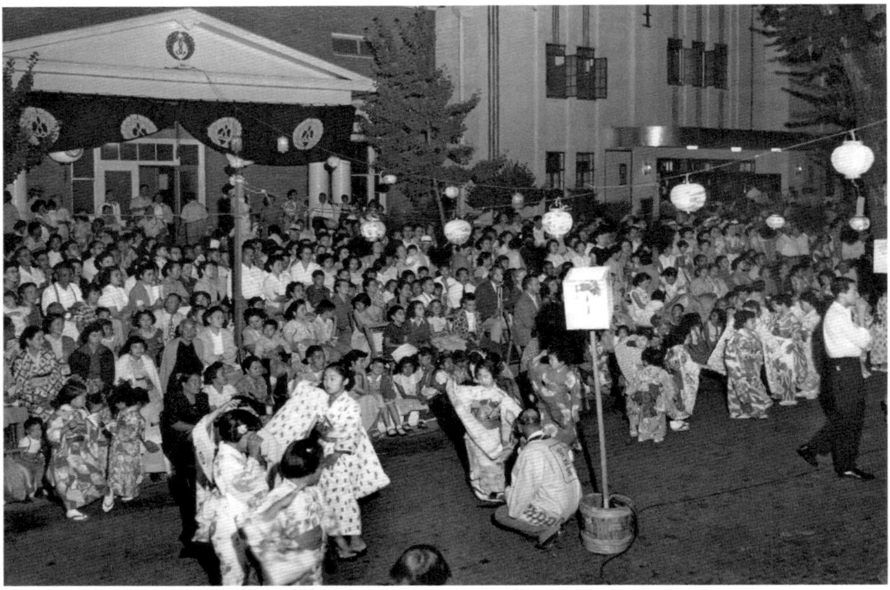

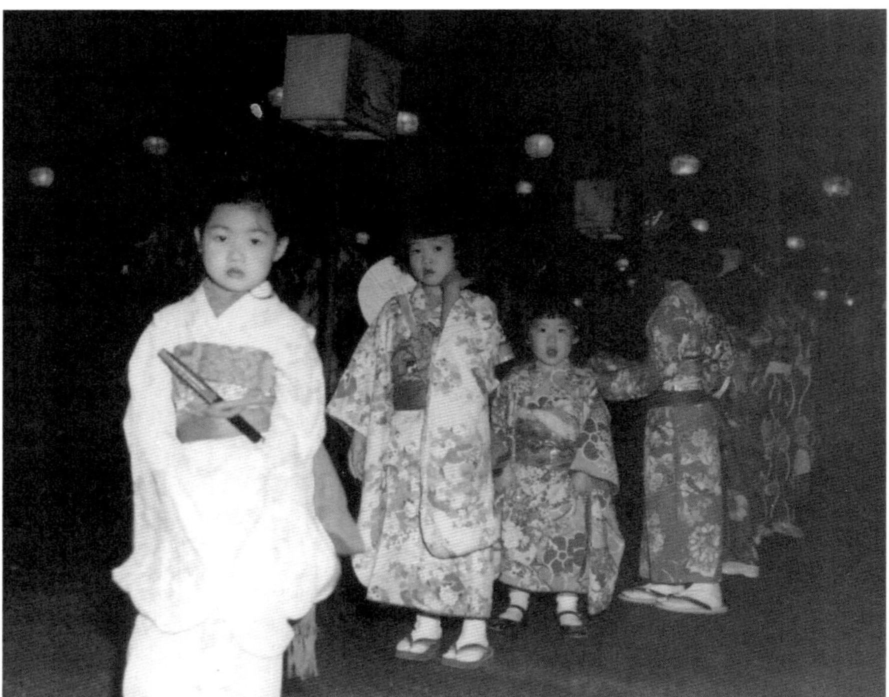

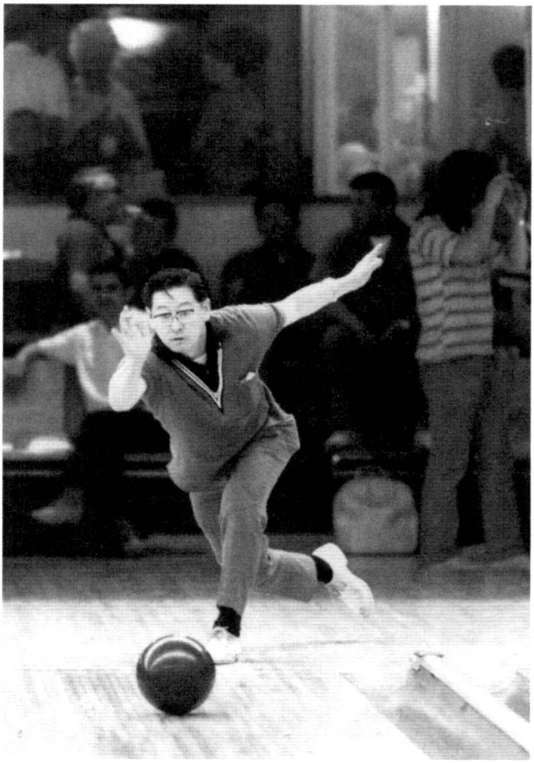

Opposite, top: Obon festival in front of Buddhist Church on O Street between Fourth and Fifth Streets, early 1950s. *Courtesy Keiko Komura.*

Opposite, bottom: Obon festival in front of Buddhist Church on O Street between Fourth and Fifth Streets, early 1950s. *Left to right*: Keiko Komura, Jane (Nishijima) Komure, Bonnie (Nishijima) Okamoto. *Courtesy Keiko Komura.*

Left: Kanji Nishijima. *Courtesy Jane (Nishijima) Komure.*

> *"Stags" which is comprised of select players from various rival teams in Sacramento. Toko Fujii, the "man behind the men" as he is referred to in Sacramento, is a public spirited human dynamo who initiates and conducts sports and recreational activities in the community. Plump and jovial Toko finds time from his hotel business to form bowling and basketball leagues, plan bazaars, and has his head and hands full in every form of youth activity. He is himself the father of two children. Toko realized more than anyone else the dire need of assisting the kids not only to find wholesome recreational outlets but to instill in them a sense of responsibility and individual initiative.*[244]

But just when many had replanted permanent roots and begun to heal from the physical, emotional and economic hardships inflicted by the wartime experience, the community faced a second and far more devastating blow to Sacramento's historic Japantown: the Capitol Mall Redevelopment project.

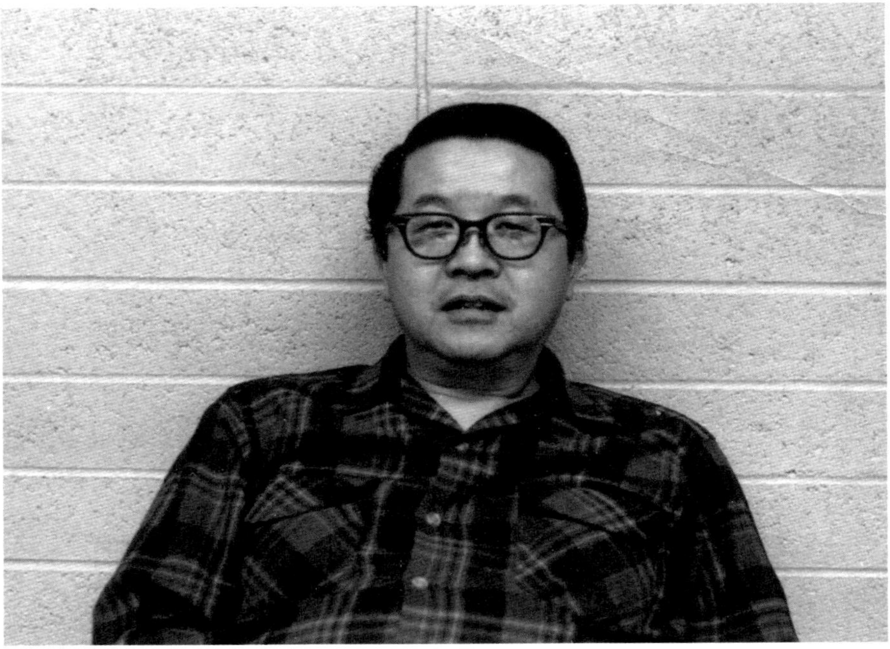

Toko Fujii. *Courtesy Terry (Fujii) Kornelly.*

Under the guise of "civic progress," this project replaced Japantown and many other structures of historic significance to other minority communities with monumental public buildings and upscale high-rises. As a result, the Capitol Mall project disrupted the Japanese American economy and way of life through another forced evacuation and eliminated historic Japantown from Sacramento's landscape, physically erasing forever from public memory the part Japanese Americans had played in the city's history.

However, the Capitol Mall project did not arise out of a calculated plan by civic leaders to break up the ethnic enclaves of the West End, although the ethnic composition of the area may have influenced some people to support the plan without hesitation or concern for those who would be displaced by, and suffer losses from, the project. The origins of the Capitol Mall project stretch back almost to the turn of the century, when civic leaders began looking at plans to create a grand thoroughfare leading from the riverfront to the Capitol building. But because of various financial and legal problems, the city was unable to begin the Capitol Mall project until after World War II. In the early 1940s, the desire to develop the West End of the city gained greater momentum and force as the area both physically and socially deteriorated as a result of the Depression and because of the allocation of new investment away from the city's core and increasingly toward Sacramento's burgeoning suburbs. After the war, James S. Dean, the director of state finance and an architect by profession, revived interest in creating a Capitol Mall when he appeared before the City Council in September 1945 with a "Report on Grouping of Public Buildings on Capitol Avenue."[245] In 1950, the City Council formed the Sacramento Redevelopment Agency (SRA) with Joseph T. Bill as executive director to oversee the West End project.[246]

To address the problem of growing slum conditions in the West End, the City Council of Sacramento began discussing improvement projects much larger in scope than just the beautification of Capitol Avenue. The City Planning Commission launched a series of studies, beginning in 1949, on the extent of deterioration in the entire West End. Architectural studies revealed that between 1937 and 1949, the value of the area's land primarily from Seventh to Front Streets and I to R Streets had decreased an average of 30 percent. Therefore, the area's tax scale was abating as the public debt was increasing. Additional studies found that the West End occupied 8 percent of the city's area and represented 20 percent of the city's population, 26 percent of the building fires, 36 percent of the juvenile delinquencies, 42 percent of adult crimes and 76 percent of tuberculosis cases. As one reporter commented, the area had become a "haven for the elderly, the service workers, and the unattached floater…One out of every three retail stores had an alcohol license."[247] Jerome Lipp, the first chief land agent who was in charge of property acquisition for the Capitol Mall project and who, in 1958, held the position of executive director of the SRA, recalls the horrid conditions of the area: "It was one of the worst slums in the country. The area had become a real cesspool. I remember people out in the middle of the street with their eyes closed all dreamy dancing around. I had to go into some of these buildings to acquire and inspect them for appraising. The filth was something you can't even conceive. It was not just blight in the narrow, legal sense. This was a full-blown, three-dimensional, horrible, filthy slum."[248]

By 1950, two goals coalesced to form the shape and scope of the Capitol Mall project: first, the long-held dream of creating a grand Capitol Mall thoroughfare, and second, the hope of eradicating the awful blight found in many sections of the entire West End. City officials combined these aims to form the basis of the Capitol Mall project. The beautification proposals of the early twentieth century, once limited in scope and long-held, were now studied as a comprehensive urban renewal program.

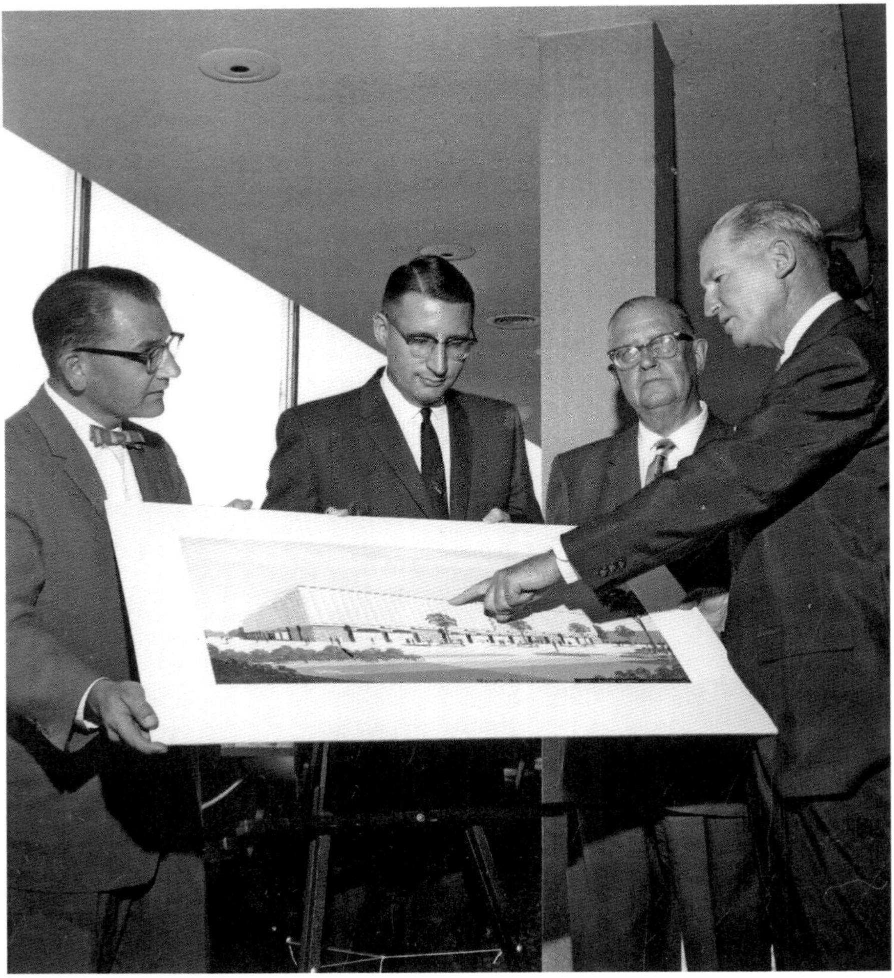

Sacramento Redevelopment Agency and city officials discussing the Capitol Mall project and location of new Macy's department store. *Courtesy Center for Sacramento History, James E. Henley Collection, 1997/046/370.*

After four years of debate and legal clarification between the public, the City Council and the SRA, the council in early 1954 approved the SRA's tentative "Capitol Mall Plan" to be publicly debated and discussed before the council voted to include in the November election a $1.5 million bond to procure the necessary one-third cost of the project, with the remaining two-thirds to be financed by the federal government. The SRA's plan, which covered fifteen square blocks between Fourth and Seventh Streets and K and P Streets, was extremely vague. It called for, over a two-year period, the acquisition of property through the powers of eminent domain, the wholesale demolition of most of the area's structures, the relocation of residents, the rehabilitation of a few historic landmarks and the sale of project property to private investors. The plan made no mention of rehabilitating or preserving existing private structures, nor did it provide any specific information on property acquisition procedures or guarantees for assistance in rehousing or relocation compensation for West End businesses and residents.[249] The tentative plan, the first in a three-phase project that covered the entire West End, clearly reflected the entrepreneurial vision shared by the SRA. On July 1, 1954, San Francisco developer Ben Swig, with the enthusiastic support of the Chamber of Commerce and the SRA, proposed that the entire Capitol Mall project be dedicated to the construction of a modern business and office complex, a K Street shopping plaza and public parking lots. In other words, the project called for Japantown and the blocks around it to be replaced with government buildings, shopping malls and parking structures.[250]

Public announcement of the Capitol Mall project received optimistic and exuberant applause throughout the city. But for the 2,652 residents in the project area, the response was closer to outrage and dismay. Many West End residents, property owners and merchants joined organizations that either outright opposed the plan or fought for guaranteed relocation assistance to be included in the plan before citizens voted in November on whether to finance the project. Merchant Sal Anapolsky, chairman of the West Side Community Association, scolded the city for failing to guarantee relocation assistance and designate a relocation area for West End businesses and residents.[251] The fact that the project area consisted of 21 percent African Americans, 30 percent Asian Americans and 13 percent Latino Americans prompted many minority leaders to voice opposition to the plan because it did not include relocation assistance, suitable housing and a policy that guarded against racial discrimination in relocating residents to other parts of the city. Among the minority spokesmen were the Reverend E.C. Regalado, who spoke for the Latino Americans, and Nathaniel Colley, a prominent African American lawyer for the American Civil Liberties Union.[252] Colley, representing thirty-two black business owners, feared that "for whites only" signs on new structures built under redevelopment would replace the present unsightly conditions with a "Blight of Bigotry."[253] He lamented, "We'd like to be able to support this program, but you can't expect us to take it and love it and lose. There are people in the West End who will suffer tremendous losses, and they should have some compensation for them."[254] However, the Capitol Mall project proposed by the SRA had equally profound implications to the Japanese Americans in Sacramento. It was in effect a call for the eradication of Japantown and a second forced evacuation and relocation, but this time under the guise of "civic progress" rather than "military necessity." Publication of the Capitol Mall project sent a shock wave throughout the Japantown community, even prompting the *Pacific Citizen* newspaper to declare, "Sac'to Nipponmachi [Japantown] Doomed by Capitol Redevelopment."[255] "Doomed" Japantown was, for the project called for the wholesale clearance of 80 percent of the city's Japanese-owned and -operated business and residential area, splitting Japantown down the center along Fourth Street. The second phase of the project, slated for early 1960, threatened to raze the remaining western half of the community.[256] Further, the fifteen-block project comprised 496 Japanese, of whom 65 were property holders owning 25 percent of the property parcels in the project area, and some 300 businesses and professional firms, including the Buddhist Church and its community auditorium, the Japanese Baptist Church and the Konko Temple.[257]

The older, first generation within the Japanese American community may have simply acquiesced to the city's authority. As Marian Uchida said, "The Issei generation didn't know what civil disobedience was. If the government told you to do something, you just did it."[258] That submission to authority is captured in a common Issei phrase: "*Shikata ga nai* (There's nothing we can do about it)." However, the younger, American-born Nisei leaders of Sacramento were determined to confront city leaders to ensure the protection of property and civil rights for those in their community. Immediately following the California Supreme Court's decision in April 1954 that confirmed the legality of Sacramento's Capitol Mall plan, representatives of the JACL, the Nisei Veterans of Foreign Wars (NVFW) and other Japanese American community leaders, merchants, property owners and residents convened in the Buddhist auditorium and organized the Japanese-American Redevelopment Study Association (JARSA). With a $6,000 defense fund and a fifteen-member advisory board, including Dr. Akio Hayashi and lawyers Henry Taketa, Mamoru Sakuma and Dean Itano, operating as its spearhead, JARSA sought to, in the words of Henry Taketa, "seriously study the plan, gather information to give our people, coordinate representation on possible negotiations, and do everything in our means and power to protect and preserve the economy and welfare of persons of Japanese ancestry."[259] Merchant and president of the

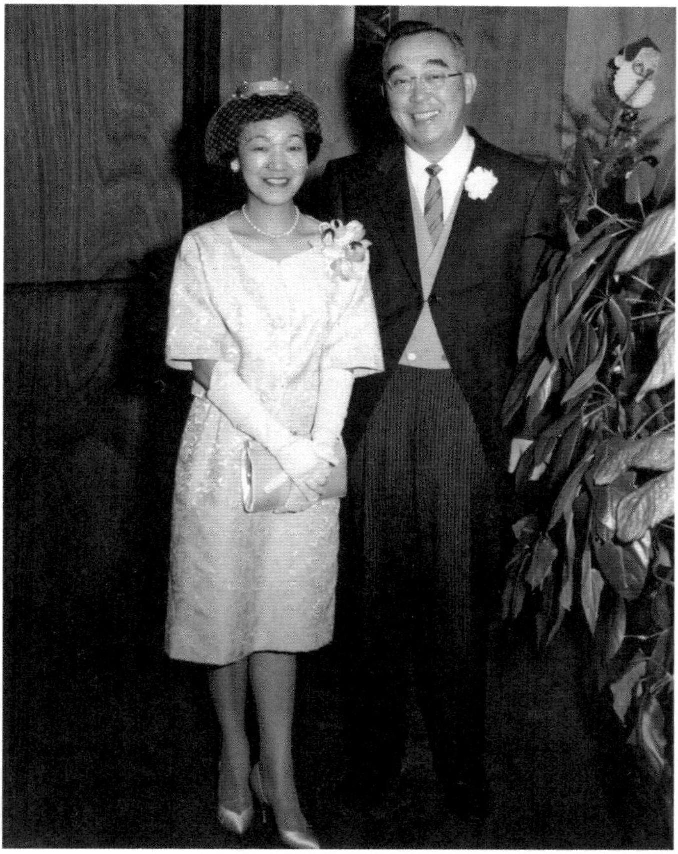

Alice and Akio Hayashi. Dr. Hayashi was a member of the Japanese American Redevelopment Study Association. *Courtesy Sybil (Hayashi) Miyamoto.*

Sacramento JACL at the time Toko Fujii remembers, "We were all fairly active in [JARSA]. We did not know whether we could fight redevelopment or not, but we formed the association to study redevelopment and what they were going to do to us."[260] Fresh out of law school, Dean Itano, executive director of the association, recalls, "I was fairly new to the practice at the time this [redevelopment] deal came up. [Japantown merchants] felt that they should have somebody more or less to coordinate all the activities and call meetings if necessary and to implement whatever plans were adopted by the group and make the views of the Japanese American community known to the city government."[261]

The SRA avoided incorporating into the master plan any concrete proposals for compensation assistance, believing that hardships would remain minimal because the plan called for a block-by-block clearing of the land over two years, a slow process that would provide West Enders enough time to find new areas to which to move. Further, the SRA desired to keep the cleared area open for big capital private investors who had the finances to turn the West End into a burgeoning economic center.[262] The immediate concern shared by Japanese Americans was the economic hardship that Japantown residents and merchants would experience. Japanese American representatives, as well as other West Enders, argued that such a callous tentative plan would inflict undue hardship on those who would be forced to move.

During a series of City Council meetings in the summer of 1954, Japanese American representatives from JARSA, the NVFW and JACL, and over one hundred Japanese American supporters in attendance, battled with the Redevelopment Agency and the City Council over the Capitol Plan's objectives, attempting to persuade the SRA to incorporate provisions in the plan that would avoid another evacuation, safeguard the economic vitality of Japanese American businesses in the area and, possibly, even preserve a section of Japantown's business center.[263] Toko Fujii presented an official statement to the city that offered support to the city's efforts to remove the more blighted sections of downtown but emphasized the economic hardship this would inflict on residents of the area if not done fairly, especially those who traditionally have experienced racial intolerance. Fujii reinforced his claim by citing a Redevelopment Agency report that acknowledged the economic loss racial minorities in the area would experience. Fujii closed his statement with these words: "Japanese Americans, as a particular minority group, are just barely recovering from the tragedy of the recent mass evacuation of World War II. Because of our experiences, we hope that safeguards will be insured for every resident of Sacramento regardless of his economic status and that the City Council will defend the needs and rights of every person regardless of race or color."[264] In his opening remarks to the City Council and the SRA, Henry Taketa stated:

> *There is a misunderstanding about our position on the plan. We are 100% citizens and residents of this community. We have our whole heart and soul in what will take place here. Our fathers and mothers came here in their youth, and now they are reaching the twilight years of their lives. But in the meantime, they have worked hard, industriously, and provided a foundation for us, for the young generation. We have a considerable fondness for our community. For that reason, after our wartime dislocation, we always dreamt of coming back here. I would say 90% of us have returned.*

> *Since coming back, for our own interests and perhaps also for our own self-respect, wherever Japanese-Americans have gone and taken a premises, occupied a building or a home, I think that you have seen an appreciation of property, rather than depreciation. For example, our little community on Fourth Street, since our return, has improved considerably.*[265]

Frank Yoshimura, representing the NVFW, characterized the SRA's plan as an "abuse of power of eminent domain and un-American." "The Redevelopment Agency proposes to remove the small businesses out, demolish a fifteen square block area, and sell it to big private investors," protested Yoshimura. He closed his remarks by pointing out the fact that the area comprises a large number of racial minorities that would confront intolerance and resistance in trying to relocate their businesses and homes to other areas of the city. In the same tone, Arthur Mitsutome of Senator Lions Club expressed support for the idea of "community improvement," but from his perspective, the city's plan fell short of achieving this goal. "We believe in the American democratic way of life," Mitsutome stated, "and feel that fair play should be accorded to all. Progress in the redevelopment of our great Capitol city with utter disregard to the rights of the individuals concerned will not be progress in the right direction nor can it be classified as true redevelopment."[266]

What made the Capitol Mall project appear much more alarming to the Japantown community was its resemblance to another forced evacuation. And it was on this point that Taketa set the tone of Japanese American concerns:

> *Why are we so concerned with this project? Most of us do live in this project area. As a result of our wartime evacuation, we were forcibly kicked out from our residences and places of business. We by experience know that you take a lot of losses when you have to move out and then move back in. We know by experience that there are considerable financial risks involved in the matter of relocation or dislocation.*[267]

But beneath all the practical concerns of relocation and economic hardship lay perhaps something more valuable to the Japanese American community in the West End: the desire to preserve a sense of place and maintain a neighborhood long ago established by the first generation, a desire particularly shared by the Issei. For one such Issei, Giichi Aoki, owner of Aoki Music, the future of Japantown was "very dark and gloomy." Representing the feelings of many in his generation, Aoki appealed to the sentiments of experience:

> *I came to Sacramento in 1909 and started a business on Fourth Street between L and M, selling Victor and Columbia talk machines and records...and other merchandise our countrymen wanted...The entire Japanese population suffered great hardship both mentally and economically. Evacuation during this peace time is entirely different from the last in its nature and scope. Many of our businesses are very old, being on average 65 years or older. We will not be able to withstand another evacuation within so short a time unless provision is made to compensate for our economic losses. Without such help, I sincerely believe that individuals like myself will be unable to make a living. On behalf of Japanese American businessmen like myself I appeal to your essence of justice and fairness.*[268]

Another longtime resident, Mr. Sugiyama, went so far as to say that the Capitol Mall project was like "putting salt on a deep wound just beginning to heal." Speaking before the City Council, he pleaded:

> *The area you have chosen for* [redevelopment]*...has been known to us as Japantown for over fifty years. These people have invested everything they had so they could have enough money to retire on. Most of the shopkeepers are well along in years. It has been only eight years since they started life all over again. These are the same people who once before gave up everything they had* [during the war]*—their homes, their businesses, education of their children—everything they struggled to work for when they evacuated... What other people have had to take so much as the Japanese? It is easy to say that the Japanese merchant should move out and start someplace else. You forget we are Japanese and face discrimination. We have restrictions on where we can buy a home, where we can work, and what position we can fill in any business.*[269]

As already mentioned, the Nisei generation, who were Americans by right of birth, assimilated more into the mainstream of American society; therefore, Japantown was not as vital to their livelihood as it was to their parents.[270] Nisei attorney Dean Itano clearly observed the difference in generational responses concerning the demise of Japantown: "I think the older people had a stronger desire to keep the ethnic community together. Naturally, they were more concerned about moving into areas where they might be isolated from other Japanese people. There was probably less concern with my generation [the Nisei] and younger [Sansei] people."[271] Businessman Jerry Miyamoto also acknowledged this different generational response: "It was harder on the older people that had to move. There was some security that they had, but then they were [being] forced out of it."[272]

Japanese American merchants also criticized the project for its indiscriminate wholesale razing of entire blocks, including the more salient sections, in order to clean up blighted areas. Pharmacist Fred Ouye exclaimed, "From the outside, it may have looked like [blight]. But if you're in there doing business, you think, 'Hell, this is great!' There were exaggerations. I think for the people that lived there you don't feel quite like you are living in [blight]."[273] Appliance store owner Kanji Nishijima also disagreed with city officials and was reluctant to move his business out of what he thought was a "good location." "It was the entry to Sacramento and right in front of the Capitol. I would not have called it a slum area. I think they publicized it that way and exaggerated. Most of the people in that area kept their houses clean."[274] The Redevelopment Agency acknowledged JARSA's criticism that the plans would destroy many of the more salutary sections of the West End. In fact, city planners had intentionally designed the Capitol plan to begin where few or no slums existed. The strategy and philosophy of the SRA and the city was to start in the relatively "healthy" neighborhoods in the east and develop westward, thereby pushing the blight into the river. Jerome Lipp, chief land agent and former executive director of the SRA, acknowledged the criticism by many West End merchants and residents but thought that if redevelopment had not been approached with this philosophy, the city would not have achieved one of its main goals: the elimination of blight in the city's core area. The former executive director provides some insight into the reasoning behind the SRA's redevelopment philosophy:

> *Many criticized* [the redevelopment plan] *correctly and said, "Most of the slums are down on First and Second Streets. Why are you beginning at Sixth and Seventh Streets? Why don't you go down to where the slums really are?" But the original plan was if we began at the river, we would spread the slums and the blight ahead of us as we bought property, and* [the blight] *would encroach further east into the healthy tissue of the community.* [The West End slum] *was like a cancer. It was marching east into other areas and buildings. Nobody wanted to build around Seventh and Eighth Streets because of the filth that was spreading into the area. If you take it out of there, the whole area starts to come back.* [Therefore,] *we began easterly and began moving west to drive it into the river. That* [is how] *we were able to clear out* [the blight].[275]

By the third City Council meeting, Japanese American representatives were convinced that redevelopment was a foregone conclusion.[276] As a last resort, they proposed the only alternative plan to the tentative Capitol Mall project, a compromise between the city's desire for a wholesale demolition of the West End and their constituents' desire to remain within the area and preserve Japantown. They proposed that if the SRA did not include compensation as part of the redevelopment plan or concrete guarantees that property owners could repurchase land in their area, then a "rehabilitation" program would be implemented instead, where the city allowed residents to "refurbish" and "modernize" present buildings to meet specified standards without destroying existing buildings or erecting others. With this plan proposed by Japanese American leaders, the city could achieve its redevelopment objectives of erasing the rundown sections of downtown while preserving the healthier areas and eliminating undue hardship for property owners.[277] Attorney Mamoru Sakuma asked, "Why not look into self-redevelopment before a plan of such as this is put into effect? I think that there would be no opposition to the plan if that is done. I'm definitely opposed to Redevelopment unless some compensation is given to the people who will be hurt, or if they are not given an opportunity to redevelop themselves."[278] However, such a proposal fell on deaf ears.[279] In fact, JARSA attorney Dean Itano could name only one councilman, Clarence Azevedo, who showed any interest in JARSA's counter proposal of self-rehabilitation. The attorney recalls, "There were some pretty strong feelings for redevelopment. We considered Councilman Clarence Azevedo a friend. I guess there was conflict [in the council] because of Clarence's sympathy for our group. He took a lot of abuse from his fellow councilmen."[280]

Another proposal by JARSA was to preserve a section of one block for a smaller Japantown where Japanese American merchants could run their businesses. But the agency quickly hedged on making any guarantees that such a project as a "Japanese Center" could be incorporated in the master plan. As Fred Grum, chairman of the SRA, argued, such a proposal would jeopardize their strategy for a successful redevelopment operation. In order to entice private investors to move into the West End, entire blocks must be preserved for large-scale construction. Such a project as a "Japanese Center" might be possible but only after the Redevelopment Agency's primary objective was fulfilled.[281] The SRA's first priority was with large-scale private investors, who would purchase one or two blocks at a time. The SRA used this same argument with the historic landmark preservationists who adamantly maintained that the wholesale clearance approach failed to

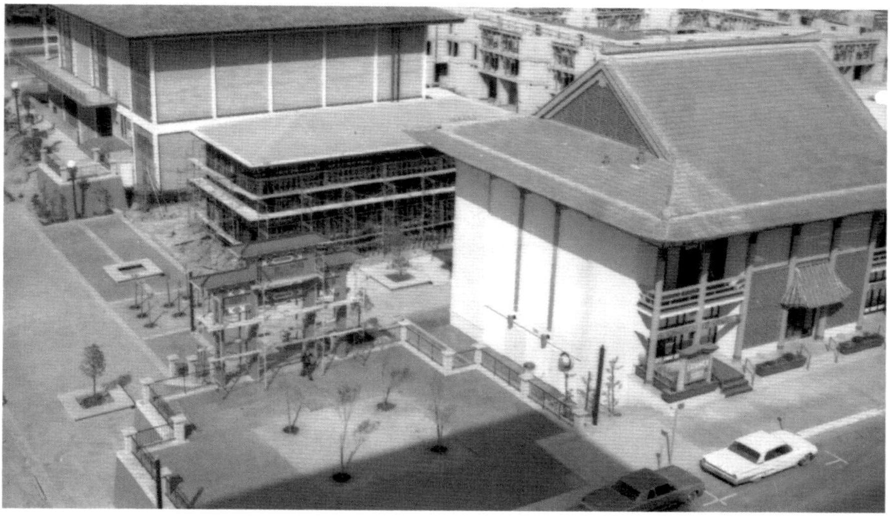

Sacramento's Chinatown was eventually incorporated into the city's redevelopment master plan. *Courtesy Center for Sacramento History, James E. Henley Collection, 1997/046/0445.*

preserve a sufficient number of important landmarks, a criticism shared by Eleanor McClatchy and the *Sacramento Bee*. But Lipp explained:

> *My objective at that time was to try to create an environment that would not only attract* [major corporations] *but also to encourage future development of that quality and to have other major buildings go into that area by requiring certain things...that would create an attractive approach to our state capitol. If I did not get big buildings down there, redevelopment would not have been successful. We would have never been able to turn that area around. You can't leave a historic landmark unless it's on the periphery. You can't put a Macy's on a* [piece of a block]. *They needed a full block, and the same applied to Crocker Bank, IBM and* [large, upscale apartments] *such as the Capitol Tower apartments.*[282]

According to the agency, plans to acquire entire blocks from West End residents and merchants and reserve them for large business and government structures were vital to a successful redevelopment project. The City Council and the SRA stood firm on this principle.

But despite the continuous protests made by Japanese American leaders over the lack of concrete provisions to safeguard the welfare of those in the project area, the SRA persisted with a policy of vagueness, promising nothing so as to leave the plan flexible with as few obligations as possible and as much land to sell to big investors.[283] Many became irate with the SRA's uncompromising stand and constant use of vague terms when discussing compensation. Standing frustrated before the City Council and Redevelopment Agency, attorney Mamoru Sakuma publicly lambasted the Capitol Mall project as simply "no plan at all":

> *The thing that bothers many people in the area is that—the constant employment of the terms by the Agency like "perhaps," "gradual," "maybe," and such things as "the details will be worked out,"* [and] *when you say, "this building might stay." We are not interested in might. We want to know what it is that you plan now.* [But] *you have been so evasive about it. If the plan you propose here consists of commercial and public buildings, multiple residential buildings,* [and an area] *for shopping, how is it that you are going to be able to continue with this overall master plan if you start talking in terms of a so-called Japanese community? You have no plan* [for a Japantown]. *I just can't see this redevelopment program as it is presently constituted, where there's no serious attempt to at least adjust some of the economic hardships...Frankly, as an individual, I am sick and tired of all this talk about nothing.*[284]

With a $1.5 million redevelopment bond issue slated for the November elections, an initiative that, if passed, would allow the SRA to proceed with the Capitol Mall plan, West End residents continued to speak out, calling it "a ruthless development plan that ignores human rights and property rights."[285] The pre-election debates pitted renewal advocates—the City Council, Mayor Henderson, the Chamber of Commerce, business organizations and the local media—against wary West End residents and business owners.[286] The issue to civic leaders and the business community was "progress" and the elimination of blight in the state's capital. But a great number of local merchants and residents in the West End believed the city's plans reflected a callous disregard for the people in the area. Jack Shelby, who owned a hardware store on Fifth Street between K and L Streets, and who later was elected to the City Council, deftly organized his effort to kill redevelopment as chairman of the Sacramento Business and Taxpayers Association. During his campaign for the City Council, Shelby tried to rally anti-redevelopment support within the West End by placing full-page ads in local newspapers, characterizing the plan as "a cold-blooded economic program" designed to improve downtown business conditions "at the expense of 4,000 American citizens."[287] In one such article, Shelby wrote, "Redevelopment, as presently constituted, is not true progress, nor is it redevelopment. No agency has the right to dislocate several thousand citizens merely to improve the downtown business area for the personal profit [of] a few big business interests."[288]

However, Shelby's campaign failed to win over all West End business owners and sometimes even collapsed under the SRA's pressure. Recalling Shelby's tenacious anti-redevelopment reputation, Jerome Lipp explained how the agency defeated some of Shelby's efforts at mobilizing support:

> *To put it mildly, he gave me a few problems. My board of directors and agency members told me, "We have to be careful with this guy Shelby." He was very much anti-redevelopment. He was trying to get all the people around him where his hardware store was to band together against me. What I did is send my negotiators out and* [gather pro-redevelopment support] *one by one around him. So when he finally started to look around to get support, he found that they had already decided to sell.*[289]

In a move to gain support for the bond issue and ease the worries of property owners, Mayor Henderson, City Manager Bartley M. Cavanaugh and SRA executive director Joseph T. Bill visited Washington, D.C., in September 1954 to request that money be made available for moving expenses of businesses and families displaced by the redevelopment project. Although it was not a direct result of Sacramento's delegation, Congress amended the Federal Housing Act of 1949, making available up to $100 for moving expenses for families and $2,500 for businesses and nonprofit institutions. This was increased to $3,000 by 1958.[290]

Despite the token relocation assistance provided by the new law, property owners still fought the plan the SRA was proposing. Because Sacramento's Japanese American population composed the largest number of people who would be devastated by the SRA's plan and Japanese American leaders were some of the first well-organized and outspoken critics of the project, they became the target for some redevelopment advocates who implied they were "obstructionists" in plans to improve the city.[291] The day after Henry Taketa publicly criticized the plan, the *Sacramento Bee* wrote, "Any community leader who would reject such an opportunity [for redevelopment] might properly be called the representative of blight."[292] Many who lived in the West End found the *Sacramento Bee*'s advocacy for redevelopment and the bond measure understandable and not much different than the opinions of most of the city spokesmen who viewed compromise as simply a lost opportunity for developing Sacramento into one of the greatest cities in the nation. As Toko Fujii said, "The *Sacramento Bee* did not really care about reporting our concerns. Who [cared] about a few of us in the West End with such an opportunity facing the city?"[293] For the *Sacramento Bee*, the choice was simply between "blight or bloom." Responding to the criticisms expressed by Japanese American leaders during City Council meetings, the newspaper wrote, "The cries arise from [a small group who say] that dislocation and relocation would be costly. While they do not fight the Redevelopment Project outright, some of the conditions they want met are impossible under law and under conditions of fair play...But some of the city's leaders may mistake these minority [views]...for the will of the whole city."[294]

Some residents began to question the agency's lack of concern for underrepresented racial minorities. Some felt that perhaps city officials targeted the West End for redevelopment precisely because of its sizable minority population, a group that, at that time, had little representation in government and therefore would provide few obstacles to the city's efforts at redevelopment. For example, the agency's first attempt to acquire property for a pilot project in the area bound between Third and Fifth Streets and I and J Streets, an area well known for its sizable Chinese population, found stiff resistance from social organizations such as the Chinese Benevolent Association. The latter organization claimed that the project was unfair because thirty-eight of the fifty-two lots were owned by Chinese merchants.[295] Toko Fujii, felt that, in general, redevelopment efforts probably took advantage of the large minority population in the West End: "In some ways, this was racial because I think they probably considered people of color not as adept at replying or not quite as aggressive at demanding their rights."[296] Pharmacist Fred Ouye shared a similar feeling: "The government probably did not expect us minorities to cause too much commotion over their demands."[297] Considering the racial intolerance that existed at that time, the city and the agency may have been minimally concerned about populations that lacked any real political power or influence in the community. But the existence of blighted areas in parts of the West End was what the SRA kept the city focused on to build support for the plan.

The city's long-held dream of creating an imposing Capitol Mall thoroughfare and wiping out the slums of the West End stumbled on Election Tuesday, November 2, 1954, when Proposition B, the redevelopment bond issue, failed to receive the two-thirds vote necessary for approval. From the *Sacramento Bee*'s perspective, the bond defeat "kills, for the time being, plans for the beautification of the West End."[298] But for others, including some five hundred Japantown residents, there was "considerable jubilation" over the election results. They had won a temporary victory.[299]

And a temporary victory it was. Just a few days after the election, the Redevelopment Agency and the City Council quickly resurrected new hope for the Capitol Mall plan by changing funding strategies. Basing the bond issue's failure on fears of increased taxes, rather than criticisms of the city's lack of concern for displaced property owners, the Redevelopment Agency solved the local funding problem by issuing its own bonds with city-guaranteed profits based on the increased value assessments of redeveloped land. As one city spokesman argued, the new redevelopment strategy "won't cost the taxpayers a cent."[300] On May 5, 1955, the city received news that the federal government had approved its redevelopment funding plan.[301] With the finances now available, the SRA and the city could ignore the West End's criticisms and continue unabated with their plans to acquire, clear and sell the fifteen blocks to large-capital investors. The only dissenting councilman, Clarence Azevedo, resigned from the Council's Redevelopment Committee out of disgust with the city's disregard for the outcome of the bond referendum.[302]

The federal decision quickly terminated six months of "jubilation" for West End property owners and especially for the Japanese American community. Their worst fears since the bombing of Pearl Harbor had materialized. "We called it our second evacuation," said former JACL president Toko Fujii. "This was 100 percent the feeling of the community."[303] Pharmacist Fred Ouye concurred: "We had to go to the first relocation, come back, get started and then here comes another blow, we had to move again."[304] Another Japantown merchant, Kanji Nishijima, expressed the same feeling:

> *We were relocated when the war broke out in 1942. We were just sent to camp like we were incarcerated. Then after the war, we came back and here we start building up our businesses again and bang, the redevelopment comes, and we get chased out again. This time they used that famous word "eminent domain." It was too soon. We came back in 1946, and within ten years we are going to the redevelopment hearings. It was too soon of being kicked around again. We got kicked around in 1942 and then we got kicked around again.*[305]

However, controversy between the Japanese American community and the city did not end with the approval of the Capitol plan. A major issue for property owners in Japantown centered on fair land acquisition procedures and property compensation. Some became skeptical of the Redevelopment Agency's honesty and fairness in property appraisals after one significant condemnation case. Nishijima bought a twelve-unit apartment building near Seventh and O Streets a few years after returning from internment. To appraise the property for government acquisition, the Redevelopment Agency hired Jerome Lipp as chief land agent. In 1955, Lipp's appraisal staff surveyed the apartment property and set the appraisal figure just under the original purchase price. Disturbed by the low figures the SRA offered, the owner refused to sell his property to the agency, forcing the agency to declare the property condemned under the powers of eminent domain. Represented by attorney Mamoru Sakuma, who would later become a Superior Court judge, Nishijima prepared to challenge the Redevelopment Agency in court. The day before the trial, the chief land agent called Sakuma over the phone and offered to buy Nishijima's property for the same amount he had paid for it eight years earlier, explaining that his appraisal staff had "made a few mistakes" during their survey. Although feeling that the agency was still trying to avoid paying fair market value and afraid of the court costs and lost business that would result if he went to trial, Nishijima decided to settle his case outside court and accept the agency's proposal.[306] He recalls:

> *I had to hire Sakuma as my lawyer, and we were going to go to court on a Monday. But Sunday Sakuma gets a call from Jerome Lipp, and Lipp told him he would get me a higher figure. It was about the same as what I originally bought it for. What they offered us was way out of line. But Sakuma advised me that what's going to happen is that by the time you end up you'll...have to pay all the lawyers' fees and you'll slow down in business and it would cost you money. So he advised not to go to court and just accept what they give* [me]. *We went along. But to this day, I* [am] *not happy with what they offered.*[307]

News of this incident spread throughout the Japanese American community. Attorney Henry Taketa confronted the Redevelopment Agency, protesting its procedures. Although he had previous meetings with the agency to ensure that property owners would be dealt with in a fair manner, the Nishijima case caused Taketa and the Japanese American community at large to grow suspicious and dubious of the SRA's policies. Lipp recalled the controversy:

> *Henry Taketa was clearly, in my judgment, the leader of the Japanese. He was suspect of what redevelopment was going to do to his clients, to people of his ancestry, understandably. Nishijima's situation…spread throughout the Japanese community, and many became suspect of me and a lot of them thought, "Gee, I sold at the price they offered. Maybe I should have held out and I would have gotten a lot more money." What happened after that, of course, is that I went back to all my appraisers and said, "I want you to go back and check your figures. If any of them are wrong, tell me now. Don't wait until I schedule something for trial." That's the only instance in which that happened. There were maybe four or five other condemnation trials, though.*[308]

This incident cast suspicion particularly on Jerome Lipp, placing him at the center of the community's frustration. "I think most in the West End felt this way," expressed Nishijima. "But they felt that they could not do much about it."[309] Even many of the community leaders were distrustful of the agency. "Slippery" is how attorney Dean Itano characterized working with the SRA.[310] The community's negative image of the SRA prompted some to publicly protest Lipp's appointment as executive director of the agency in 1958. Lipp clearly acknowledged his position as an outlet of frustration for many Japanese American property owners in the area and a symbol of the entire Capitol Mall affair: "My hands were tied by federal requirements, but they still looked to me because I was the chief land agent, and some of them were upset and did not want me in that executive director job."[311] In an effort to "smooth over some of the bad feelings," Lipp, after he was appointed, had $50,000 of the agency's funds deposited in the Sumitomo Bank. "I was concerned that many of the Japanese people, who indirectly fought my appointment…would feel that I was unsympathetic to their concerns. I wanted to send a signal that 'hey, I am not mad at anybody. Let's see if we can't get along.'"[312]

Nishijima's condemnation case was a pivotal moment in the clash with the city because it cast doubt in the minds of many Japanese American property owners whether they would receive fair market value for their property and confirmed the fears of many who believed that redevelopment was a callous undertaking with little concern for those who wielded little political power. Moreover, the Nishijima case was also significant because it may have set a precedent for future appraisals by showing the agency that Japanese Americans would not stand for "any raw deals." As Fujii expressed it, "After his case, all the other appraisals became more realistic.

So Kanji and Mamoru actually saved a lot of money for the rest of the property owners who later on had to deal with the agency as far as appraisals were concerned."[313]

Another controversy between the city and the Japanese American community surfaced over land acquisition procedures. Fujii's experience stands as an illustration of what many had to contend with. Fujii made a proposal to the Redevelopment Agency that would allow the government to buy his apartment building but where he would still remain in business until construction of the new buildings was ready to start, a process that was expected to begin a few years later. He thought that his proposal was reasonable since it would allow the government to collect rent from his business while his services remained open. "We knew there was not going to be any wholesale tearing down of the buildings and removal for years to come because it just takes time," said Fujii. "Our proposal to them was to let them buy the building, let us stay there until [they] get ready to tear it down, then we will move."[314] But the agency declined his proposal, and he was required to move out of the area even though new construction did not start until years later. Fujii recalls his frustration:

> *It must have been at least two or three years before they actually tore the buildings down. So what they did was they took away our income for that period of time unnecessarily. The Redevelopment Agency could have been getting rent from us. That would have made it better for them. We would have gotten that income out of it and that would have been better for us. But government actions being unyielding, and a lot of times illogical, forced that type of situation to exist. All that time the buildings were boarded up and no income for the agency and no income for us.*[315]

Not until September 1956 did the Redevelopment Agency begin to acquire the first three blocks of the project area, forcing many business owners to relocate to other sections of the city. With the project in full motion, Japanese American leaders decided to take the opportunity to start a project that they had been dreaming of since their return from incarceration: the creation of a Nisei War Memorial and Community Center. The idea first appeared with Masao Taketa, a leading Sacramento Valley pioneer and father of Henry Taketa. He felt so strongly about a living memorial to Japanese Americans in Sacramento and those who distinguished themselves in service that he and his family purchased property on T Street, across from the Japanese Parkview Presbyterian Church, for the JACL and VFW Post on which to build a Japanese

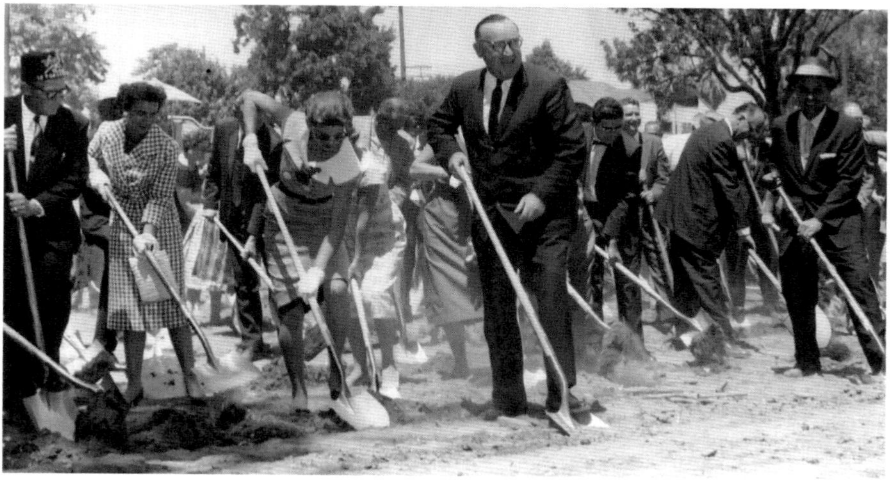

Governor Pat Brown with other city representatives at the Capitol Mall Redevelopment project opening ceremony, 1959. *Courtesy Center for Sacramento History, Frank Christy Collection, 1998/722/1427.*

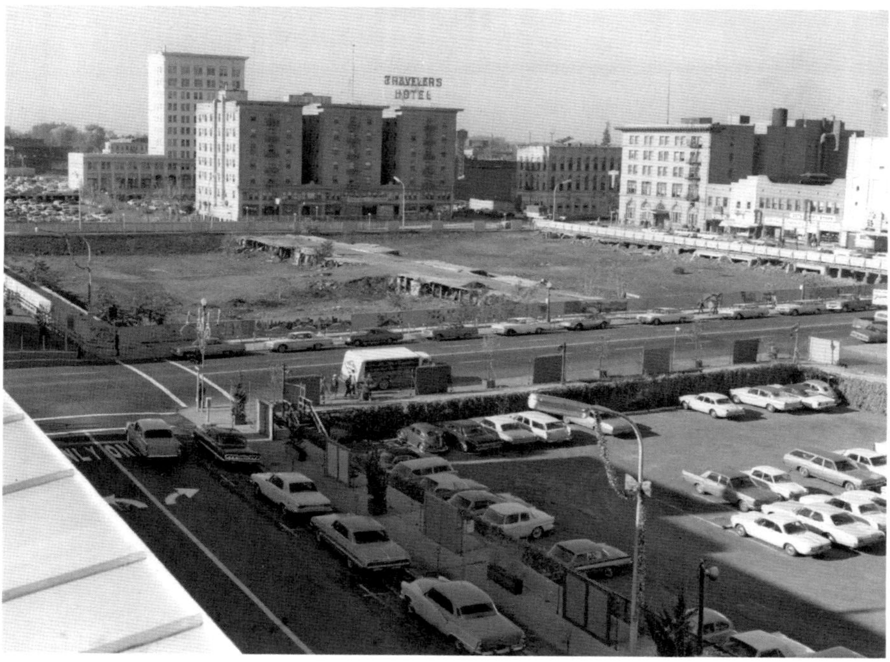

The first phase of the city's demolition. *Courtesy Center for Sacramento History, Frank Christy Collection, 1998/722/1298.*

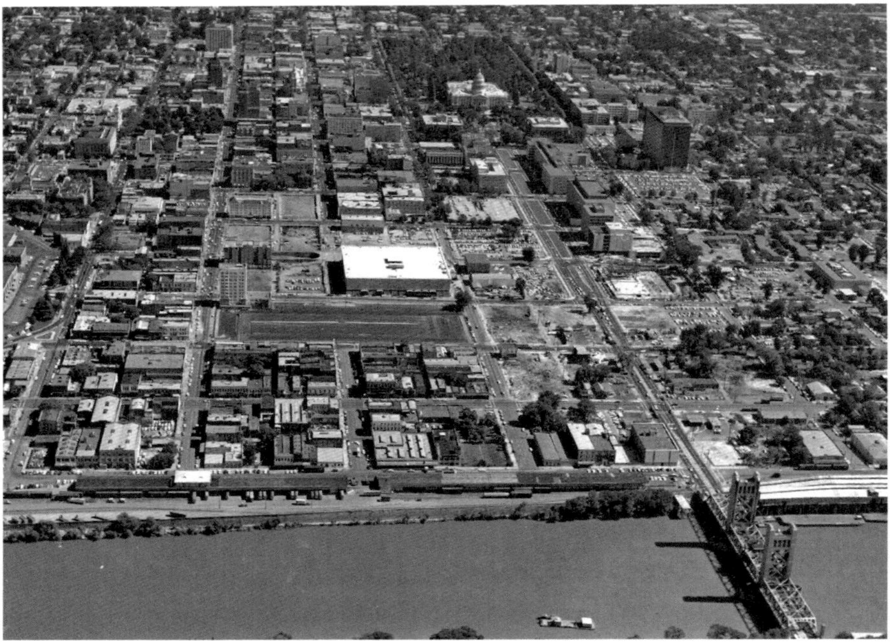

Sections of the city bulldozed, 1960. Japantown once stood within these desolate blocks. *Courtesy Center for Sacramento History, Frank Christy Collection, 1998/722/1417.*

American community hall. Unfortunately, the elder Taketa died before he could see his dream come true. In 1952, the two organizations appointed a fourteen-man building committee. But the Capitol Mall project disrupted the program in 1953–54, years that were to have been used for soliciting of contributions from Japanese American merchants situated in the heart of the redevelopment area. But soon after the city decided to ignore the defeat of the bond and implement the project, the Nisei Memorial Committee, with Henry Taketa and Dr. Yoshizo Harada leading the way, decided to move ahead with construction plans. The pending destruction of Japantown prompted the committee to purchase the Flower Garden Restaurant at 1515 Fourth Street, a location just outside the redevelopment area but centrally located near the historic district of Japantown. The memorial was completed by early 1956, marking the culmination of a community-wide effort that would serve not only as a lasting monument for Nisei veterans but also as a small, lonely reminder of Sacramento's once thriving Japantown community.[316] The memorial still stands.

CHAPTER 5

CONCLUSION

Between 1956 and 1960, Japantown slowly collapsed under the wrecking ball.[317] Some merchants relocated to a residential area along Tenth Street between W and T Streets where a sizable Asian population already existed in an attempt to create a new Japantown to accommodate their clientele. However, this new enclave hardly compared in either size or diversity of businesses to historic Japantown. Many moved south between R Street and Broadway or Sutterville Heights, while others relocated along the boulevards of Riverside, Freeport and Fruitridge, with a small number grouped together in the Oak Park area off Twelfth Avenue. By 1958, a Nisei-dominated firm, the Meadowville Land Company, had begun constructing over one thousand homes on a 260-acre subdivision. Many of these houses became occupied by former residents of Japantown.[318] The passage of Fair Housing laws in the 1960s and '70s, coupled with the rising affluence of Japanese Americans in the postwar era, opened up opportunities for Japanese Americans to occupy some of the new housing areas in south Sacramento, such as South Park, Fruitridge Road, Freeport Boulevard, Pocket Road and Greenhaven.[319]

With the beginning of the Capitol Mall project, a dream long held by many Sacramento residents, also came the end of a community held dear by Sacramento's Japanese Americans. Japanese Americans in Sacramento have experienced a series of hardships throughout their history, and the demolition of Japantown stands as one of the most shattering. To most, the Capitol Mall project was a triumphant step toward progress without any loss to the city. But to the Japanese American community, the project upset their economic and social stability by throwing them into another forced evacuation. However, their redevelopment evacuation was not so much a "blitz" out of "military necessity" as it was a slow demolition for "progress." There is a general feeling shared among Japanese Americans that the Redevelopment Agency carried out the project in an uncompromising and highhanded manner. Apart from this feeling, some agree that redevelopment has both economically and aesthetically enhanced Sacramento.[320] As Frank Hiyama said, "From an engineering standpoint, redevelopment was good for Sacramento. [But] Japanese families living in that area sacrificed the most."[321]

From a historical perspective, features of the Capitol Mall project plan may not have been as good for the city as one might think. In 1940, 3,500 persons of Japanese descent were living in the city of Sacramento, operating almost five hundred businesses in or around Japantown. For many, Japantown cultivated a sense of community solidarity within a racially hostile world and shaped their unique identity not only as Japanese pioneers in America but as Japanese Americans of Sacramento. But the Capitol Mall project completely erased the physical traces of this distinctive and unique past from Sacramento's public landscape, devastating much of the city's public history because it failed to consider the cost of sacrificing a rich cultural and social heritage for the aggregate gain of physical and economic urban renewal. As urban historian Dolores Hayden persuasively argues, identity is intimately tied to memory, and urban landscapes are storehouses for collective social memories. When such physical features are carelessly eliminated without any attempt at preservation, important collective memories are lost, memories that at once remind us of America's unique identity as a culturally rich and ethnically diverse nation and strengthen our sense of common struggle, and hence our common membership in a predominantly urban society.[322] Although Sacramento's wholesale demolition approach, which the city rigorously followed in the pre-1960 period of the project, eliminated the downtown slums, it also ruthlessly demolished many urban features that had been standing since the turn of the century, including historic ethnic landmarks important to the Japanese American community and other minority groups.[323] Enticed by futuristic business and consumer-oriented plans, civic leaders demonstrated a careless disregard for the city's historic past, including the contribution Japanese Americans had made to the history of Sacramento.

It is unfortunate that Sacramento civic leaders did not recognize the historical value in such places as Japantown or some of the other ethnic

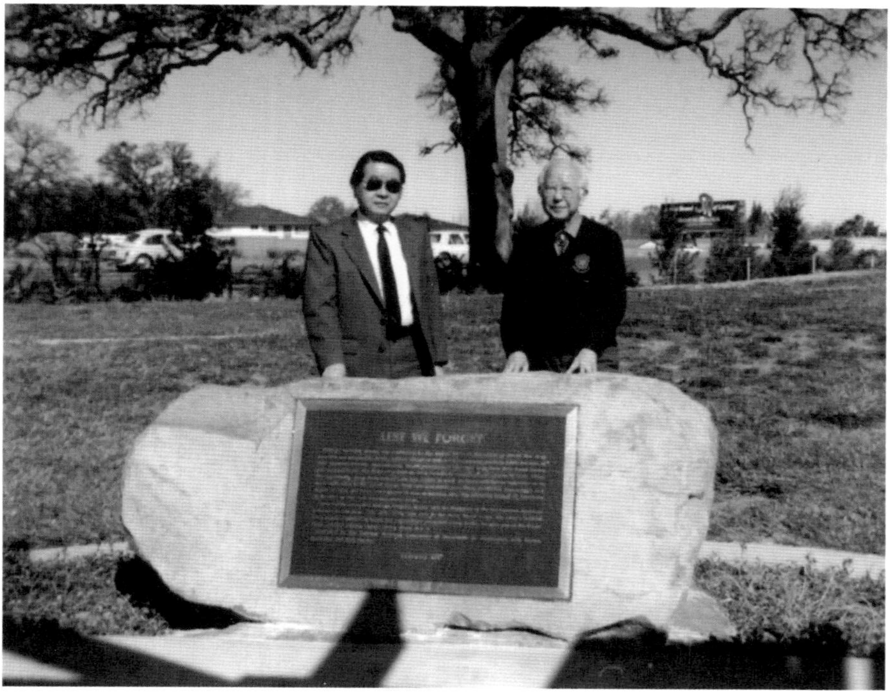

Toko Fujii and Henry Taketa at Walerga Temporary Detention Center Memorial. *Courtesy Center for Sacramento History, Henry and Sally S. Taketa Collection, 2003/016/0188.*

enclaves and vernacular features of the city. However, to fault the city on these grounds would be unfair. Only recently have Americans started to reassess the value of collective life in the poorer neighborhoods of the inner cities and the role these public places have played in shaping the history, character and development of an urban area. As Hayden forcefully writes:

> *Ghettos, barrios, Chinatowns, Little Tokyos, Little Manilas, and Little Italys are places imbued with bitter memories, such as slavery, internment, deportation, and segregation, as well as more positive stories of hard work and community organization. A new American sense of identity is emerging as we begin to recognize a diverse society where cultural differences are respected. With acceptance of diversity can come a new sense of place. Americans are just starting to realize the need for public places to celebrate the history of ordinary citizens and the collective significance of our working lives. When we know our own engaging and difficult history as a nation*

> *of women and men, drawn from many ethnic backgrounds, we can begin to create public places, in all parts of our cities, to mourn and to celebrate who we really are.*[324]

Although vanished from Sacramento's landscape, Japantown still remains in the private and shared memories of the Japanese American community in Sacramento. The Capitol Mall project destroyed Japantown, but it did not shatter the community's spirit. Although dispersed from the city's core, members of the community gather together for volunteer fundraisers; community service events; the annual Japanese American film festival; basketball tournaments; educational programs for children and adults that teach Japanese culture, language and the Japanese American experience; and the fall food and cultural bazaars. The bazaars are spirited events that regularly feature traditional Japanese and other Asian cuisine, flower arrangement, tea ceremony and *taiko* drum concerts. Most of these activities are sponsored by the various Japanese American–based churches. Members of the Sacramento and Florin chapters of the JACL remain vigilant in promoting civil rights issues and education. As the former Sacramento JACL president Toko Fujii commented, "The Japanese community is a close-knit community. So redevelopment kind of destroyed the fabric of the Japanese American community as it was known, but the Japanese community spirit remained and is still present today."[325]

APPENDIX

SACRAMENTO'S JAPANTOWN BUSINESS ESTABLISHMENTS, 1940*

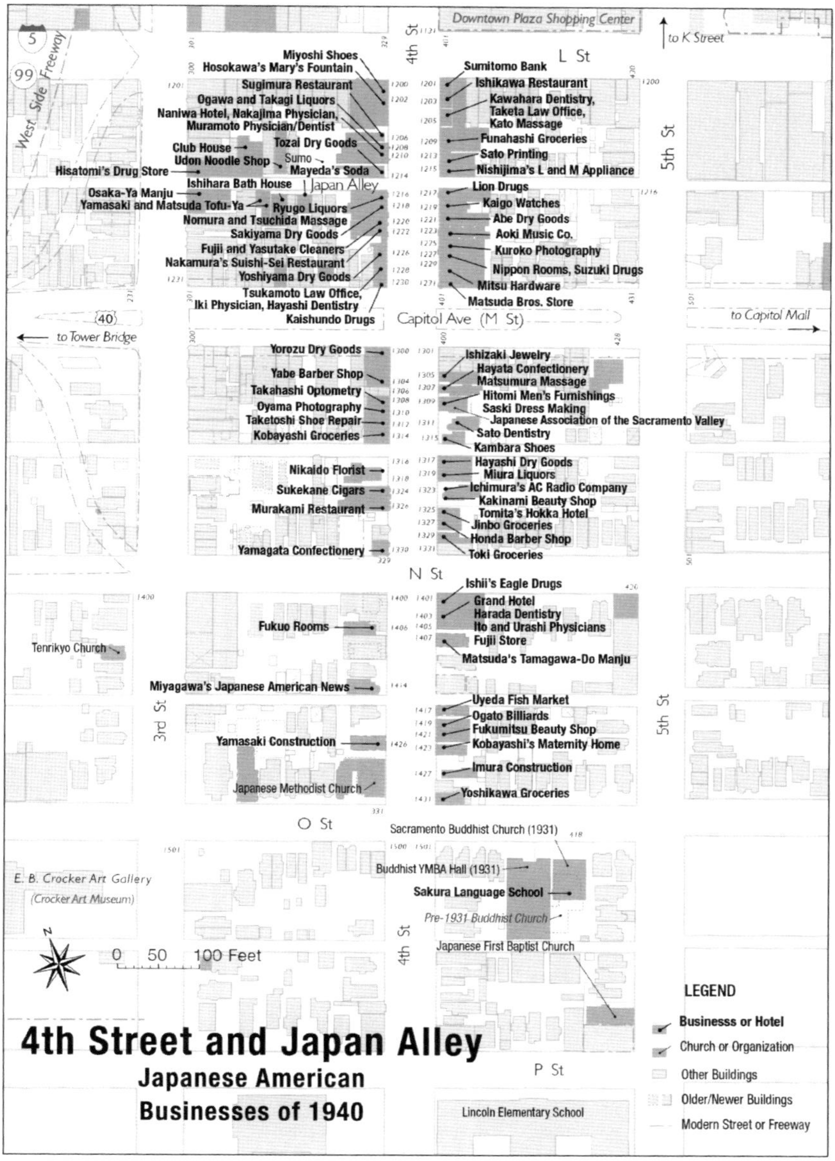

7/7/13 v35

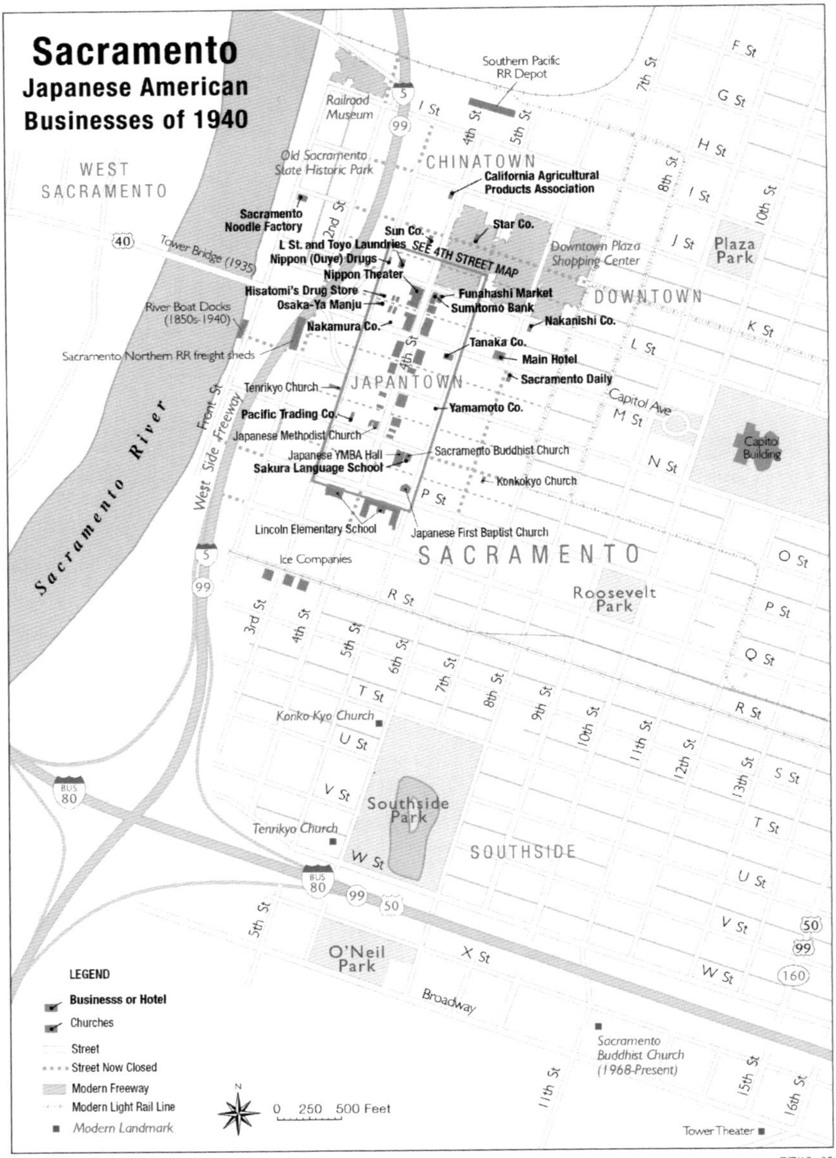
Sacramento
Japanese American
Businesses of 1940
WEST
SACRAMENTO
Southern Pacific
RR Depot
Railroad
Museum
Old Sacramento
State Historic Park
CHINATOWN
California Agricultural
Products Association
Sacramento
Noodle Factory
Star Co.
Sun Co.
L St. and Toyo Laundries
SEE 4TH STREET MAP
Nippon (Ouye) Drugs
Nippon Theater
Downtown Plaza
Shopping Center
Tower Bridge (1935)
Hisatomi's Drug Store
Osaka-Ya Manju
Funahashi Market
Sumitomo Bank
DOWNTOWN
River Boat Docks
(1850s-1940)
Nakamura Co.
Nakanishi Co.
Tanaka Co.
Main Hotel
Sacramento Northern RR freight sheds
Sacramento Daily
Tenrikyo Church
JAPANTOWN
Capitol Ave
Pacific Trading Co.
Yamamoto Co.
Japanese Methodist Church
Capitol
Building
Japanese YMBA Hall
Sakura Language School
Sacramento Buddhist Church
Konkokyo Church
Sacramento River
West Side Freeway
Front St
Lincoln Elementary School
Japanese First Baptist Church
SACRAMENTO
Ice Companies
Roosevelt
Park
Plaza
Park
Konko-Kyo Church
Southside
Park
Tenrikyo Church
SOUTHSIDE
O'Neil
Park
Broadway
Sacramento
Buddhist Church
(1968-Present)
Tower Theater
F St
G St
H St
I St
J St
K St
L St
M St
N St
O St
P St
Q St
R St
S St
T St
U St
V St
W St
X St
2nd St
3rd St
4th St
5th St
6th St
7th St
8th St
9th St
10th St
11th St
12th St
13th St
15th St
16th St
LEGEND
Businesss or Hotel
Churches
Street
Street Now Closed
Modern Freeway
Modern Light Rail Line
Modern Landmark
N
0 250 500 Feet

7/7/13 v35

<u>Third Street</u>

L Street Intersection

Kodakari Restaurant
Shimada's U.S. Hotel
Takejiro Barber Shop
Shimoda Restaurant
Sendai Hotel
Kaku Billiards
Tsutsui's Mikado Fish Market
Hisatomi Drug Store
Sendaikan Rooms
Wakashino Osaka-Ya
Inada Fish Market
Harada Shoe Store
Mashikiya Hotel
Fujisada Barber Shop
Higoya Hotel
Takemoto Drug Store
Takagaki's Wakanoura Restaurant
Harada Physician
Imura Brothers Barber Shop

Capitol Avenue Intersection

Honda Grocery Store
Nakatani Bath House
Hashisaka Brothers Gas Station

N Street Intersection

<u>Fourth Street</u>

L Street Intersection

Miyoshi Shoes
Hosokawa's Mary's Fountain
Ishikawa's Maruzen Restaurant
Kato Massage
Goichi Kawahara Dentistry
Taketa Law Office
Sugimura Restaurant
Ogawa and Takagi Liquors
Funahashi Groceries
Naniwa Hotel
Muramoto Dentistry
Muramoto Physician's Office
Nakajima Physician's Office
Sato's Hokka Printing
Waukita Dry Goods
Nishijima's L and M Appliances
Ryugo Liquors
Nomura and Tsuchida Massage
Miyahara Senbei Store
Lion Drugs
Sakiyama Dry Goods
Kaigo Watches
Fujii and Yasutake Cleaners
Abe Dry Goods
Nakamura's Sushi-Sei Restaurant
Aoki Music Co.
Kuroko Photography
Yoshiyama Dry Goods
Suzuki Drugs
Nippon Rooms
Akio Dentistry
Iki Physician's Office
Tsukamoto Law Office
Mitsu Hardware
Kaishundo Drugs
Matsuda Brothers Groceries

Capitol Avenue Intersection

Yorozu Dry Goods
Riichiro Barber Shop
Yazo Jewelry
Hayata Confectionery
Matsumura Massage
Takahashi Optometry
Hitomi Men's Furnishings

Japanese Association of the Sacramento Valley
Sasaki Dress Making
Oyama Photography
Sato Dentistry
Taketoshi Shoe Repair
Kobayashi Fish Market
Kambara Shoes
Nikaido Royal Florist
Hayashi Dry Goods
Miura Liquors
Ichimura's AC Radio Company
Kakinami Beauty Shop
Tomita's Hokka Hotel
Sukekane Cigars
Jinbo Groceries
Murakami's Kats Nikko-Ro Restaurant
Honda Barber Shop
Toki Groceries
Yamagata Confectionery
N Street Intersection
Ishii's Eagle Drugs
Harada Dentistry
Ito Physician
Urashi Physician
Fujii Store
Fukuo Rooms
Matsuda's Tamagawa-Do Manju
Japanese Americans Newspaper
Uyeda Fish Market
Ogata Billiards
Fukumitsu Beauty Shop
Japanese Americans Maternity Home
Kobayashi Midwife
Yamasaki Construction
Imura Construction
Yoshikawa Groceries
O Street Intersection

Fifth Street
L Street Intersection
Takeda's American Poultry
M Street Intersection
Nagano Auto Repair
N Street Intersection
Yamamoto Groceries
Asahi Auto Repair
Kakinami Beauty Shop
O Street Intersection

L Street
Third Street Intersection
Nippon (Ouye) Drugs
Morimoto Cleaners
Matsumoto Billiards
Kurotori's L Street Laundry
Toyo Laundry
Hasegawa Restaurant
Kimura Liquors
Kyono Barbers
Nakashima Confectionery
Katsumata Groceries
Nippon Theaters
Hamada's Corner Cafe
Fourth Street Intersection
Sumitomo Bank
Okamoto Rooms
Sakai Furnished Rooms
Kano Beauty Shop
Higaki Laundry
Fifth Street Intersection

Capitol Avenue
Third Street Intersection
Kyotani Liquors
Ogata Candies
Hayama Barber Shop
Bishu Hotel

Nishita Candies
Yamamoto Restaurant
Nakamura Radio Shop
Nishiguchi Billiards
Nichibei Hotel
Fujimi Hotel
Okabe Restaurant
Toyasaki Physician
Dote Confectionery
Ota Restaurant
Inada Candies
Yoshida's Five and Ten Cents Store
Itano Insurance
Hara Auto Shop
Yamada Fishing Goods
Dote Liquors
Togasaki Physician
Okamoto's M Street Laundry
Fourth Street Intersection
Nakayama Seeds
Kajitani Bakery
Honda Dentistry
Ito's Center Hotel
Mitsuji's Okayama Hotel
Tanaka Liquors
Taketa's State Market Groceries
Fifth Street Intersection

N Street
Third Street Intersection
Iwata Groceries
Fourth Street Intersection
Toriumi Dress Making
Fifth Street Intersection

O Street
Third Street Intersection
Japanese American Language School
Yuriko Date's Dress Making
Fujii and Yasutake Star Cleaning Company
Japanese American Methodist Episcopalian Church
Fourth Street Intersection
Sakamoto and Nishimura Groceries
Matsunaga Rooms
Sakura Japanese American
Language Institute
Buddhist Church
Takaka Dress Making
Saruwatari Midwife
Fifth Street Intersection

Japan Alley (Between L Street and Capitol Avenue, Third and Fourth Streets)
Yamasaki Tofu-ya
Matsuda Tofu-ya
Tokyo Club
Iroha and Yoshikawa Restaurant and Udon Noodle Shop
Ishihara's Sakura Bath House
Mayeda's Sunrise Soda Company

*Sources used: 1940 Sacramento City Directory with assistance from Marian Uchida, April Adachi, Fred Matsuda and Amy Wong.

NOTES

CHAPTER 1

1. Wilson and Hosokawa, *East to America*, 21, 29; Kendis, *Matter of Comfort*, 16.
2. *U.S. Census Population: 1930*, Table 17, 33.
3. Kendis, *Matter of Comfort*, 17; *U.S. Census Population: 1930*, Table 17, 266.
4. U.S. Immigration Commission, *Immigrants in Industries*, vol. 24, part 25, 326–27; Kendis, *Matter of Comfort*, 17–18.
5. U.S. Immigration Commission, *Immigrants in Industries*, vol. 24, part 25, 345, 351–53; Wilson and Hosokawa, *East to America*, 105.
6. Nisuke Mitsumori interview, in Sarasohn, *Issei Christians*, 132.
7. Riichi Satow interview, in Sarasohn, *Portrait of a Pioneer*, 25.
8. Kubo interview by author.
9. Hata and Hata, "George Shim," 55; U.S. Immigration Commission, *Immigrants in Industries*, vol. 24, part 25, 347.
10. Hiyama interview by author; Daniels, *Politics of Prejudice*, 13.
11. U.S. Immigration Commission, *Immigrants in Industries*, vol. 23, part 25, 33–34.
12. Ibid., vol. 24, part 25, 353–54; Daniels, *Politics of Prejudice*, 13–14; Kendis, *Matter of Comfort*, 17–18; See also Ichioka, "Amerika Nadeshiko," 339–75.
13. *U.S. Census Population: 1930*, Table I, 233.
14. Kane Kozono interview, in Sarasohn, *Portrait of a Pioneer*, 83–84.
15. U.S. Immigration Commission, *Immigrants in Industries*, vol. 24, part 25, 286–87, 298–99; Higgs, "Wealth of Japanese American Tenant Farmers," 493.
16. Hiyama interview by author.

17. U.S. Immigration Commission, *Immigrants in Industries*, vol. 24, part 25, 324–28.
18. Ibid., 321, 331.
19. Ibid., 341, 327.
20. Ibid., 331, vol. 23, part 25, 249.
21. Ibid., 351–52; Osuke Takizawa interview, in Sarasohn, *Portrait of a Pioneer*, 102; Takae Washizu interview, in Sarasohn, *Portrait of a Pioneer*, 112.
22. Takizawa interview, in Sarasohn, *Portrait of a Pioneer*, 102.
23. U.S. Immigration Commission, *Immigrants in Industries*, vol. 24, part 25, 327.
24. Matsuda interview by author.
25. U.S. Immigration Commission, *Immigrants in Industries*, vol. 23, part 25, 249.
26. Ibid., 321–25, 328–31.
27. Itawa, *Planted in Good Soil*, vol. 1, 238.
28. U.S. Immigration Commission, *Immigrants in Industries*, vol. 24, part 25, 341–42, 356.
29. Ichioka, "Japanese American Immigrant Response," 162.
30. Hayashi interview by author; Yagi interview by author.
31. Kendis, *Matter of Comfort*, 17–18; Thompson, *Yellow Peril*, iii.
32. Shoichi Fukuda interview, in Sarasohn, *Portrait of a Pioneer*, 64; Maeda, *Continuing Traditions*, 15.
33. Hiyama interview by author.
34. Daniels, *Concentration Camps*, 9.
35. *U.S. Industrial Commission on Immigration*, 754.
36. Takaki, *Strangers from a Different Shore*, 199–201; Maeda, "Alien Land Law," 101.
37. Takaki, *Strangers from a Different Shore*, 199–201; Maeda, "Alien Land Law," 101.
38. *U.S. Census Population: 1920*, Table 16, 65; Higgs, "Landless by Law," 210–13.
39. Wilson and Hosokawa, *East to America*, 126.
40. Ichioka, *Issei*, 99–101, 133–40.
41. Gothberg, "Press Reaction," 672.
42. Yuji Ichioka, "Japanese American Immigrant Response," 177–78.
43. U.S. Department of Labor, *Labor Unionism*, 50–54; Itawa, *Planted in Good Soil*, 417–19.
44. Daniels, *Politics of Prejudice*, 2; Kendis, *Matter of Comfort*, 18.
45. *U.S. Census Population: 1940*, Table 12, 684; Higgs, "Landless by Law," 221.

Chapter 2

46. U.S. Immigration Commission, *Immigrants in Industries*, vol. 23, part 25, 249–50, 258.
47. Ichihashi, *Japanese Americans in the United States*, 116.
48. U.S. Immigration Commission, *Immigrants in Industries*, vol. 23, part 25, 454; *U.S. Census Population: 1930*, Table 17, 266.
49. U.S. Immigration Commission, *Immigrants in Industries*, vol. 23, part 25, 251.
50. Ibid., 249.
51. Fujii interview by author.
52. Hiyama interview by author.
53. Hayashi interview by author.
54. U.S. Immigration Commission, *Immigrants in Industries*, vol. 24, part 25, 249–51.
55. Maeda, *Continuing Traditions*, 11; U.S. Immigration Commission, *Immigrants in Industries*, vol. 23, part 25, 249, 250, 253, 266.
56. U.S. Immigration Commission, *Immigrants in Industries*, vol. 23, part 25, 249–50.
57. Ai Miyasaki interview, in Sarasohn, *Portrait of a Pioneer*, 126.
58. Toshiko Igarashi interview, in Sarasohn, *Portrait of a Pioneer*, 126.
59. Bonacich and Modell, *Economic Basis*, 47–48.
60. U.S. Immigration Commission, *Immigrants in Industries*, vol. 23, part 25, 262.
61. Ibid., 250.
62. Maeda, *Continuing Traditions*, 12.
63. Takahashi interview by author.
64. Toshiko Igarashi interview, in Sarasohn, *Issei Christians*, 196.
65. U.S. Immigration Commission, *Immigrants in Industries*, vol. 23, part 25, 249, 253; Cole, "Portrait," 4.
66. U.S. Immigration Commission, *Immigrants in Industries*, vol. 23, part 25, 253.
67. Ibid., 260, 267–68.
68. Ibid., 260–61; Cole, "Portrait," 9.
69. *Sacramento City Directory*, 1915; Wilson and Hosokawa, *East to America*, 102.
70. *Sacramento Daily Union*, 7 July 1892, 3.
71. Mills, "Anti-Asian Bias."
72. *Sacramento Daily Union*, 26 February 1894, 1; 9 April 1894, 1; 7 August 1894, 1.

73. Wilson and Hosokawa, *East to America*, 106.
74. *Sacramento Bee*, 2 June 1895.
75. U.S. Immigration Commission, *Immigrants in Industries*, vol. 23, part 25, 120–21, 259–60.
76. Ibid., 259, 269, 127–28.
77. Ichihashi, *Japanese Americans in the United States*, 224–26; Ichioka, "Japanese American Associations," 409–37.
78. Report of State Board of Control of California to Governor William D. Stephens, *California and the Oriental: Japanese, Chinese, and Hindus*, June 19, 1920, 104; Bonacich and Modell, *Economic Basis*, 38; Light, *Ethnic Enterprise*, 10; Kendis, *Matter of Comfort*, 18; Daniels, *Concentration Camps*, 9, 22–23.
79. Report of State Board, 104; Ichihashi, *Japanese Americans in the United States*, 128; Daniels, *Politics of Prejudice*, 16–30.
80. Ichihashi, *Japanese Americans in the United States*, 124; *U.S. Census Population: 1920*, Table 1, 106: Cole, "Portrait," 7–10.
81. *U.S. Census Population: 1940*, Table 6, 518.
82. Ichihashi, *Japanese Americans in the United States*, 128.
83. Modell, "Japanese-American Family," 75.
84. U.S. Immigration Commission, *Immigrants in Industries*, vol. 23, part 25, 268.
85. Bonacich and Modell, *Economic Basis*, 62.
86. Kubo interview by author.
87. Light, *Ethnic Enterprise*, 66.
88. Wataru Ishisaka interview, in Sarasohn, *Portrait of a Pioneer*, 148.
89. Sacramento Japanese American United Methodist Church, *Our History*, 10.
90. Ibid.
91. *Buddhist Church of Sacramento*, 1–2; Maeda, *Continuing Traditions*, 14.
92. *History of the Tenrikyo Church*, 108–9; Maeda, *Continuing Traditions*, 14.
93. Konko Church, *25th Memorial Service*, 20; Oya interview by author.
94. Sacramento First Japanese American Baptist Church, *Our Church History*, 1; Toshiko Igarashi interview, in Sarasohn, *Issei Christians*, 197–98.
95. Isamu Nakamura interview, in Sarasohn, *Issei Christians*, 170.
96. Ibid.; Maeda, *Continuing Traditions*, 13.
97. U.S. Immigration Commission, *Immigrants in Industries*, vol. 23, part 25, 260–61; Maeda, *Continuing Traditions*, 15.
98. *Sacramento Bee*, 7 May 1942, 14.
99. Uchida interview by author; Cole, "History," 63.

100. *Sacramento Bee*, 24 January 1942, 21; U.S. Immigration Commission, *Immigrants in Industries*, vol. 23, part 25, 267–68.
101. U.S. Immigration Commission, *Immigrants in Industries*, vol. 23, part 25, 256; Maeda, *Continuing Traditions*, 11.
102. Girdner and Loftis, *Great Betrayal*, 90.
103. State of California Superintendent of Banks, "Annual Report," 313–16.
104. Kubo interview by author; Report of State Board, 80; Light, *Ethnic Enterprise*, 48; Girdner and Loftis, *Great Betrayal*, 90.
105. Kubo interview by author; Report of State Board, 80–81.
106. Light, *Ethnic Enterprise*, 48.
107. Ibid., 27–28.
108. Kubo interview by author.
109. U.S. Immigration Commission, *Immigrants in Industries*, vol. 23, part 25, 261–62, 265.
110. Bonacich and Modell, *Economic Basis*, 48; Miyamoto, "Social Solidarity," 75; Kitano, *Japanese-Americans*, 19–20.
111. O'Brien and Fugita, "Middleman Minority Concept," 193; Light, *Ethnic Enterprise*, 76.
112. U.S. Immigration Commission, *Immigrants in Industries*, vol. 24, part 25, 453, 457–58.
113. Yagi interview by author.
114. Kubo interview by author.
115. U.S. Immigration Commission, *Immigrants in Industries*, vol. 24, part 25, 453–58; Hiyama interview by author.
116. U.S. Immigration Commission, *Immigrants in Industries*, vol. 24, part 25, 455.
117. Hiyama interview by author; Yagi interview by author; Cole, "Portrait," 4–5.
118. *Sacramento City Directories*, 1908–1942.
119. Girdner and Loftis, *Great Betrayal*, 90.
120. Toshiko Igarashi interview, in Sarasohn, *Issei Christians*, 197.
121. Chikaji Teramoto interview in Cole, "History," 178.
122. *U.S. Census Population: 1930*, Table 17, 226; *U.S. Census Population: 1940*, Table 41, 103.
123. *Sacramento City Directory*, 1935, 1939, 1942, 1947.
124. Cole, "History," 66.
125. Toshiko Igarashi interview, in Sarasohn, *Issei Christians*, 197, 199–200.
126. Kubo interview by author.

127. Eaton, *Beauty Behind Barbed Wire*, 123–24.
128. Takahashi interview by author.
129. Wong interview by author.
130. Uchida interview by author.
131. Fujii interview by author.
132. Ibid.
133. Takahashi interview by author; Wong interview by author; Matsuda interview by author.
134. Lee interview by author; Cole, "History," 71.
135. Lee interview by author.
136. Cole, "History," 175–76.
137. Takahashi interview by author.
138. Wong interview by author.
139. Lee interview by author; Yagi interview by author; Kubo interview by author; Nishijima interview by author.
140. Kubo interview by author; Shibata interview by author; Maeda. *Continuing Traditions*, 16.
141. Matsuda interview by author.
142. Spickard, "Nisei Assume Power"; Kendis, *Matter of Comfort*, 17–19.
143. Recollections of Grace (Sakata) Sugiyama and Sachiko (Hori) Yamamoto. Document courtesy of Christine Umeda.
144. Maeda, *Continuing Traditions*, 16–17.
145. Ibid.
146. Kendis, *Matter of Comfort*, 18–19; Takaki, *Strangers from a Different Shore*, 219–20.
147. Takaki, *Strangers from a Different Shore*, 222.
148. JACL minutes, October 31, 1931, March 2, 1935, reprinted in *Pacific Citizen*, 20 December 1957, section C, 15; *Pacific Citizen*, 21 December 1958, 18-A.
149. JACL minutes, 1 February 1936, reprinted in *Pacific Citizen*, 20 December 1957, Section C, 15.
150. *Pacific Citizen*, 21 December 1956, 18-A; Spickard, "Nisei Assume Power," 153.

Chapter 3

151. Daniels, *Decision to Relocate*, 10.
152. Kumamoto, "Search for Spies," 58–67; Daniels, *Decision to Relocate*, 10; *Sacramento Bee*, 10 December 1941, 27.

153. *Sacramento Bee*, 1 December 1991.
154. Ibid.
155. Isamu Nakamura interview, in Sarasohn, *Issei Christians*, 171–72.
156. Ibid.
157. *Sacramento Bee*, 29 December 1941, 26; 30 December 1941, 25; 2 January 1942, 3.
158. Ibid., 8 December 1941, 1; 13 December 1941, 13; *Sacramento Union*, 8 December 1941, 1–2; *Sacramento City Directory*, 1941.
159. Nakamura interview, in Sarasohn, *Issei Christians*, 171.
160. Nishijima interview by author.
161. Takahashi interview by author.
162. Kubo interview by author.
163. *Sacramento Bee*, 13 December 1941, 1; Hayashi interview by author.
164. Nakamura interview, in Sarasohn, *Issei Christians*, 173; *Sacramento Union*, 10 December 1941, 2.
165. *Sacramento Union*, 10 December 1941, 2; *Sacramento Bee*, 9 December 1942, 1.
166. *Sacramento Union*, 10 December 1941, 2.
167. *Sacramento Bee*, 13 December 1941, 12.
168. Spickard, "Nisei Assume Power," 154–59; *Sacramento Bee*, 12 January 1942, 3; 23 January 1942, 3; 30 January 1942, 1; 31 January 1942, 1.
169. *Sacramento Union*, 8 December 1941, 1–2; 9 December 1941, 1–2.
170. *Sacramento Bee*, 8 December 1941, 8.
171. Ibid., 10 December 1941, 27; 3 January 1942, 3; *Sacramento Union*, 12 December 1941, 1.
172. Riichi Satow interview, in Sarasohn, *Portrait of a Pioneer*, 157; *Sacramento Bee*, 24 January 1942, 20; 30 January 1942, 8.
173. *Sacramento Union*, 9 December 1941, 2; 10 December 1941, 10; *Sacramento Bee*, 13 December 1941, 1.
174. *Sacramento Union*, 12 December 1941, 1.
175. Ibid., 12 December 1941, 9.
176. *Sacramento Bee*, 30 December 1941, 25.
177. Ibid., 30 December 1941; 19 January 1942, 18.
178. Minejiro Shibata interview, in Sarasohn, *Portrait of a Pioneer*, 160; *Sacramento Bee*, 26 December 1941, 8; 29 December 1941, 6; 1 January 1942, 6.
179. Adachi interview by author.
180. *Sacramento Union*, 15 May 1942, 1.
181. *Sacramento Bee*, 10 December 1941, 27; 30 December 1941, 4; *Sacramento City Directory*, 1942.

182. *Sacramento Bee*, 8 December 1942, 4; *United States, War Relocation Authority*, 160–62.
183. *Sacramento Bee*, 1–15 May 1942, Classified section; 15 May 1942, 1; *Sacramento Union*, 1–15 May 1942, Classified section.
184. *Sacramento Bee*, 7 May 1942, 1.
185. Toshiko Igarashi interview, in Sarasohn, *Issei Christians*, 203.
186. *Sacramento Union*, 8 May 1942, 10.
187. *Sacramento Bee*, 9 May 1942, 24.
188. *Sacramento Union*, 1 May 1942, 14; 3 May 1942, 17; *Sacramento Bee*, 9 May 1942, 24
189. Nakamura interview, in Sarasohn, *Issei Christians*, 172.
190. Shoichi Fukuda interview, in Sarasohn, *Portrait of a Pioneer*, 172.
191. *Sacramento Union*, 15 May 1942, 1.
192. Ibid., 8 May 1942, 1; 10 May 1942, 10.
193. Miyamoto interview by author.
194. Kubo interview by author.
195. Nakamura interview, in Sarasohn, *Issei Christians*, 172.
196. Hayashi interview by author.
197. *United States, War Relocation Authority*, 162.
198. *Sacramento Bee*, 10 December 1941, 1; 23 May 1942, 7; *Sacramento Union*, 11 May 1942, 1.
199. *Sacramento Bee*, 7 May 1942, 14; *Pacific Citizen*, 11 June 1942, 2.
200. *Sacramento Union*, 8 May 1942, 1; 13 May 1942, 1; 15 May 1942, 1; 27 May 1942, 15.
201. Ibid., 8 May 1942, 15.
202. Riyo Orite interview, in Sarasohn, *Portrait of a Pioneer*, 175.
203. Riichi Satow interview, in Sarasohn, *Portrait of a Pioneer*, 178.
204. *Sacramento Union*, 8 May 1942, 15.
205. Nakamura interview, in Sarasohn, *Issei Christians*, 173.
206. *Sacramento Union*, 8 May 1942, 15.
207. *Pacific Citizen*, 4 June 1942, 6.
208. Maeda, *Continuing Traditions*, 29.
209. Daniels, *Decision to Relocate*, 4.
210. *Sacramento Union*, 15 May 1942, 1.
211. Ibid., 14 May 1942, 1.
212. Ibid.

CHAPTER 4

213. Sarasohn, *Portrait of a Pioneer*, 235.
214. *Pacific Citizen*, 3 June 1943, 7.
215. *Sacramento City Council Minutes*, 28 May 1943.
216. *Pacific Citizen*, 13 May 1943, 3; 10 June 1943, 8; 8 January 1944, 7; 3 March 1945, 8; 21 April 1945, 2.
217. Ibid., 6 November 1943, 7.
218. Sarasohn, *Portrait of a Pioneer*, 237, 241, 251, 253.
219. *Pacific Citizen*, 6 November 1943, 7.
220. Sarasohn, *Portrait of a Pioneer*, 237; Ouye interview by author; Caesar, "Historical Overview," 161.
221. *Pacific Citizen*, 21 May 1949, 8.
222. Sarasohn, *Portrait of a Pioneer*, 251, 258.
223. Sarasohn, *Issei Christians*, 183.
224. Ibid., 207.
225. Takahashi interview by author.
226. *Sacramento City Directory*, 1947.
227. *Pacific Citizen*, 20 December 1957, C-17; Henry Taketa interview by Debbie Roberts, *Florin Japanese American Citizen League*, 51–57.
228. *Pacific Citizen*, 7 April 1945, 2; 20 December 1957, C-17.
229. Nishijima interview by author.
230. Frank Hiyama interview by author.
231. Adachi interview by author; Matsuda interview by author; Uchida interview by author.
232. Ouye interview by author; Sarasohn, *Portrait of a Pioneer*, 249.
233. *Pacific Citizen*, 23 April 1954, 2; *Japanese American Business Directory*, 1955, as cited in Maeda, *Sacramento Ethnic Survey*, 145–46.
234. Sarasohn, *Portrait of a Pioneer*, 248.
235. *Sacramento City Directory*, 1949.
236. *Pacific Citizen*, 23 April 1954, 2; 22 July 1955, 3; *City Directory*, 1954.
237. *City Directory*, 1954.
238. *Sacramento City Property Map Book.*
239. *City Directory*, 1954; Ouye interview by author.
240. Kendis, *Matter of Comfort*, 18–20; Boyd, "Oriental Immigration," 59.
241. *City Directory*, 1954; Hiyama interview by author.
242. *Pacific Citizen*, 21 May 1949, 5.
243. Ibid., 5 April 1947, 8; 15 April 1950, 7; 16 December 1950, 8; 3 March 1951, 7; 31 March 1951, 7.

244. Ibid., 21 May 1949, 5.
245. *History of State Offices*, 4–5; *Sacramento Bee*, 3 August 1940.
246. Gaywood, *Planning*, 5–7.
247. Leonard, "Sacramento Redevelopment," 1; Wise, "Future of Urban Renewal," 7.
248. Lipp interview by author.
249. Sacramento City Council Minutes, Special Meeting, 15 June 194, 7; *Sacramento Bee*, 23 July 1954, 1; 25 October 1954, 21; Sacramento City Council Minutes, Special Meeting, 29 June 1954, 71–72.
250. *Sacramento Bee*, 1 July 1954, 1.
251. Ibid., 6 July 1954, 10.
252. Sacramento City Council Minutes, 15 June, 29 June, 20 July, 1954.
253. *Sacramento Bee*, 21 July 1954, 1; Sacramento City Council Minutes, 20 July 1954.
254. Sacramento City Council Minutes, 15 June 1954.
255. *Pacific Citizen*, 23 April 1954, 2.
256. Ibid.
257. Ibid., 23 April 1954, 2; 22 July 1955, 3; *City Map Book*, 1954–55.
258. Uchida interview by author.
259. Sacramento City Council Minutes, 15 June 1954, 5–7; *Pacific Citizen*, 23 April 1954, 2; 4 June 1954, 5.
260. Itano interview by author.
261. Ibid.
262. *Sacramento Bee*, 16 June 1954, 1: Sacramento City Council Minutes, 29 June 1954, 72–73.
263. *Council Minutes*, 15 June 1954, 6; *Sacramento Bee*, 16 June 1954, 1; Kanji Nishijima interview.
264. *Pacific Citizen*, 18 June 1954, 5.
265. Sacramento City Council Minutes, Supplement Statements, 15 June 1954, 6.
266. Ibid., 70–75.
267. Ibid.
268. Ibid., 75–78.
269. Ibid., 77–79, 74–75.
270. Nishijima interview by author; Fujii interview by author.
271. Itano interview by author.
272. Miyamoto interview by author.
273. Ouye interview.
274. Itano interview by author; Fujii interview by author; *Pacific Citizen*, 9 July 1954, 5.

275. Lipp interview by author.
276. Itano interview by author; Fujii interview by author; *Pacific Citizen*, 9 July 1954, 5.
277. Sacramento City Council Minutes, 20 July 1954, 19–21; *Sacramento Bee*, 21 July 1954, 1.
278. Itano interview by author; *Sacramento Bee*, 16 July 1954, 6 July 1954.
279. See responses by Fred Grum and Joseph Bill in Sacramento City Council Minutes, 20 July 1954.
280. Itano interview by author.
281. Sacramento City Council Minutes, 29 June 1954, 71–73; Lipp interview by author.
282. Lipp interview by author.
283. *Sacramento Bee*, 16 June 1954, 1; Sacramento City Council Minutes, 29 June 1954, 72–74.
284. Sacramento City Council Minutes, 29 June 1954, 75–80.
285. *Bee*, 23 July 1954, 1; 21 October 1954, 3.
286. *Sacramento Shopping News*, 14 October 1954, 1; 28 October 1954, 1; *Sacramento Bee*, 21 October 1954, 1; 25 October 1954, 21.
287. *Sacramento Shopping News*, 29 October 1954, 10.
288. Ibid.
289. Lipp interview by author.
290. Fred Grum, "Letter to Councilman Marty," 1; Leonard, "Capital Mall Project," 9; Fujii interview by author; Oyue interview by author.
291. *Pacific Citizen*, 9 July 1954, 5.
292. *Sacramento Bee*, 6 June 1954, editorial page.
293. Fujii interview by author.
294. *Sacramento Bee*, 1 July 1954, 1.
295. Ibid., 14 November 1952, 8.
296. Fujii interview by author.
297. Ouye interview by author.
298. *Sacramento Bee*, 3 November 1954, 1.
299. *Pacific Citizen*, 12 November 1954, 1; *Sacramento Shopping News*, 11 November 1954, 1.
300. *Sacramento Bee*, 25 November 1954, 1; see also Roberts, "Sacramento Since World War II," 77.
301. *Sacramento Bee*, 5 May 1955, 1.
302. Ibid., 25 November 1954, 1.
303. Fujii interview by author.
304. Ouye interview by author.

305. Nishijima interview by author.
306. Ibid.; Lipp interview by author.
307. Nishijima interview by author.
308. Lipp interview by author.
309. Nishijima interview by author.
310. Itano interview by author.
311. Lipp interview by author.
312. Ibid.
313. Fujii interview by author.
314. Ibid.
315. Ibid.
316. *Pacific Citizen*, 13 May 1955, 5; 4 November 1955, 1; 25 November 1955, 5; 29 March 1957, 3.

CHAPTER 5

317. *Pacific Citizen*, 21 September 1956, 1; 12 July 1957, 8; 13 February 1959, 4.
318. Ibid., 4 April 1958; 27 February 1959, 3.
319. Maeda, *Ethnic Survey*, 150; "Final Report on Relocation," 3; Grum, "Letter to Councilman Marty," 1; Leonard, "Final Relocation Report," 8–9.
320. Nishijima interview by author; Ouye interview by author; Fujii interview by author; Okada interview by author; Hiyama interview by author; Cole, "History," 121.
321. Hiyama interview by author.
322. Hayden, *Power of Place*.
323. *Pacific Citizen*, 12 July 1957, 2.
324. Hayden, *Power of Place*, 237–38.
325. Fujii interview by author.

BIBLIOGRAPHY

SECONDARY SOURCES

Bonacich, Edna, and John Modell. *The Economic Basis of Ethnic Solidarity: Small Business in the Japanese-American Community*. Berkeley: University of California Press, 1980.

Boyd, Monica. "Oriental Immigration: The Experience of the Chinese, Japanese, and Filipino Population in the United States." *International Migration Review* (Spring 1971): 59.

Buddhist Churches of America: Sacramento, 75 Year History, 1899–1974. Chicago: Nobart Publishing, 1975.

Caesar, Clarence. "An Historical Overview of the Development of Sacramento's Black Community, 1850–1983." Master's thesis, California State University–Sacramento, 1985.

Cole, Cheryl. "A History of the Japanese American Community in Sacramento, 1883–1972." Master's thesis, California State University–Sacramento, 1971.

———. "A Portrait of Sacramento's Japanese American Community, 1883–1972." *Golden Notes* (Spring 1975): 1–13.

Daniels, Roger. *Concentration Camps: North America, Japanese American sin the United States and Canada During World War II*. FL: Robert E. Krieger Publishing Company, 1981.

———. *The Decision to Relocate the Japanese-Americans*. Philadelphia: J.B. Lippincott Company, 1975.

———. *The Politics of Prejudice: The Anti-Japanese American Movement in California and the Struggle for Japanese American Exclusion*. Berkeley: University of California Press, 1963.

Eaton, Allen H. *Beauty Behind Barbed Wire: The Arts of the Japanese Americans in Our War Relocation Camps*. New York: Harper and Brothers Publishing, 1952.

Gaywood, Grant D. *Planning for "Core Area" Development in Sacramento: California's Capital City*. Sacramento, CA: Redevelopment Agency of the City of Sacramento, 1957. Sacramento Central Library, Sacramento Room.

Girdner, Audrie, and Ann Loftis. *The Great Betrayal: The Evacuation of the Japanese Americans During World War II*. London: Macmillan Company, 1969.

Gothberg, John A. "Press Reaction to Japanese American Land Ownership in California." *Journalism Quarterly* 47 (Winter 1970): 670–76.

Greer, Scott. *Urban Renewal and American Cities: The Dilemma of Democratic Intervention*. Indianapolis, IN: Bobbs-Merrill Company, 1965.

Hata, Don, and Nadine Hata. "George Shim: The Potato King of California." *Journal of the West* (January 1986): 47–53.

Hayden, Dolores. *The Power of Place: Urban Landscapes as Public History*. Cambridge, MA: MIT Press, 1995.

Higgs, Robert. "Landless by Law: Japanese American Immigrants in California Agriculture to 1941." *Journal of Economic History* (March 1978): 210–13.

———. "The Wealth of Japanese American Tenant Farmers in California, 1909." *Agricultural History* (April 1979): 490–94.

History of State Offices in Sacramento. Sacramento: State of California, Department of General Services, Office of Architecture and Construction, 1969, California State Archives.

The History of the Tenrikyo Church in America. Los Angeles: Mission Headquarters in America, 1984.

Ichihashi, Yamato. *Japanese Americans in the United States: A Critical Study of the Problems of the Japanese American Immigrants and Their Children*. Stanford, CA: Stanford University Press, 1932; reprint, New York: Arno Press, 1969.

Ichioka, Yuji. "Amerika Nadeshiko: Japanese American Women in the United States, 1900–1924." *Pacific Historical Review* (May 1980): 339–75.

———. *The Issei: The World of the First Generation Japanese American Immigrants, 1882–1924*. New York: Free Press, 1988.

———. "Japanese American Associations and the Japanese American Government: A Special Relationship, 1909–1926." *Pacific Historical Review* (August 1977): 409–37.

———. "Japanese American Immigrant Response to the 1920 California Alien Land Law." *Agricultural History* (April 1984): 162.

Itawa, Masakazu. *Planted in Good Soil: The History of the Issei in the United States Agriculture*. New York: Peter Land Publishing, 1992.

Kendis, Kaoru Oguri. *A Matter of Comfort: Ethnic Maintenance and Ethnic Style Among Third Generation Japanese-Americans*. New York: AMS Press, Inc., 1989.

Kitano, Henry H.L. *Japanese Americans: Evolution of a Subculture*. NJ: Prentice-Hall, 1976.

Konko Church of Sacramento. *The 25th Memorial Service for the Late Reverend Yasumura, December 1993*. Sacramento, CA: Konko Church of Sacramento, 1993.

Kumamoto, Bob. "The Search for Spies: American Counterintelligence and the Japanese-American Community, 1931–1942." *American Journal* (Fall 1979): 56–69.

Lastufka, Ken. "Redevelopment of Sacramento's West End, 1950–1970: An Historical Overview with an Analysis of the Impact of Relocation." Master's thesis, California State University–Sacramento, 1985.

Light, Ivan H. *Ethnic Enterprise in America: Business and Welfare Among Chinese, Japanese, and Blacks*. Berkeley: University of California Press, 1972.

Lord, Myrtle Shaw. *A Sacramento Saga*. Sacramento, CA: Sacramento Chamber of Commerce, 1946. Sacramento Central Library, Sacramento Room.

Maeda, Wayne. "Alien Land Law of 1913: Institutional Racism Against the Japanese." Master's thesis, California State University–Sacramento, 1976.

———. *Continuing Traditions: Japanese-Americans, Story of a People, 1869–1992*. Sacramento, CA: Sacramento History Museum, 1992.

———. *Sacramento Ethnic Survey: Japanese*. Sacramento, CA: Sacramento Archives and Museum Collection Center, May 1987.

McGowan, Joseph A. *History of the Sacramento Valley*. Vol. II. New York: Lewis History Publishing Center, 1961.

Mills, Patricia A. "The Anti-Asian Bias in Editorial Cartoons Featured in the *Sacramento Bee*, 1900–1945." Master's thesis, California State University–Sacramento, 1990.

Miyamoto, Frank. "Social Solidarity Among the Japanese Americans in Seattle." In *University of Washington Publications in the Social Sciences*. Seattle: University of Washington Press, 1939.

Modell, John. "The Japanese-American Family." *Pacific Historical Review* (February 1968): 69–78.

O'Brien, David J., and Stephen S. Fugita. "Middleman Minority Concept: Its Explanatory Value in the Case of the Japanese Americans in California Agriculture." *Pacific Sociological Review* (April 1982).

Ogawa, Dennis M. *From Japs to Japanese: The Evolution of Japanese-American Stereotypes*. Berkeley, CA: McCutchen Publishing Corporation, 1971.

Roberts, Brian. "Sacramento Since World War II: From Small Town to Megalopolis in Less than Fifty Years." Master's thesis, California State University–Sacramento, 1989.

Sacramento First Japanese American Baptist Church. *Our Church History*. Sacramento, CA: Japanese American First Baptist Church, 1993.

Sacramento Japanese American United Methodist Church. *Our Church History*. Sacramento, CA: Japanese American United Methodist Church, 1994.

Sowell, Thomas. *Ethnic America: A History*. New York: Basic Books, Inc., 1981.

Spickard, Paul R. "The Nisei Assume Power: The Japanese American Citizens League, 1941–1942." *Pacific Historical Review* (May 1983): 144–61.

Takaki, Ronald. *Strangers from a Different Shore: A History of Asian Americans*. Boston: Little Brown and Company, 1989.

Thompson, Richard Austin. *The Yellow Peril: 1890–1924*. New York: Arno Press, 1978.

Wilson, Robert A., and Bill Hosokawa. *East to America: A History of the Japanese Americans in the United States*. New York: William Morrow and Company, 1980.

Wilson, William H. *The City Beautiful Movement*. Baltimore, MD: Johns Hopkins University Press, 1989.

Yasui, Barbara. "The Nikkei in Oregon, 1834–1940." *Oregon Historical Quarterly* (September 1975): 248–56.

Yatsushiro, Toshio. *Politics and Cultural Values: The World War Two Japanese American Relocation Centers and the United States Government*. New York: Arno Press, 1978.

Zimmer, Basil G. *Rebuilding Cities: The Effects of Displacement and Relocation on Small Business*. Chicago: Quadrangle Books, 1964.

PRIMARY SOURCES

Bill, Joseph T. "Work Progress: Narrative Report 40, September 1954." Sacramento, CA: Redevelopment Agency of the City of Sacramento, 1954. Frank B. Durkee Collection, Sacramento Archives and Museum Collection Center.

"Final Report on Relocation of Householders from Capitol Mall Project Area." Sacramento, CA: Redevelopment Agency of the City of Sacramento, 1960. Frank B. Durkee Collection, Sacramento Archives and Museum Collection Center.

Grum, Fred. "Letter to Councilman Albert M. Marty, November 28, 1956." Frank B. Durkee Collection, Sacramento Archives and Museum Collection Center.

Hegemann, Werner G. "Report of Dr. Werner Hegemann on Sacramento, 1913." Sacramento, CA: Sacramento Central Library, Sacramento Room.

Japanese-American Citizens League. "Sacramento Chapter Minutes—October 1931–May 1942." Reprint, *Pacific Citizen*, 20 December 1957, C15–C19.

Leonard, Howard B. "Capital Mall Project: Relocation Report Nisei." Sacramento, CA: Redevelopment Agency of the City of Sacramento, 31 May 1961. Frank B. Durkee Collection, Sacramento Archives and Museum Collection Center.

———. "Final Relocation Report: Capitol Mall." Sacramento, CA: Redevelopment Agency of the City of Sacramento, 1 March 1963. Frank B. Durkee Collection, Sacramento Archives and Museum Collection Center.

———. "Sacramento Redevelopment." Frank B. Durkee Collection, Sacramento Archives and Museum Collection Center.

McEntire, Davis. "Relocation Plan: Slum Area Labor Market Area, Sacramento." Sacramento, CA: Redevelopment Agency of the City of Sacramento, January 1959. Frank B. Durkee Collection, Sacramento Archives and Museum Collection Center.

"A New Sacramento: Progress and Promise." Sacramento, CA: Redevelopment Agency of the City of Sacramento, 1967. Frank B. Durkee Collection, Sacramento Archives and Museum Collection Center.

"Old Sacramento and Redevelopment Reports: 1958–1970." Sacramento, CA: Museum of History Division. Sacramento Archives and Museum Collection Center.

Pacific Citizen, 13 May 1943, 3; 3 June 1943, 7; 10 June 1943, 8; 6 November 1943, 7; 8 January 1944, 7; 3 March 1945, 8; 7 April 1945, 2; 21 April 1945, 2; 21 May 1949, 8; 23 April 1954; 4 June 1954; 18 June 1954; 9 July 1954; 12 November 1954; 13 May 1955; 22 July 1955; 23 September 1955; 4 November 1955; 25 November 1955; 21 September 1956; 21 December 1956; 29 March 1957; 12 July 1957; 20 December 1957; 4 April 1958; 30 May 1958; 24 October 1958; 13 February 1959; 27 February 1959; 22 July 1960; 3 March 1961; 23 June 1961; 30 June 1961.

Sacramento Bee, 3 August 1940; 8–19 December 1941; 26 December 1941; 29–30 December 1941; 1–3 January 1942; 12 January 1942; 19–20 January 1942; 23–24 January 1942; 30–31 January 1942; 1–15 May 1942, Classified Section; 7 May 1942; 9 December 1942; 24 January 1942; 17 July 1949; 19–30 November 1949; 1–10 December 1949; 10 October 1952; 14 November 1952; 27 April–1 May 1953; 6 June 1954; 16 June 1954; 1–23 July 1954; 21–25 October 1954; 25 October 1954; 28 October 1954; 3 November 1954; 12 November 1954; 25 November 1954; 14 January 1958; 3 April 1960; 2 June 1985; 1 December 1991.

Sacramento City Council Minutes, 28 May 1943; Special Meeting: 15 June 1954; 29 June 1954; 20 July 1954. Sacramento, CA: Sacramento Archives and Museum Collection Center.

———. City Minutes 2680: 5 June 1955. Sacramento, CA: Sacramento Archives and Museum Collection Center.

———. City Minutes 2878: 7 July 1955. Sacramento, CA: Sacramento Archives and Museum Collection Center.

Sacramento City Property Map Book, 1941–1942, 1954–1955. Sacramento, CA: Sacramento Archives and Museum Collection Center.

Sacramento Daily Union, 7 July 1892, 3: 26 February 1894, 1; 9 April 1894, 1; 7 August 1894, 1.

Sacramento Directory Company. *Sacramento City Directory*, 1909–1956.

Sacramento Shopping News, 14 October 1954, 1; 28 October 1954; 11 November 1954.

Sacramento Union, 3 August 1940; 8–13 December 1941; 1–15 May 1942, Classified Section; 17 July 1949; 19–30 November 1949; 1–10 December 1949; 23 October 1954.

State of California Superintendent of Banks. "Annual Report, 1910." Sacramento: California State Government Printing Office, 1910.

United States Bureau of the Census. *U.S. Census Population: 1920, State Compendium, California*. Washington, D.C.: U.S. Government Printing Office, 1922.

———. *U.S. Census Population: 1930, Vol. III, Characteristics of the Population, Reports by States, California*. Washington, D.C.: U.S. Government Printing Office, 1932.

———. *U.S. Census Population: 1940, Vol. II Characteristics of the Population, California*. Washington, D.C.: U.S. Government Printing Office, 1902.

———. *U.S. Census Population: 1950, Vol. II, Characteristics of the Population, California*. Washington, D.C.: U.S. Government Printing Office, 1952.

United States Department of Labor. *Labor Unionism in American Agriculture, Bulletin 836*. Washington, D.C.: U.S. Government Printing Office, 1945. Reprint, New York: Arno Press, 1975.

United States Immigration Commission. *Immigrants in Industries, Part 25, Vol. 23, 24, 25. Japanese Americans and Other Immigrant Races in the Pacific and Rocky Mountains*. Washington, D.C.: U.S. Government Printing Office, 1913.

United States Industrial Commission on Immigration, Reports, Vol. XV. Washington, D.C.: U.S. Government Printing Office, 1932.

United States, War Relocation Authority: A Story of Human Conservation. Washington, D.C.: U.S. Government Printing Office, 1946.

Wise, Harold F. "The Future of Urban Renewal in California, an Address at the 67th Convention of the California Savings and Loan League." Frank B. Durkee Collection. Sacramento, CA: Sacramento Archives and Museum Collection Center.

Interviews and Oral History Projects

Adachi, April. Interview by author, 19 June 2013.

Florin Japanese American Citizen League Oral History Project. Sacramento University Archives and Special Collections, California State University, Sacramento, 1987.

Fujii, Toko. Interview by author, 12 December 1994; 6 October 1997.

Hayashi, Alice. Interview by author, 1 October 1997.

Hiyama, Frank. Interview by author, 18 February 1995.

Itano, Dean. Interview by author, 22 June 1995.

Kubo, James. Interview by author, 16 October 1997.

Lee, Sooky. Interview by author, 26 September 1997.

Lipp, Jerome. Interview by author, 15 March 1995.

Matsuda, Fred. Interview by author, 19 June 2013

Miyamoto, Jerry. Interview by author, 19 June 1995.

Nishijima, Kanji. Interview by author, 18 March 1995.

Okada, Eugene. Interview by author, 16 September 1997.

Ouye, Fred. Interview by author, 10 December 1994.

Oya, Yomisu. Interview by author, 11 March 1998.

Sanui, Ken. Interview by author, 14 January 1997.

Sarasohn, Eileen S., ed. *Issei Christians: Issei Oral History Project*. Sacramento, CA: Parkview Presbyterian Church, 1973.

———. *Issei: Portrait of a Pioneer, An Oral History.* Palo Alto, CA: Pacific Books, 1983.
Shibata, Victor. Interview by author, 25 June 2013.
Takahashi, Michiko. Interview by author, 13 June 2013
Uchida, Marian. Interview by author, 19 June 2013.
Wong, Amy. Interview by author, 19 June 2013.
Yagi, Kerri. Interview by author, 3 October 1997.

INDEX

A

Adachi, April 95, 122
Alien Land Act 26, 40
anti-Chinese immigration laws 16
anti-Japanese movement 25, 38, 118
Aoki, Giichi 70, 85, 143
Asiatic Exclusion League 18, 26, 27
Azevedo, Clarence 146, 151

B

Baptist Church 44, 119
bathhouses 32, 72
Buddhist Church 42, 61, 85, 119, 132

C

Capitol Mall Redevelopment project 135
Chinatown 150
Chinese Exclusion Act of 1882 21
City Council 13, 118, 137, 146
Colley, Nathaniel 139

D

Delta 23, 30
Delta farmers 20

E

Executive Order 9066 95

F

First Japanese Baptist Church 32, 61, 98
Fujii, Toko 30, 83, 133, 141, 142, 150, 151, 154, 160
Funahashi family 119

G

Gentlemen's Agreement 18, 26
Great Depression 42, 55

H

Hamatake, Ichiro 86
Harada, Yoshizo 156

Hawaii 15, 17, 23
Hayashi, Akio 140
Hayashi, Alice 23, 31, 105
Hayashi, Florence 112
Hiyama, Frank 17, 20, 25, 31, 122
Home Front Commandos 118

I

Igarashi, Kenzaburo 32, 98
Igarashi, Toshiko 32, 35, 57, 60, 98
Iki, George 91, 107
Imazaki, Howard 112
Ishii, Ed 86
Itano, Dean 140, 144, 146

J

Japan Alley 72, 132
Japanese American Citizens League 81, 91, 95, 128
Japanese-American Redevelopment Study Association 140
Japanese Association 25, 39, 55, 85, 90
Japanese banks 49, 57, 86
Japanese hospital 35
Japanese language schools 46
Japanese Methodist Church 42
Japanese newspapers 32, 85
Japanese Town Alley 14

K

kenjinkai 23, 36, 41, 51
Kodomo Shibai 78
Koimori family 55
Konko Church 44
Kozono, Kane 19
Kubo, James 17, 41, 49, 52, 54, 74, 86, 104
Kuroko family 55
Kurotori, Unosuke 98

L

Lincoln School 31, 46, 106
Lipp, Jerome 137, 145, 149, 152

M

Matsuda family 55
Matsuda, Fred 23, 51, 70, 123
Matsuho family 55
Matsui, Shigezu 90
McClatchy, Eleanor 147
McClatchy, V.S. 39
Methodist Church 119, 132
Mitsumori, Nisuke 16
Mitsutome, Arthur 143
Miyagawa, F.J. 85
Miyaki, Shig 60
Miyamoto, Jerry 104, 144
Miyamoto, Sumio 112
Miyasaki, Ai 14, 32
Morimitsu, Art 112
Muramoto, George 91
Muramoto, Goro 112, 120

N

Nagata, Jean 93
Nakamura, Isamu 84, 85, 90, 99, 104, 112
Nakamura, Jobo 112, 119, 128, 133
Nakatani family 90
Nakatani, Soichi 66
National Origins Immigration Act of 1924 28, 40, 57
Native Sons of the Golden West 118
Nippon Theater 66, 90
Nisei Bowling League 133
Nisei generation 75
Nisei sports 78
Nisei War Memorial 154
Nishijima, Kanji 85, 122, 145, 151, 152, 153
Nishimura family 55

O

Obon 61, 132
Okada, Eugene 128
Orite, Riyo 107
Osuga, Peter 119
Ouye, Fred 123, 124, 127, 145, 151

P

Pearl Harbor 83
picture brides 18
Presbyterian Church 46, 119

R

Resolution 207 118

S

Sacramento Bee 90, 93, 147, 149
Sacramento Redevelopment Agency 145
Sacramento Union 90, 98, 113
Sakamoto, Stirling 128
Sakatachi, Yoshiro 95
Sakata, Frank 23
Sakuma, Mamoru 140, 146, 148
Satow, Riichi 17, 85, 107
Shelby, Jack 148
Shiba, Nori 112
Shima, George 17
Shimoda, Yuki 72
sumo 72, 132

T

Takahashi, George 112, 120
Takahashi, Michiko 35, 66, 72, 84, 85, 119
Taketa, Henry 13, 91, 112, 119, 140, 142, 149, 152, 156
Takizawa, Osuke 21
Tambara, Masao 86
Tambara, Yasuno 86
tanomoshi 41, 50
Tenrikyo Church 44
Teramoto, Chikaji 14, 57
Tokyo Club 71
Tsukamoto, Mary 84
Tsukamoto, Walter 91, 112

U

Uchida, Marian 46, 61, 123, 140

W

Walerga 98, 107
War Relocation Authority 95
Wong, Amy 61, 66, 72
World War I 23, 56

Y

Yabe, Fumiko 92
Yagi, Katti 53
Yoshimura, Frank 143

ABOUT THE AUTHOR

Kevin Wildie grew up in Sacramento, California. He teaches United States and Asian American history as an adjunct history professor at Cosumnes River College in Sacramento, California, and Yuba College in Marysville, California. He earned a BA (1995) and MA (1998) in history from California State University–Sacramento. Between 2000 and 2002, he traveled with his wife, Vanessa Yajima-Wildie, through Asia and taught English in Japan for two years. His wife's auntie, Michiko Takahashi Ho (featured in the book), grew up in Sacramento's Japantown. He lives in Roseville with his wife and daughters, Maddie and Allie.